E-business
Principles and Practice

Jennifer Rowley

palgrave

© Jennifer Rowley 2002

First published 2002 by
PALGRAVE
Houndmills, Basingstoke, Hampshire RG21 6XS and
175 Fifth Avenue, New York, N.Y. 10010
Companies and representatives throughout the world

PALGRAVE is the new global academic imprint of
St. Martin's Press LLC Scholarly and Reference Division and
Palgrave Publishers Ltd (formerly Macmillan Press Ltd).

ISBN 0–333–94913–7 hardback
ISBN 0–333–94914–5 paperback

This book is printed on paper suitable for recycling and
made from fully managed and sustained forest sources.

A catalogue record for this book is available
from the British Library.

Library of Congress Cataloging-in-Publication Data
Rowley, J. E.
    e-business: principles and practice / Jennifer Rowley.
        p. cm.
    Includes bibliographical references and index.
    ISBN 0–333–94913–7 (cloth)
    1. Business–Data processing. 2. Electronic commerce. I. Title.
    HF5548.2 .R69.2002
    658.8'4–dc21   2001059006

Copy-edited and typeset by Povey–Edmondson
Tavistock and Rochdale, England

10   9   8   7   6   5   4   3   2   1
11   10   09   08   07   06   05   04   03   02

Printed in Great Britain by
Antony Rowe Ltd
Chippenham, Wiltshire

Dedication
This book is for my mother and father,
Isabel Betsy Praill and Reginald Joseph Praill

Acknowledgements
I am grateful to all of the entrepreneurs and organisations
that have contributed to the creation of the fascinating new digital
world that adds another dimension to our lives

Contents

List of figures

Acknowledgements

The author and publishers wish to acknowledge the following for permission to reproduce copyright material in the form of screenshots: The Co-operative Bank; Yahoo! Inc. © 2000 by Yahoo! Inc. (YAHOO! and the YAHOO! logo are trademarks of Yahoo! Inc.); HSBC Holdings plc; H & R Johnson Tiles Ltd, Stoke on Trent ST6 5JZ © 2001, all rights reserved; Toys Я Us; *The Guardian* newspaper; Digital Wellbeing Limited; rightmove.co.uk; mail: acrew. Every effort has been made to contact all the copyright-holders but if any have been inadvertently omitted the publishers will be pleased to make the necessary arrangement at the earliest opportunity.

Introduction

E-business, which embraces business relationships in the supply and distribution chain, through to relationships with the customer, is challenging long-established business models, principles and practices. Designed to fill the gap in the marketplace for an accessible textbook, this book offers an overview of key concepts in e-business. The book is informed by current research and practice in e-business and longer-established models and concepts in marketing, information systems and business strategy.

The chapters in the book are organised to reflect an emphasis on the customer experience. Thus, embedded in the heart of the book are three key chapters on marketing communication, customer service and customisation, and online communities. In the context of marketing communication, the Internet poses the real challenge of channelling communication through a small screen (which is even smaller in the case of mobile technologies, such as mobile phones). Search engines, banner ads and URLs are just three of the new terms that the Internet brings to marketing communication. The customer service experience is very different when delivered by a machine rather than by a person, but there is a unique opportunity to build customer profiles and to customise the product or service offering on the basis of those profiles. Relationship marketing has been extended into the arena of online communities. Whilst virtual business communities have existed in a number of contexts for some years, online consumer communities challenge conceptualisations of organisations and offer new perspectives and challenges.

The chapters on customers and the customer experience are preceded by three chapters that set out the context for e-business. Chapter 1 explores the business opportunities presented by e-business, and the nature of internet business as a new channel through which customers can be reached. Options for business models are also reviewed. This is followed by a summary of the key features of the technological landscape that facilitates e-business. One key aspect of the technological context is websites. Website design and development, and the use of websites by customers in searching for information and products are explored in Chapter 3.

In order to fulfil customers' expectations, businesses need to organise, to address issues such as systems, distribution, payment arrangements and, in general to understand how to operate effectively as virtual organisations. In order to move their engagement with e-business forward, businesses need to formulate strategy and undertake planning. E-business strategy is discussed in Chapter 8. Key considerations in formulating strategy are an understanding of the nature of the marketplace, and the creation of effective alliances. Finally, a range of issues associated with making both businesses and customers confident in engaging in e-business are reviewed under the chapter title 'Protecting online communities and societies'. Privacy, security, intellectual property and regulation are important elements of community and societal infrastructure.

The e-marketplace is changing quickly, and it would be unrealistic to expect this book to do any more than to take a snapshot at the time of writing. Further, electronic business, as a research area and as an area of business activity, is still in its infancy. This book will not cover every technological or business innovation that is developing or might develop on the Internet. Rather, (the book is designed to create an awareness and understanding of e-business models and issues, and an ability to identify, analyse and evaluate those issues in future generations of the e-marketplace.)

The book takes as its guiding principles a small group of themes that are interwoven throughout the text:

1. E-business is concerned with global marketplaces, but many of the communities that will be associated with an e-business will, for a variety of cultural, historical, economic, political and logistical reasons, be constrained in space and might be described as local. Indeed, differentiation in a global marketplace may rely heavily upon such factors. Businesses will need to focus on achieving global reach but local customisation.
2. E-business offers many opportunities for the customisation of the marketing exchange in respect of the dimensions associated with communication, product, delivery, price and relationships.
3. Business processes and models need to be aligned to succeed in this new marketplace.
4. Most businesses and business sectors will use e-commerce to complement their other channels in a variety of different ways and, therefore, understanding the integration of e-business into an established enterprise is essential.
5. There is considerable uncertainty as to the potential impact of e-businesses on markets, business processes and customer bases. This unpredictability derives from the relative novelty of e-business and, particularly in the consumer marketplace, from uncertainties about consumer behaviour and response.

The book features:

1. *Case Cameos.* Short case examples of e-business activity give a perspective on how issues have been resolved in practice.
2. *Exploratory Activities.* These encourage the reader to pause and think about the ideas in the text. Many ask the reader to visit websites to collect additional information. Since information on websites is volatile, the reader can collect an up-to-date picture from the website.

3. *Group Discussion Activities.* These pose a series of questions to form a basis for group discussion and analysis of a topic. They are useful for informal group work or group reflection in a class setting. They may be used as a preparation for assessment. Several of the Group Discussion Activities are based on Case Cameos or figures within the text of the book.

4. *Assessment Questions.* At the end of each chapter there are a number of examination-type assessment questions that encourage readers to reflect on the material in that chapter and to test their retention of the material. These assessment questions also flag the key issues that are addressed in each chapter. Although the questions are focused on the material in this book, better answers will include material from reading and engagement with the Exploratory and Group Discussion Activities.

5. *Group Assessments.* Two or three Group Assessments are included at the end of every chapter.

6. *Learning Outcomes.* Study objectives are identified at the beginning of each chapter

7. *Chapter Summaries.* These draw together the key themes that have been developed in each chapter.

8. *Key Concepts.* Brief definitions of the key concepts covered within each chapter are revisited.

AUDIENCE

This textbook is designed to support students studying e-business on MBA courses, Masters' courses in Business and Management Studies, Marketing, Public Relations, Communication Studies and Information Systems. In addition, the accessible approach adopted in this book will appeal to final-year undergraduate students on courses in these areas. Whilst designed primarily for the academic market, the topicality of the subject matter is also likely to attract interest from professional managers, information systems designers, information managers, knowledge engineers and others who need to reflect on the impact that e-business may have on their organisation and to implement e-business solutions.

Frameworks for e-business

In five years' time all companies will be Internet companies,
or they won't be companies at all (Symonds, 1999)

After reading this chapter you will:

■ Be able to define e-business and e-commerce

■ Be aware of the four stages of e-commerce development

■ Appreciate some of the threats and opportunities associated with e-business

■ Understand the key differences between *consumer* and *organisational* e-marketplaces

■ Have considered the nature of the Internet as a channel

■ Appreciate the diversity of e-business models

INTRODUCTION

Most introductions to e-business open with a history of the growth of the Internet, and predictions for the growth of e-commerce and e-business. Even historical statistics are difficult to interpret, and predictions communicate even less about the real impact that e-business is likely to have on the world in which we live. For those who have a predilection for such statistics, some websites that give up-to-date versions of these figures are listed at the end of this chapter.

Nevertheless, there is no denying that there is considerable excitement and media interest around the concept of e-business (or cybermarketing), e-commerce, online communities, v-business, World Wide Web marketing (or Internet business). Even the terms used to describe the e-business revolution inject a sense of novelty and excitement. Add to this media enthusiasm for reporting new initiatives in e-business, the extent of promotion of e-business ventures through all media, and the concern of governments about the potential impact of the Internet on societies and economies, there can be no doubt about the level of interest in e-business. Yet, how can a few messages on a small screen in our homes or offices have any real impact on our lives and the way in which we do business? After all, we can choose to use the PC, we choose what websites we visit and what Internet service we use. It would appear that the Internet, accessed through PCs, mobile technologies, kiosks and other routes is an engaging communication channel that many of us cannot resist.

SOME DEFINITIONS

The terms e-business and e-commerce are both used in this book and, whilst they are closely related concepts, the distinction is important.

E-commerce is doing business electronically across the extended enterprise. It covers any form of business or administrative transaction or information exchange that is executed using any information and communications technology. Morath (2000) views e-commerce as often taking a narrow perspective limited to specific initiatives, such as sales via the Internet, electronic procurement, or electronic payment.

E-business is a wider concept that embraces all aspects of the use of information technology in business. It includes not only buying and selling, but also servicing customers and collaborating with business partners, and often involves integration across business processes and communication within the organisation.

The model proposed in Figure 1.1 is essentially a model for e-commerce in that it focuses on the 'transaction' or service interface with the customer. E-business embraces such interfaces, but it is also concerned with business processes that are necessary to support the promise that lies behind the interface. Once organisations enter into the final two stages of the model, they can no longer treat Internet commerce as a separate entity, and need to develop integrated solutions to the use of information technologies across the business. E-commerce continues to be important at the customer interface, but without the more pervasive approach inherent in the concept of e-business it will have limited success.

EXPLORATORY ACTIVITY

Write down your own understanding of the following terms: Internet marketing, web marketing, virtual business, e-commerce, cybermarketing, e-shopping, e-retailing, and online commerce. Revisit these descriptions as you read later chapters in this book.

DEVELOPING E-COMMERCE

Figure 1.1 proposes a four-stage model of the development of e-commerce that underpins the structure and approach of the remainder of this text. Early developments are in the first stage, Contact. In this mode the Internet is simply an additional channel through which marketing communication can be delivered. Typically such sites display basic company and possibly product information; they often extend to only a few pages. Such sites are described as '**brochureware**', since they are essentially an electronic version of a publicity brochure. All organisations need some visibility in e-space, but not all organisations need to progress to the other three stages. In further development of Internet activities, organisations need to understand the types of relationships that they are seeking to establish with customers and partners, and to develop models that match those objectives.

Stage 2, Interact, is concerned with enhanced information exchange with customers and trading partners. Web pages will provide links to facilitate communication and, on the basis of that communication, it may be possible to start to target marketing efforts. Some sites in this category may run to hundreds or thousands of pages, and interaction may take the form of searching for information within the website, using search engines and other search tools.

In Stage 3, Transact, the functionality that offers order placement and other transactions is made available. Many e-shopping applications are currently in this stage of development. Financial service institutions are focusing on the opportunity to execute online transactions, but because trust and confidentiality are important prerequisites in successful financial services businesses, they need to consider moving to Stage 4 applications.

In Stage 4 two-way relationships are established, with full integration of Internet capability into the business. In consumer markets this may mean

Figure 1.1　Stages of e-commerce service development

Stage	Characteristics	Website functionality
1 Contact	Promote corporate image Publish corporate information Offer contact information	Content
2 Interact	Embed information exchange Targeted marketing effort	Communication
3 Transact	Online transactions Catalogue order/fulfilment Interaction with trading partners	Commerce
4 Relate	Two-way customer relationships Full integration of Internet capability into the business Service interface integrated with delivery and other business operations	Community

allowing consumers access to organisational databases that show stock level, order tracking, prices and discounting schemes, and other product details. In an organisation-to-organisation relationship suppliers and other partners may have access to significant elements of the organisation's databases, including valuable product and customer-profile information, through the organisation's extranets. All such information can be regarded as marketing communication, since perceptions and relationships will be influenced by:

■ Which information a partner is permitted to access, and
■ What that information communicates about the company (which may include bad news as well as good).

Careful attention needs to be given to the development of appropriate knowledge access, security, privacy and confidentiality policies and their implementation, because these all communicate something about the nature of the organisation's relationship with its customers and suppliers. Access to organisational information raises issues of trust and commitment. The challenge is, through these arrangements, to demonstrate the organisation's commitment to the relationship, to inculcate trust in the partner and, where possible, to engage customers as active co-producers.

Figure 1.2 shows the information that is exchanged as part of a two-way relationship based on an order transaction. Some of these processes, such as those that generate order-confirmation notification (probably by e-mail) and order-tracking information can be automatic. State-of-the-art systems software allows organisations to configure this interaction in terms of language, currency, stages of interaction (such as whether automatic order confirmation

Figure 1.2 Stage 4 of e-commerce service development: integration of Internet capability

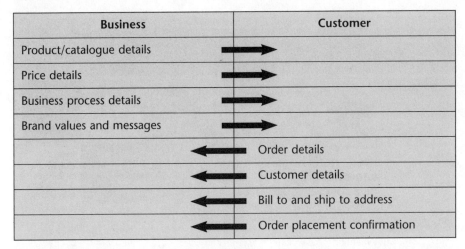

Business	Customer
Product/catalogue details ➡	
Price details ➡	
Business process details ➡	
Brand values and messages ➡	
⬅	Order details
⬅	Customer details
⬅	Bill to and ship to address
⬅	Order placement confirmation

is offered or whether a credit limit is checked) and product details shown (such as stock levels).

The final column in Figure 1.1 identifies the focus of website functionality associated with each stage of development. Content, communication, commerce, and community are widely cited as the essential prerequisites for a successful website. As businesses develop their websites through the stages they add functionality, starting with content and adding communication, commerce and, finally, community. In addition, as the website functionality increases and the extent of engagement in e-business evolves towards the Relate stage, content and communication tools are likely to become more sophisticated.

The model is a generalisation and the order of these four stages of development may vary depending on the type of company. Quelch and Klein (1996), for example, distinguish between existing major companies and Internet start-up companies. They propose that Internet start-ups are likely to introduce transaction facilities earlier than existing companies, because this is the essence of their revenue stream. Existing companies venturing into Internet activity have other established revenue streams and can afford to gain experience of the e-business environment through promotional activities, and using a website to communicate with, and offer customer service to, customers prior to launching a transaction-based service.

This model has an important role in defining the parameters for discussion elsewhere in this book. Organisations will have a variety of different types of engagement with Internet marketing and e-business. This will impact upon their approach to website design, customer relationships, customer service, community and business strategy. In addition the marketplace in which the business operates (consumer or business) and the role that the organisation plays in that marketplace will influence priorities in terms of many of the topics discussed later in this book.

Figure 1.3 Content, communication, commerce and community on a business website

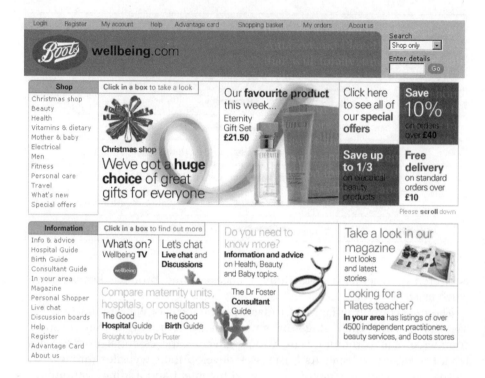

GROUP DISCUSSION ACTIVITY

Examine the website in Figure 1.3. Each member of the group is asked to write down a brief description of features on the website relating to:

- Content
- Communication
- Commerce
- Community

Share your perceptions and discuss whether this is an effective business website.

EXPLORATORY ACTIVITY

Visit a website with which you are familiar or a site referred to elsewhere in this book. Does it have all four of content, communication, commerce and community? If not, would it be appropriate for additional features to be added?

DRIVERS FOR E-BUSINESS

The media are inclined to colourful tales of the impact that e-business will have on traditional marketplaces and retailers. Dot.com companies such as Amazon and PlanetRX are cited as the upstarts that are models for businesses that will totally undermine retailing through existing channels, in surprisingly short periods of time. Such stories would encourage the more insecure managers to look over their shoulders for e-business-based competitors and drive them to contemplate how they might steal the march on any potential competitors and forge ahead in e-business. Others, including customers, managers and academics, have been immunised against media hype by long exposure and are sceptical that e-business can really have any significant impact on their life or their business. Customers ask: 'Is it secure?', 'Is it really more convenient?' and 'Is it really cheaper?'. Business sceptics prefer to believe that their customers could not possibly desert them for an arid and demanding e-business environment. The reality is that e-business will affect businesses on many different levels. E-business is challenging existing business models and is creating a climate in which established consumer behaviour, attitudes and relationships may all be subject to re-evaluation and change. Change will probably be slower than the enthusiasts would like us to believe, and its rate and nature will be different in different organisational and business sectors. E-business offers an opportunity to rethink a whole range of assumptions about how businesses operate, how they relate to their customers and suppliers, and their role and position in the wider marketplace.

This section summarises some of the oft-quoted drivers for e-business. These can be divided into threats and opportunities. The threats mostly arise from the need to respond to change and to remember that if an organisation does not rise to the challenge then 'the competition is only a click away'. Opportunities arise from the redefining of traditional business models, business sectors and customer loyalties.

Threats

1. *Increasing customer expectations about choice*, especially in relation to a wide product range, the opportunity to undertake comparison shopping, and 24-hour availability.
2. *Pressure on product margins*. In markets which already have pressure on product margins, additional pressures will arise from an additional channel of delivery.
3. *Barriers to entry are minimal*. It takes only a relatively short period of time to implement web presence and thereby to launch a new e-business. This is likely to lead to increased and different competition, with different business models.
4. *Size does not matter* and, indeed, small to medium-sized enterprises may be more flexible and able to adapt.
5. *Disintermediation* may lead to the removal of retailers and closer direct relationships between manufacturers and customers in some sectors (Peterson, 1997).

Opportunities

1. *The opportunity to choose a business model.* Some organisations – such as Prudential Assurance with Egg and the Co-operative Bank with Smile – have launched separate Internet businesses, and have taken the opportunity to establish a new brand which might be more representative of their vision for the future of the business, than stale long-standing brands. For other organisations, the marketing communication may be undifferentiated between delivery channels, but differentiation may take place at the operations level. For example, whilst Tesco has chosen to deliver from existing stores, Sainsbury's and Asda have differentiated their e-commerce delivery activities by building dedicated picking centres from which deliveries will be made.

2. *Redefinition of business relationships.* For example, Compaq, in coming to an agreement with the developers of the Millennium Dome for e-ticketing facilities, did not simply offer a transaction based on the provision and maintenance of a computing capability, but rather opted to be paid on the basis of ticket receipts. This means that they have a continuing relationship with their customer and, perhaps more significantly, they share the risk.

3. *Cost savings on transactions can be considerable*, because the customer takes responsibility for a large element of the service transaction. Optimum cost savings will only be achieved if the customer interface, and business processes are fully integrated.

4. *E-commerce also presents an opportunity to redefine the relationship with customers.* Routine service transactions are under the customer's control. The customer is encouraged to learn the script (for example, the process associated with placing an order); this learning increases the barriers to switching. It is supported by Frequently Asked Questions menus (FAQs). Human service agents are engaged to provide a higher level of expertise, and to give tailored customer care when required, from a call centre setting (Dawes and Rowley, 1998).

5. *Access to new global markets* (Peterson, 1997). Although, especially in niche markets, access to such global markets has provided welcome opportunities for small businesses, entering global markets also poses its challenges. There is a need to deal with issues of culture (styles of business, delivery options expected by customers), currency and delivery.

6. *Customer knowledge.* As discussed above, e-commerce transactions embed the collection of customer contact data. Customers are known by name and various addresses. It is also possible to profile customers by tracking what they order. Banks, in particular, are in a strong position to collect such transaction data. This data can form the basis of targeted marketing strategies, more effective segmentation, and targeted marketing spend. Ultimately, provided customers do not resent the manipulation and intrusion that they might perceive to be implied through such an approach, there is the potential for increased levels of customer loyalty and benefits.

GROUP DISCUSSION ACTIVITY

Banking and financial service organisations have developed e-banking and associated services as an additional channel through which they can communicate with and deliver services to their customers. Discuss the potential relevance of each of the features in Figure 1.4 to e-banking. Rank these in order of importance for the financial services industry. Do you think that different rankings might be appropriate for different parts of the industry, such as insurance companies, and banks and building societies?

Figure 1.4 Features of e-commerce

Key feature	Implication
Availability	24-7 and immediate access
Ubiquity	It can be assumed that all organisations and customers will soon have Internet access
Global	Leaving delivery on one side, our mental map of near and far will radically change
Local	Internet is also a good medium to reinforce local physical presence and local person-to-person business relationships
Digitisation	Business will increasingly be happening in information space. This will lead to: ■ Convergence of telecommunications, broadcasting and other information industries ■ Different economic laws operating, with increasing rather than decreasing returns to scale
Multimedia	Provides new opportunities for information provision during buying and selling and provides new opportunities in consultancy, design and entertainment
Interactivity	An opportunity to improve customer service at an affordable price
One-to-one	Using data processing and customer profiling, one-to-one marketing is a natural consequence of doing business on the Internet. It may also be a necessity to overcome the anonymity of Internet business relationships
Network effects and network externalities	Low cost and fast growth in the number of relationships enable business models that require a significant number of parties in the network and whose benefits increase faster with a growing number of parties – that is, these business models exhibit network effects and/or network externalities
Integration	The value of combined information across steps of the value chain is more than the sum of its parts. The Internet now provides at least part of the technology for value-chain functional and information integration. Advanced electronic commerce companies show how to exploit the added value

Source: Based on Timmers (1999).

CONSUMER AND ORGANISATIONAL E-MARKETPLACES

It is important to understand that whilst there may be some characteristics of e-commerce and e-business that impact across many different sectors, there are also significant differences between organisational and consumer markets, and the impact of e-business on specific market sectors. In organisational markets there is a history of e-business based on EDI. The difference between electronic data interchange (EDI) and the Web is the ubiquitous platform that removes the technological constraints that tied organisations to a set of specified suppliers. In organisational contexts in particular, e-business also embraces knowledge management within the organisation in support of effective business processes, and learning. Figure 1.5 summarises some of the key differences between organisational and consumer e-commerce. In organisational markets there are typically fewer, but more high-value, customers, and there are established relationships with those customers.

In consumer markets the impact and penetration of e-business varies between sectors. In particular, the relative sources of competitive advantage of e-business, as compared with traditional retailing, are unique to specific sectors. So, for example, in gambling, the source of competitive advantage was initially associated with the avoidance of UK gambling taxes, which leads to larger winnings and larger profits. For air-travel booking, lower transaction costs have been passed on to customers in the form of lower fares. For banks, lower transaction costs strengthen the banks' competitive position by allowing them to offer higher interest rates for investors. Supermarkets, on the other hand, are seeking differentiation on the basis of a more personalised service and the convenience of remote ordering and home delivery, and expect to be able to charge customers for this service.

Figure 1.6 is one list of the most-visited e-commerce sites. The ranking is not important, and has probably changed since the data was compiled but it does give a view of the kinds of activities that consumers are performing online, and some of the significant online brands. Note that the list of sites is

Figure 1.5 Comparing organisational and consumer markets

Organisational markets	Consumer markets
Fewer customers and known customers	Lots of customers necessary for success
Fewer transactions	Large number of transactions
Each transaction of larger value	Relatively low-value transactions
Net worth of key customers is high	Cannot predict growth rate
Regular transactions	Less regular transactions with individual customers
Credit rating known	Credit rating often not known.

Figure 1.6 Most-visited e-commerce sites

United Kingdom	Germany	United States
Streetsonline.co.uk *Music, literature*	Amazon.de *Music, literature*	Amazon.com *Music, literature*
Amazon.co.uk *Music, literature*	Comdirect.de *Broking, finance*	Priceline.com *Marketplace*
Egg.com *Banking, mortgage, insurance*	Bahn.de *Transport*	Disney.com *Entertainment*
Lastminute.com *Travel and tourism*	t-versand.de *Telecommunication*	Shopnow.com *Mall*
Amazon.com *Music, literature*	Primus-online.de *Mall*	Webshots.com *Photography*
Jungle.com *Computer hardware*	Bol.de *Music, literature*	Pch.com *Mall*
Barclays.co.uk *Banking, mortgage, insurance*	Consors.de *Broking, finance*	Expedia.com *Travel and tourism*
Tesco.co.uk *Supermarket*	Adobe.de *Software*	Barnesandnoble.com *Music, literature*
Ugo.com *Games*	Dig-online.de *Computer hardware*	Nestcard.com *Banking, mortgage, insurance*
Expedia.com *Travel and tourism*	Deutsche-bank-24.de *Banking, mortgage, insurance*	Travelocity.com *Travel and tourism*

Source: Based on Connectis (November 2000), pp. 6–7.

quite different for the different countries listed, although the activities are comparable. Figure 1.7 gives examples of a few e-marketplaces and portals for B2B e-commerce.

NEW CHANNEL?

The sceptics in both business and academia declare that the Internet is 'just another channel' or, in other words, just another way of doing business. They assert that customer benefits and the value of the customer to the business remain the platforms for successful business. Customer satisfaction will continue to derive from quality services and products and these can only be created through effective partnerships and alliances, and an understanding and leverage of the business processes inherent in specific industries.

Figure 1.7   B2B e-marketplaces and portals

www.paperx.com	PaperX brings together Europe's paper manufacturers, merchants, publishers and printers. Buyers respond to offers posted on the site by sellers. The London-based B2B marketplace checks that the traders are authorised to buy and sell paper, and handles payment and credit verification. Sellers are charged a transaction fee.
www.buyingpower.com	Buyingpower is an independent Irish energy broker that targets small and medium-sized enterprises in the UK. Businesses register with the site and submit requirements for gas and electricity. The site pools businesses from the same region into 'powergroups' and invites suppliers to bid for their energy requirements. The supplier with the lowest bid wins.
www.bizdirect.pt	Bizdirect is aimed at small and medium-sized businesses wishing to buy or sell office equipment, consumables and services. The site is a joint venture between Sonae, a Portuguese telecommunications and internet services provider, Aitec, a Portuguese internet business accelerator, and Banco Portugues de Investimento, the Portuguese bank.
www.constructeo.com	Constructeo is an Internet portal launched by French construction company Vinci-GTM in partnership with purchasing specialists Masai and Eyrolles. Site features include industry news, online catalogues, and e-procurement services, financial market trends and technical information. The site also hosts extranets or private networks for sharing correspondence, inspection certificates, blueprints and engineering documents.
www.comdaq.net	Comdaq is a London-based commodities exchange for trading sugar, coffee and cocoa. Because of price fluctuations, only Category A members (that is, established producers and consumers) are allowed to take part in instant trade. Category B members must contract with each other after trading to reconfirm transactions.

May (2000) identifies two uses of the word **channel**, and suggests that e-commerce is subtly blending these together. These two uses emerge from different prior professional and academic groups, each of which has previously been able to own and define the concept for its own purposes. Commerce is forcing a reconsideration of such fundamental concepts. May suggests that:

- In the *media world*, a channel is a branded carrier of entertainment or information to an audience; the purpose of the channel is to send content to an audience.
- In the *marketing world*, channel means any permanent route to a group of customers. Channels are conduits for a company's products and services with consuming populations fitted at their outlets.

In the traditional media world there is a differentiation between those who provide primary content for the channel (such as television) and those who use it to send commercial messages. For marketers, content generates audiences for commercial messages and can help to deliver suitable demographics. Authors and producers tend to regard advertising as a layer superimposed on the chief purpose of the channel in order to contribute to commercial viability. Marketers also deal with various channels that are purely commercial in orientation, such as publicity and mail-order catalogues.

The website must combine a mix of these functions. It must be a route to a market, but at the same time it is an information and entertainment medium. The Web is a place where stories are told, dialogues are initiated and information is discovered. Further, it is largely text-based and users are readers and often writers. The development of the Web as a channel requires an understanding of the way in which information, entertainment and commerce can be melded together.

In using the Web to communicate, consumer response to business offerings will be crucial. Consumers will place themselves along a spectrum, which at one end involves the engagement and fostering of intimate relationships with a business over a period of time and at the other end involves 'rational decision-making behaviour' in which they will seek the best economic value from each individual transaction. Tools exist to support either of these approaches. Figure 1.8 summarises some of the characteristics of each of

Figure 1.8 Consumer economic behaviour

Loyal customer relationships	Customers pursue best value
More likely in B2B, although improved information on alternative trading partners may undermine existing relationships	More likely in B2C, but search cost might outweigh perceived benefits and lead to inertia and apparent loyalty
Businesses need to understand the unique glue for relationships in their sector	Search tools need to be efficient and effective to encourage evaluation and comparison of offerings
Important for transactions in which trust and confidence are factors.	Suitable for commodity marketplaces
Customisation based on customer profiles gathered over the period of a relationship	Standard product, offered at a competitive price. Auctions and shopping agents are tools that support identification and selection of product for purchase
Community encourages tighter identification with the business and the customers that form its community	Transaction-focused with little development or learning and customer satisfaction based on individual transactions
Differentiation on the basis of relationship	Cost leadership

these opposing poles. Ultimately customers in both organisational and consumer markets will decide where they sit on this spectrum, in respect of the different products and services that they acquire. For some products, customers will tend to cluster at one or the other end of the spectrum, but for others the customer group will be more widely spread through the spectrum.

EXPLORATORY ACTIVITY

Find a friend who engages in e-shopping. Ask her to explain what she buys and why she buys these products or services from this channel, rather than through established channels.

E-BUSINESS MODELS

There has been much discussion of new business models for the digital economy. Timmers (1999) defines a business model thus:

> An architecture for product, service and information flows, including a description of the various business actors and their roles, a description of the potential benefits for the various business actors, and a description of the sources of revenue.

Embracing both consumer and business marketplaces and covering a wide range of business sectors, there is a wide range of different models available to e-businesses. Most of the business models that exist in other business contexts are mirrored in the e-business context. However the digital environment is likely to have two effects:

- Fundamental impact on the significance, role in the marketplace and operation of a given business model. It may also impact on the success of a specific business model for a business, but the overall range of business models remains relatively stable. For example, there remains a role for financial service intermediaries or advisers, but the execution of this role may be informed by a much more powerful knowledge base, and customisation of communication between the adviser and the customer may be possible on a much larger scale than previously.
- Businesses may need continually to re-evaluate the business model that is most effective for them, and to consider some of the remodelled approaches presented by the web, such as portalling, auctions, and communities.

Since the e-marketplace is so diverse it is challenging to categorise the business models available, and there are many approaches to the categorisation of business models on the Internet. Figure 1.9 shows one such model proposed by Hanson (2000). Hanson views business models from the

CHANGING BUSINESS MODELS

zShops is a new syndication venture for Amazon. Under the zShops scheme, Amazon hosts hundreds of small e-commerce providers on its site. These shops gain access to Amazon's 13 million customers, as well as sophisticated tools for online ordering. In return they pay Amazon a listing fee for each item, plus a commission on each sale. With zShops Amazon becomes a distributor of online shops. Apart from additional revenue the other attraction for Amazon is the extra traffic from customers visiting the niche zShops. In this model, Amazon's core assets are the ordering system and established customer base.

Figure 1.9 Web business benefits

Improvement-based business models	Revenue-based business models
Enhancement, including brand building, category building and quality *Efficiency* – cost reduction *Effectiveness* – dealer support, supplier support, information collection	*Provider Pays* – sponsorship, alliance, advertising, prospect fees, sales commissions *User Pays* – product sales, per use (for information and access services), subscriptions, bundle sales

Source: Based on Hanson (2000).

Figure 1.10   Revenue-generating business models

Revenue-generating model	Description
Additive channel	Sell more of our traditional lines to new markets
New offer channel	Invent a new product or service for the e-commerce channel
Subscription	Charge for access to content
Advertising	Sell advertising space on the site
Sponsorship	Apply a brand to a content offering
Licensing	Restrict a channel to paying carriers
Portalling	Charge destinations for sending users there
Commission	Take a percentage on transactions effected through the channel
Tolling	Take a percentage on transactions effected through your mechanism.

Source: Based on May (2000).

perspective of the benefits to be accrued to the business. He embraces the category of revenue-generating business models, discussed by May (2000) (as summarised in Figure 1.10), and also recognises the benefits to be derived from business improvement. These arise from enhancement to existing brands and products and services, increases in efficiency and increases in effectiveness, particularly in relation to communication with suppliers, dealers and retailers, and customers. To experience the benefits in this second category a business does not need to engage in e-commerce. Many of these benefits are achieved through a holistic approach to the penetration of e-business through the organisation. In addition, some of these benefits may be particularly appropriate to public-sector organisations, in which enhanced service and information provision is often a more important performance indicator than success with revenue generation.

Figure 1.11 offers an alternative categorisation of business models on the basis of the function or role played by businesses in the e-marketplace. This is useful in offering perspectives on the type of activity in this marketplace. It also identifies some of the business functions that are new, or at least have been significantly redefined in the e-marketplace. Most of these roles can be fulfilled by '**pure play** Internet business' or by existing businesses, which in the retailing sector are often described as '**bricks-and-mortar**' stores. E-commerce is associated with most of these options, but many roles can on occasion be performed with motives other than direct revenue generation. This second categorisation aims to emphasise the value added by the business to the marketplace, whereas categorisation on the basis of a revenue-generating model indicates how businesses can draw value or revenue from the marketplace. These are two complementary perspectives.

CHAPTER SUMMARY

This chapter has explored the nature of e-business and e-commerce from a variety of different angles. After encouraging reflection on definitions, the four stage model of e-commerce development was introduced to emphasise that not all e-business activity involves transactions. Websites can also be used for content, communication, and community building. Drivers towards engagement in e-business can be seen in terms of threats and opportunities. Although it is possible to identify key features of the Internet that can provide businesses with market advantage, these features impact differentially in different sectors. One major distinction is between consumer and organisational, or business, marketplaces. In consumer marketplaces the concept of the Internet as a channel provides a useful perspective. Consumer economic behaviour is an important factor in business success. There are a number of different categorisations of business models. Together these emphasise the diversity of e-business ventures and activity.

Figure 1.11 Business function-based business models

Business model	Comment
Digital information delivery	Digital information can be easily customised and delivered without delay. Production and distribution have become much more tightly coupled. Businesses involved with the creation and distribution of music, electronic magazines, information and advice, e-books, video and radio have been significantly affected and face a real challenge in finding the most effective business model. Issues of intellectual property and control of copying are fundamental to continued business opportunities
E-service delivery	Concerned with the delivery of a service over the Internet. Typical sectors in this group include: financial services, estate agency, banking, gambling, travel agency and theatre bookings. These are often information-based services, in which transactions are conducted and a record of those transactions maintained. In some cases the Internet just provides ticketing or contracting (for example, travel agency) and the actual service (flights and accommodation) is separated from the ticketing operation. Transactions are typically much cheaper than through traditional channels
Retailing	Retailing also embraces a service element, but the primary concern is the sale of a product or a service (but not its delivery). Typical industry sectors include: toys, CDs and printed books, computer hardware, supermarkets, flowers and clothes. Retailers may have access to more geographically scattered markets and customers can compare offerings from several outlets
Intermediaries or aggregators	Intermediaries add value in the chain between the manufacturer and the consumer. Retailers are a special kind of intermediary. Others include third-party marketplaces (that support e-procurement), sourcing operations that provide information about business performance, portals, shopping malls, and cybermediaries
Infrastructure support providers	Infrastructure support providers are businesses that offer the hardware and software, and telecommunications platforms that underpin e-business. They include businesses such as Dell, Microsoft, IBM, many of the Internet Service Providers and telecommunication systems providers. This group stands to gain the most through growth in e-business. The more businesses participate and invest, the higher the revenues to this sector
Marketing communications agencies	Media and communications agencies have a major role to play in supporting business communication on the Internet, and about e-business offerings in other media. In addition to the traditional skills exercised by, for instance, advertising and promotions agencies, services are offered in website design, placement and design of banner advertisements, networking and registering with search engines

KEY CONCEPTS

e-commerce is doing business electronically across the extended enterprise

e-business embraces all aspects of the use of information technology in business

Brochureware are websites that are electronic versions of printed publicity brochures

Dot.com, or **pure play**, companies are businesses whose primary market presence and business activities operate through the Internet.

ASSESSMENT QUESTIONS

1. Why is it useful to differentiate between e-commerce and e-business?
2. Why is the four-stage model of e-commerce development useful?
3. Why do businesses need to think about the Internet in their present and future business plans?
4. Make a list of some of the differences between consumer and organisational marketplaces. Why are both important in e-business?
5. In what senses is the Internet a new business channel?
6. Review and critically analyse some of the ways of categorising e-business models.
7. Explain the difference between e-retailing, e-service delivery, and e-business intermediaries.

GROUP ASSESSMENT 1 – WEB STATISTICS AND GROWTH

Choose a business sector, such as travel, mobile phones or car manufacturing and distribution. Visit the websites that offer web statistics (see the end of this chapter for some suggested sites). Select statistics appropriate to your sector and produce a report that summarises the statistical indicators of the potential impact of e-commerce over the next five years. Suggest some of the possible business consequences of these predictions.

GROUP ASSESSMENT 2 – NEW CHANNELS

Britain is still the most expensive place to buy a car in Europe. British car buyers may be able to cut the cost of car purchase by 10–20% or more. This anomaly makes online car purchase an interesting option for both consumers and online businesses. Visit five of the following sites and make a note of the price for which you can buy each of three different models of car: www.jamjar.com, www.broadspeed.com, www.carbusters.com, www.autobytel.co.uk, www.virgincars.com, www.kelko.com.

REFERENCES

Note: Only a few of the sources listed below are referred to in the text of this chapter. The list has been compiled to include many of the recently published texts in e-business and related fields.

Aldrich, D (2000) *Mastering the digital marketplace*. Chichester: Wiley.

Berners-Lee, T (1999) *Weaving the web*. London: Orion Business.

Bickerton, P, Bickerton, M and Pardesi, U (2000) *Cybermarketing: how to use the Internet to market your goods and services*. Oxford: Butterworth Heinemann.

Bickerton, P, Bickerton, M and Simpson-Holey, K (1998) *Cyberstrategy: business strategy for extranets, intranets and the internet*. Oxford: Butterworth Heinemann.

Chaffey, D, Mayer, R, Johnston, K and Ellis-Chadwick, F (2000) *Internet marketing*. Harlow: Pearson Education.

Chesbrough, H W and Teece, D J (1996) When is virtual virtuous? Organising for innovation, *Harvard Business Review*, Jan–Feb, 65–71.

Cram, C M (2001) *E-commerce concepts*. Boston: Thomson Learning.

Cunningham, P and Froschi, F (2000) *Revolution: opportunities and challenges in the 21st century*. Springer Verlag.

Daum, B and Scheller, M (2000) *Success with electronic business: design, architecture and technology of electronic business systems*. Boston: Addison-Wesley.

Dawes and Rowley (1998) Enhancing the customer experience: contributions from information technology, *Management Decision*, **36**(5), 350–7.

De Kare-Silver, M (2000) *e-shock: the electronic shopping revolution: strategies for retailers and manufacturers*. 2nd edn. Basingstoke: Macmillan Business.

Ellsworth, J H and Ellsworth, M V (1997) *Marketing on the Internet*. 2nd edn. New York: Wiley.

Evans, P B and Wurster, T S (1999) Getting real about virtual commerce, *Harvard Business Review*, Nov-Dec, 84–94.

Financial Times (1999) Electronic business survey, 20, Oct, 1-12.

Gabay, J J (2000) *Successful cyberm@rketing in a week*. Abingdon: Hodder & Stoughton.

Griffel, F, Tu, T, and Lamersdorf, W (2000) *Electronic commerce*. Dpunkt.

Hanson, W (2000) *Principles of Internet marketing*. Cincinnati, Ohio: South-Western College Publishing.

Hardaker, G and Graham, G (2001) *Wired marketing: energizing business for e-commerce*. Chichester: Wiley.

Kalakota, R and Robinson, M (1999) *E-business: roadmap for success*. Boston: Addison-Wesley.

Kleindl, B A (2001) *Strategic electronic marketing: managing e-business*. Cincinnati, Ohio: South Western College Publishing.

May, P (2000) *The business of ecommerce; from corporate strategy to technology*. Cambridge: Cambridge University Press.

Morath, P (2000) *Success @ e-business*. London: McGraw-Hill.

Peterson, R A (1997) *Electronic marketing and the consumer*. Thousand Oaks, London: Sage Publications.

Quelch, J and Klein, L (1996) The Internet and international marketing, *Sloan Management Review*, Spring, 61–75.

Seybold, P (1998) *Customer.com*. Times Books.

Siebel, T M and House, P (1999) *Cyber Rules: strategies for excelling at e-business*. Currency-Doubleday.

Sterne, J (1999) *World Wide Web marketing*. 2nd edn. New York: Wiley.

Symonds, M (1999) Business and the Internet: survey, *Economist*, 26 June, 1–44.

Tapscott, D (1997) *Growing up digital*. London: McGraw-Hill

Timmers, P (1999) *Electronic commerce: strategies and models for business-to-business trading*. Chichester: Wiley.

Turban, E, Lee, J, King, D and Chung, H M (2000) *Electronic commerce: a managerial perspective*. New Jersey: Prentice Hall.

Wigand, R T (1997) Electronic commerce: definition, theory, and context. *The Information Society*, **13**(1), 1–16.

Web statistics

www.commerce.net/research/stats/stats.html (Internet Demographics and eCommerce Statistics)

www.webreference.com/internet/statistics.html

www.nua.ie/surveys/index.cgi (Internet surveys)

www.forrester.com (Forrester research)

Case studies on e-commerce are available at www.ecch.cranfield.ac.uk. These are useful examples, and can be used as a basis for discussion.

Technologies

After reading this chapter you will:

- Understand that although the Internet and the Web are key technologies in driving e-business, other parallel technologies, such as mobile technologies and digital television also contribute to e-business

- Be familiar with some of the key Internet and Web protocols

- Appreciate the structure of URLs

- Understand the role of HTML and other mark-up languages

- Be aware of the role of Web browsers

- Be able to differentiate between Internet service providers (ISPs) and application service providers (ASPs)

- Explain the relationships between the Internet, intranets and extranets

- Recognise the Internet tools that support communication and file transfer

- Access technologies

▌INTRODUCTION

Without communication and networking technologies there would be no e-commerce. Technology both facilitates and constrains the development of e-business. This chapter reviews the technological landscape against which e-business is developing. As well as exploring the nature of the Internet and the Web, it reviews other contributing technologies, such as mobile communications, kiosks and digital television. The effectiveness of networks depends crucially on network standards.

▌PARALLEL TECHNOLOGIES

Most of the excitement around e-business is integrally associated with the potential of the Internet, and more specifically the Web. Whilst these technologies are central, it is important to take a more holistic perspective and to recognise that e-business, especially in business-to-consumer applications, is concerned with allowing customers access through whichever channel they choose. This might include mobile phones and personal digital assistants (PDA) with WAP display or public access kiosks in airports, railway stations and shopping centres. In other words, consumers will demand the option of consulting information on the move, as well as through fixed machines in their office, home or even their train seats. The main limitation of e-shopping for goods is that the product cannot be touched, smelt, seen, manipulated and, in general experienced. One way in which consumers can maximise the information available to them in the purchase-decision process is to visit a real shopping mall armed with their mobile phones or to use a public access kiosk located in the mall. They could then experience the actual product, collect information from other consumers, check detailed product features information and compare prices with similar products, possibly available through other retailers in the same shopping mall or over the Internet. This scenario illustrates the need to be imaginative when considering the application of Internet and linked technologies.

Whilst the respective roles of technologies are likely to change over the years, different technologies and combinations of technologies are likely to be useful for different purposes. Figure 2.1, developed from Morath (2000), illustrates how the constraints and strengths of different technologies may be exploited to advantage in meeting the needs of different consumer groups.

Figure 2.1 illustrates that different technologies will be appropriate for different tasks, and be popular amongst different market segments. Ultimately it is likely that many consumers and business users will employ more than one technology and will choose between them for specific tasks on the basis of the task and the convenience and applicability of the technology for the completion of the task. Businesses will often need to be represented in all channels and need to embrace consistency in interaction with the user across the different channels. Thus kiosks might provide access to Internet web pages, or extracts from Internet web pages that the user may have visited from a work or home PC. For example, a user might register for travel insurance either through a home PC or a kiosk; the form-based dialogue needs to be similar in these two media for two reasons:

Figure 2.1 Matching technologies to segments

Target segment	Primary equipment	Constraints	Strengths
Young consumers	PC hooked up by modem with fixed telephone link	Bandwidth restricted. Market penetration approx. 10% (Asia), 20% (Europe) and 50% (USA)	PC power, for example, to process information further (text files, calculation data, electronic interaction). Full function keyboard. Currently most widely accepted device
Big spenders, business people and professionals	Mobile phones with WAP display	Small display. Expensive connections. Dropped calls, that is, termination due to bad radio connection	Can be used to provide value added services by sending SMS news to the customers, for example, financial updates of stock performance, buy/sales triggers, special offers, airplane delays. Mobility and (potential) ubiquity
Complete mass market	TV with Internet set-top box, connected via TV cable or telephone cable.	Convenient feedback/data entry not available unless a keyboard is added; only numbers can be entered via remote control	Large screen. Very high bandwidth for real-time video transmission

Source: Developed from Morath (2000), p. 53.

1. To enhance user familiarity with the dialogue – on different occasions over a period of years, users may use different channels to complete this transaction; it is helpful if they become familiar with the information that they are asked to provide.
2. To ensure that the data collected is consistent across channels and the same contacts are forged with customers, irrespective of the channel through which the interaction took place.

In mobile phones and digital television, similarities between media may derive more strongly from consistency in the use of brand, images and other factors that communicate messages and personality to the customer, rather than the details of the transaction. Consistency in these areas is particularly important across all media.

Figure 2.1 also identifies some of the factors that will determine the applicability of the different technologies, within different market segments. These are:

■ *Lifestyle* of the market segments
■ *Penetration of technology*, both in general, within specific countries, and within specific segments
■ *Bandwidth* and other characteristics of connections
■ *Cost* of the equipment and the ongoing cost of the use of connections
■ *Reliability*, with problems most likely to be associated with connection
■ *Size of display*, which affects the information and interaction options that can be made available at one time

- *Input options*, ranging from touch screen, keypad, to full function keyboard and, ultimately, voice
- *Integration* with other functions, such as calculations, the creation and storage of local databases and documents
- Opportunity to maintain a *print record* of any transactions or information.

This list of characteristics is useful because any new technologies can be evaluated in terms of these criteria. Linking technologies together in different configurations might also provide solutions that navigate the constraints of one technology by capitalising on the strengths of another. Figure 2.1 is not a comprehensive list of all options. So, for example, linking a portable PC through a mobile phone gives many of the advantages of a PC, but also allows mobile communication. Internet cafes are becoming popular with users who do not otherwise have Internet access. Such cafes have all of the functionality of the standard PC-linked configuration, but offer access to segments where penetration in terms of ownership remains limited. On the basis of the above criteria, the PC linked to a telephone line offers maximum flexibility in terms of the range of information that can be provided and the ease of interaction. Businesses need to establish an Internet presence but some may also have potential market segments in which the penetration of digital TV is high or in which the fascination with mobile phones allows them to deliver short and sharp marketing messages, brief items of general and product news and opportunities to effect simple transactions.

CASE CAMEO

INSTRUCTIONS IN A TELEPHONE DIALOGUE FOR BOOKING CINEMA TICKETS

1. Welcome to the Cinema Information and Booking Line. If you want to book press 1, if you want programme information press 2, if you want to talk to an operator press 3 <1 PRESSED>
2. If you want to book for *Charlie's Angels* press 1, if you want to book for *Memento* press 2, if you want to book for *What Lies Beneath*, press 3, if you want to book for *Billy Elliott*, press 4 <4 PRESSED>
3. If you want to book for today press 1, if you want to book for tomorrow press 2, otherwise press 3 < 1 PRESSED>
4. If you want to book for the 5.30 pm showing press 1, if you want to book for the 8.00pm showing press 2 <2 PRESSED>
5. Use your keypad to indicate the number of Adult tickets <2 PRESSED>
6. Use your keypad to indicate the number of non-Adult tickets <0 PRESSED>
7. You have booked 2 Adult tickets for the 8pm showing of *Billy Elliott* on Saturday 25th November. This will cost £11.50. Press 0 to confirm, or 1 to exit <1 PRESSED>
8. Please use the keypad to enter your credit card number
9. Please enter the card issue number
10. Please enter the expiry date of the card
11. Your booking has been confirmed. Please collect your tickets from the ticket office

GROUP DISCUSSION ACTIVITY

With reference to the case cameo above, answer the following questions:

1. Discuss whether this dialogue is an effective interface with the customer. List advantages and disadvantages.
2. Sketch out a PC screen form that would ask for the same information.
3. Sketch out a series of screens for WAP phone Internet booking for this transaction.
4. Which technology offers the best interface for making a booking of this type? Why?

THE INTERNET AND THE WEB

The **Internet** is a collection of interlinked computer networks – or a network of networks. Currently it connects over one million different computers and the rate of increase in use and new subscribers is growing on a month-by-month basis. The impact of the Internet derives from the underlying standards, or protocols, that allow linkages between different networks and make access possible through a wide range of different user workstations. The Internet is based on a set of open standards, or **protocols** of operation, that are not owned or controlled by any one company. These open standards ensure that businesses and individuals are not locked into one company's hardware or software. Figure 2.2 summarises some of the key standards or protocols that underpin the Internet. Many of these Internet protocols are invisible to the user because they are embedded in Internet applications.

Historically, the Internet was essentially an academic network but business use is growing so that the Internet is no longer an elite network for communication between eminent research centres, but also is accessible to organisations and individuals throughout the world. The Internet is a gateway to myriad information-based online databases, commercial and government websites, software and document archives, in addition to electronic bulletin boards and newsgroups and e-mail. The Internet offers access to both a rich seam of information and commercial transactions, and many websites combine information provision (sometimes in the form of marketing communication) with commerce. Most organisations regard it as important to have a presence on the Internet, in the form of a website, since the Internet is becoming an increasingly important means of promotion and visibility.

The terms Internet and World Wide Web (the Web or WWW) are often used interchangeably. Strictly they are not the same thing. The Internet is a worldwide network of interlinked computer networks. The Internet provides global connectivity via a mesh of networks based on the TCP/IP and Open Systems Interconnection (OSI) protocols. Documents are transferred between the networks that comprise the Internet using one of a variety of Internet

Figure 2.2 Internet protocols

Protocol	Comment
TCP/IP	Transport Control Protocol/Internet Protocol – basic communications protocol
E-mail	Electronic mail – supports the transfer of text between users
FTP	File transfer – allows computer files and software to be transferred across the Internet. FTP is a feature of web browsers
TELNET	Allows a computer to connect to another computer system as if it were a terminal in the first system. This supports the transfer of packets of data between computers and would allow, for example, remote checking of stock databases
USENET	Supports online discussion in 'newsgroups' using electronic bulletin boards
ARCHIE, VERONICA, WAS	Search protocols for FTP sites which support searching on the Internet. They have now largely been incorporated into or superseded by the Web

transfer protocols, such as File Transfer Protocol (FTP) and HyperText Transfer Protocol (HTTP). The **World Wide Web** comprises those servers linked to the Internet that use HTTP.

The defining characteristic of the Web is that websites or documents are linked to one another through hyperlinks which are embedded in each site. Users move from one site to the next using hyperlinks, which are created through a combination of:

■ an addressing system that allows the location of any object stored on a networked computer to be uniquely identified by a **Uniform Resource Locator** (URL)
■ a **mark-up language** or standard format used to define the layout of web pages. This allows the authors of sites to identify particular locations within their site as the source of links, and to specify the location of the target of those links
■ a transfer protocol (**Hypertext Transfer Protocol (HTTP)**) that defines the way in which information is transmitted across the Internet and thereby allows copies of target sites stored on remote servers to be retrieved and displayed
■ a client program, or **Web browser** such as Netscape Navigator or Internet Explorer that provides the user with control over the retrieval process and over the links to be activated.

Figure 2.3 summarises these and other protocols that underpin the operation of the Web.

Figure 2.3   World Wide Web protocols

Protocol	Comment
Web	World Wide Web (WWW) – set of standards that allows hyperlinks and graphics to move through the Internet
HTTP	Hypertext Transport Protocol – supports links between sites and retrieval
HTML	Hypertext Mark-up Language – a text-based mark-up language, or set of codes, that define the design of a web page
VRML	Virtual Reality Mark-up Language – allows 3-D models to be displayed and rotated in a web page
XML	Extended Mark-up Language adds intelligence to web pages
CGI	Common Gateway Interface – interface that provides links to other programs for Web servers, such as between a database and a web form when data entry to the database is through the form. A CGI script is used to transfer information from a computer on the Internet to the host computer
URL	Uniform Resource Locator – address or code that can be used to locate a website
Java	A programming language that permits complex applications, including graphics, to be developed so that they can be accessed using a web browser

People and organisations create **home pages** to present their own information, or service. A collection of home pages, located on the same server is called a **website**. Access to these pages is via the Uniform Resource Locator (URL) using a browser. These addresses link the user to the host computer and their individual files; these are then displayed on the user's personal workstation. With the appropriate software, users can read documents, view pictures, listen to sound and retrieve information.

The combination of web browsers and mark-up languages such as HTML and XML has been responsible for establishing the widespread business use of the Internet. This derives from the following aspects of this application:

- Navigation between documents, through the use of hyperlinks and URLs is easy and consistent across all websites and applications
- Mark-up languages support a wide range of formatting, making it easy to create interesting and easy-to-read web documents
- The graphical environment supports multimedia, which is more engaging to users and which offers a visual medium for advertising
- Interactivity, that is supported through forms by which customers can supply personal details or ask questions
- Standardisation, which encourages a large and fast-growing market.

URLS AND DOMAIN NAMES

URLs are addresses that allow the location of web pages in cyberspace. Web addresses are structured in a standard way:

http://www.domain-name.extension/filename.html

1. *http* denotes the use of the HTTP protocol. All web addresses start with http, although in modern browsers it is not necessary to enter it.
2. *www* indicates that this is a World Wide Web address. Most sites are located on the WWW, but those that are not should not have www in the address.
3. The *domain name* identifies a specific computer which is connected to a specific Internet server. The domain name is often a company name or a brand name.
4. The *extension* (also known as the *global top level domain*) indicates the type of the domain. Common extensions are:

   - .com for an American or international company (or a company that aspires to be international!)
   - .co.uk for a company based in the UK (and seeking to emphasise its presence in the UK market)
   - .ac.uk for a UK-based university (for example, Dundee.ac.uk); .edu.au is used for an Australian based university (for example, murdoch. edu.au).
   - .org.uk or .org for a not-for-profit organisation (for example, oxfam.org)
   - gov.uk for a UK government organisation (for example, Lewisham. gov.uk)
   - .net for a network provider such as Tesco Net (www.tesco.net)

   Organisations that want people to be able to communicate with their staff, also use the domain name and its extension in **Internet addresses**, for example, debowski@commerce.murdoch.edu.au or p.z.murphy@dundee. ac.uk. Internet addresses are made up of two parts: the person's user name, and the domain name of the computer/server. The user name is required to validate a user account on a specific computer. The unique Internet address for a person is abbreviated automatically to an IP address. An IP address is a string of four sets of numbers.
5. The *filename.html* part of the web address refers to an individual web page. Filenames are rarely used in marketing because this would significantly impair the memorability of the address. Accordingly, web addresses are often used without filenames. When a web address is typed without a filename, the browser automatically assumes that the user is looking for the home page, which by convention has the file name index.html. The home page should, then, always have the name index.html.

WEB PAGE CONTENT AND HYPERMEDIA

Web page text needs to be formatted similarly to the way in which text is formatted in word-processing in order to lend design to a web page. The web browser creates this formatting by interpreting the formatting instructions that are contained in the file that is designed to create a web page. These instructions are most commonly written in HTML, which is used for coding text and other mark-up languages as discussed below. HTML codes typically relate to fonts, position and colours. For example, to make the heading Sony appear in bold it would be coded <B>Sony<B>.

The easiest way to create web pages is to use web page design software (otherwise known as an HTML editor). Examples of this software include Microsoft FrontPage, Adobe PageMill, and Macromedia Dreamweaver.

HTML is an international standard (see www.w3.org) intended to ensure that any web page authored in accordance with the standard will appear the same in any web browser. HTML files can be authored with most text editors, and word processors (such as Word) also have an option to save formatted information in the HTML format.

HTML handles text. In addition to text, web pages include:

1. Static graphical images
2. Animated graphical images
3. Interactive form elements, and
4. Plug-in components.

Figure 2.4 shows a web page that incorporates some of these components. Web page components require different standards for file formats and mark-up languages. GIF and JPG are common file formats for static graphics on web pages. GIF files can also be used for animated banner advertisements. Other standard mark-up languages include:

■ XML, Extensible Mark-up Language, is designed to add intelligence to web pages. It defines the actual data or content included in a web page. Using XML a web page can act as a stand-alone program so, for instance, it may collect data and automatically send and verify the data without user intervention. One of the advantages of XML is that the data can be formatted in several different ways using XML tags. This is useful for developing displays that might appear on a PC and a mobile phone. A further development of XML is XHTML.

■ XFDL, Extensible Forms Description, is an XML syntax to request complex forms.

■ DHTML, Dynamic HTML, allows movement and layering of text and can add multimedia effects.

■ VRML, Virtual Reality Modelling Language, supports the development of three-dimensional virtual worlds.

■ WML , Wireless Mark-up Language is a mark-up language that adheres to XML standards but can run powerful applications within the constraints imposed by mobile devices. WML does not assume a keyboard or mouse.

Figure 2.4 The contents of a typical web page

There are also special-purpose mark-up languages, such as MathML, Mathematical Mark-up Language. New developments such as TV Web (see p. 39), and micropayment systems (see Chapter 7) all require developments to mark-up languages.

Interactivity on a web page is created with the use of the **Java programming language**, and **Java scripts**. Using the Java programming language, programmers can write Java applets. **Java applets** are downloaded from the Internet and can run on any system. Java is platform independent. When a user requests a web page containing Java applets, both the page and the applets are downloaded and run on the user's computer. Java applets are therefore described as running client-side applications.

JavaScript is a **scripting language** that is used to provide feedback to the web surfer, to generate new web pages and to execute tasks defined by the user. Working with source code in a mark-up language, JavaScript supports the addition of dynamic content to a web page. Web pages are made up of a number of objects, such as forms, option buttons and text boxes. By defining the properties of an object and the operations to be performed on it, JavaScript supports animation and interactivity.

Interactive features such as registration and ordering forms collect customer data. In order to act on this information the server needs to insert it into a database, and match it with existing data in the database. A scripting or gateway program is necessary to take the information from the form and interpret it for the server. The most common scripting program is the **Common Gateway Interface** (CGI) script. These scripting programs are like the glue between the interface, or form, and the underlying database. When a server receives data transmitted by a CGI script, the server processes the data according to predetermined requirements as indicated by the script. For example, this might involve passing the order to the supplier and generating an acknowledgement of the order.

EXPLORATORY ACTIVITY

Visit W3C (World Wide Web Consortium) and make a list of the current developments in Web protocols, as reported on this website.

EXPLORATORY ACTIVITY

Create a page of text in a word processor, and then save it in HTML format. Examine the resultant file, and note the codes and instruction tags, such as <TITLE>, <BODY>.

WEB BROWSERS

The browser takes the information and codes and interprets them to display the requested data on screen. Browsers need to be continually updated so that they can read new codes for new applications.

Web browsers are an important means of searching, accessing and viewing information stored on the web servers that are linked together through the WWW. Common browsers are Netscape Navigator and Microsoft Internet Explorer. Specifically, the functions supported by a browser are:

1. Entering web addresses, setting up communications links with sites, and downloading web pages
2. Displaying web pages and interactive forms, and running programs such as plug-ins and Java
3. Enabling navigation between sites by using 'forward' and 'backward' options and hyperlinks
4. Recording on the hard disk a copy of sites visited and pages downloaded (caching) to enable quicker downloading and referencing in future
5. Allowing useful sites to be bookmarked for later use; this process is referred to as 'Favorites' in Microsoft Internet explorer.
6. Enabling information to be saved to disk or printed.

Plug-ins allow rich content files such as video, radio programmes, and other multimedia content to play through browsers. For example, some popular plug-ins are:

- Apple's Quicktime, for downloading and playing video
- RealNetwork's RealPlayer which streams in audio and video
- Macromedia's Shockwave, which streams in multimedia and interactive games.

EXPLORATORY ACTIVITY

Bookmark some sites and add them to your Favourites list on your browser.

WEB SERVERS AND ISPs

Web servers are used to store, manage and supply the information on the World Wide Web. The workstation from which a user accesses a server is described as a **client**, and the whole configuration is described as client-server architecture. The special feature of client-server architecture is that most of the data and programs reside on the server, and therefore most of the processing is performed by the server. This makes it possible for the server to support access from a wide variety of different types of workstations, for example, with different processing speeds, and storage capacities.

Originally a server was one large computer, but increasingly the server function is distributed across several machines. Distributing contents to servers around the globe improves the speed with which web pages are displayed. This is particularly useful for sites that are expecting a high hit rate, such as portal sites, like Yahoo!, and Alta Vista.

ISPs (**Internet Service Providers**) are intermediaries that provide home or business users with a connection to the Internet. A basic account with an ISP provides an e-mail address, and access to the Internet. Small companies might use an ISP to host their website, whereas larger companies often prefer to operate their own web server. Through this link subscribers can access the Internet, and send Internet e-mail. ISPs also host websites or provide a link from a company's web servers to enable other companies and consumers to access a corporate website. Examples are CompuServe and AOL. Providers often also offer specialised web content. If this web content is significant and links to large databases, the ISP might also be described as an information service provider, or an OSP (Online Service Provider). A number of organisations offer a free web hosting service, although users of this service are not normally allowed to conduct business through these sites. Yahoo Geocities (www.yahoo.geocities.com), Virgin (www.virgin.net) and Tesco (www.tesco.net) have introduced free services as a means of attracting users to their website or portal. Revenue is not generated by offering the service but through the commercial value of an established community, which includes advertising revenue and e-commerce transactions. Figure 2.5 summarises the criteria that should be considered in the evaluation and selection of an ISP.

Application Service Providers (ASPs) offer a more complete service support package than ISPs. They deliver and manage applications and computer services from a remote data centre to multiple users via the Internet or a private network. ASPs manage Internet and/or internal computer applications on behalf of organisations, thereby removing the need for the organisation to develop internal competence in these areas. Scheduled payment schemes may also make it easier to control the cost of technology-based applications.

Figure 2.5 Criteria for evaluating an ISP

1. Connection availability, in terms of the number of users that can access the site at one time

2. Network considerations, in relation to measures such as speed, downtime and capacity

3. Recovery reputation when things do go wrong

4. Price and pricing strategy

5. Service level agreements, in relation to the range of services that the ISP offers

6. Disk space available to the business

7. Programming support available, especially if database access or specialist programming is required to develop applications

8. E-commerce support, including, for example, online transactions, online payment and shopping carts

9. E-mail services, particularly in relation to the number of accounts that can be provided and how they are accessed

10. Security for data transfer and transactions

GROUP DISCUSSION ACTIVITY

Visit the Internet service providers listed in the following table and complete the details in the table. This will give you a current comparison of the features of these ISPs from the consumer's perspective.

ISP	Monthly fee	Helpline costs	Call costs	Overseas access	Number of e-mail addresses	Disk space	Features/ offers
AOL www.aol.co.uk							
BT Click www.bt.com							
BT Internet www.bt.com							
Freeserve www.freeserve.com							
Ntlworld www.askntl.co.uk							

INTRANETS AND EXTRANETS

Another concept that is often encountered in the Internet world is that of the intranet. An **intranet** is an organisation's internal communication system that uses Internet technology. Intranets use web browsers and graphic user interfaces. Whilst the Internet provides largely unrestricted access to its contents for almost any member of the public, intranets have strict access controls in the form of passwords and firewalls. These security devices protect corporate web pages, document databases and other information from external access. Intranets are particularly useful for large companies operating from several locations.

The boundaries of virtual organisations are fluid and collaboration with suppliers and collaborating organisations is becoming increasingly important in contributing to business success. In order to work effectively with other organisations, a business needs to offer carefully-defined access to the staff of other organisations. This can be achieved through the use of an **extranet**. An extranet is an extended intranet giving access to users beyond the organisation, such as customers, suppliers, collaborators and sometimes even competitors. Extranets also need security devices that protect information from other Internet users and define the level of access for approved users.

INTERNET TOOLS

In addition to the Web, a number of other tools have been created that help in locating, sending and receiving information across the Internet. These various tools either support business processes, such as the transfer of files and documents, or communication. Arenas in which users communicate with organisations or each other are a key component in the virtual landscape.

E-mail

E-mail is a well-established means of communication between two parties or from one person to a defined list of recipients. E-mails are typically written and read in a special e-mail software package. In large companies, the e-mail package will be part of a groupware package that supports the various interactions and shared access necessary in the large organisation. Examples of such groupware packages are Lotus Notes, Microsoft Exchange or Novell GroupWise. Other organisations may use stand-alone packages such as Microsoft Outlook Express or Pegasus mail. A number of portals have sought to attract a community by offering free e-mail facilities that do not require any special software other than a web browser. These include Hotmail (www.hotmail.com), Yahoo! (www.yahoo.co.uk) and Excite (www.excite.co.uk). Hotmail, in particular, has been very successful in attracting the student community, because students typically have more than one address and more than one location through which they might wish to access e-mails (see Figure 2.6). The advantage of not being tied to a specific workstation is

Figure 2.6 Hotmail screen

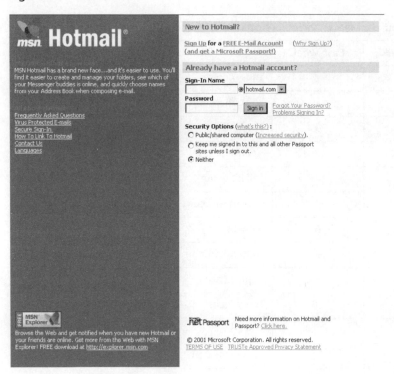

significant. E-mail is often also used as a means of communication in the customer-service context between merchants and their customers. Some traditional businesses have extended this service to provide free e-mail and Internet access as a value-added service for their customers (for example, Virgin (www.virgin.net) and BT Clickfree (www.btinternet.com).

In a marketing context e-mail is also an important push mechanism, in that targeted e-mails are used to announce new products and special offers. This is probably most effectively used in the context of personalised communication based on customer profiles (as discussed further in Chapter 5).

Chat rooms

Chat rooms, otherwise called Internet relay chat, offer real-time communication between individuals. As a user in one location types in a comment, it is simultaneously available to those around the world who are tuned in to a particular channel and they can then type in a reply. The most popular Web-based chat channels are available at 100.Hot.com (www.100hot.com/chat). Chat rooms are also established by merchants to encourage the development of online communities. Some chat rooms offer the opportunity to consult and 'talk with' an expert. The need for all participants to make an appointment to be simultaneously available limits the applicability of chat but the real-time interaction simulates real-world conversations much more effectively than an intermittent e-mail-based exchange. Figure 2.7 lists some popular chat rooms.

Figure 2.7   Chat rooms from 100hot.com

Top ranked chat sites		Updated 2 March 2001
This week	**Last week**	**Site**
1	2	Yahoo.com
2	1	Looksmart.com
3	3	Theglobe.com
4	7	Hearme.com
5	4	Talkcity.com
6	5	Classmates.com
7	6	Babylon.com
8	9	Network54.com
9	8	Topica.com
10	10	Travlan.com
11	11	Mic.com
12	14	Crossdaily.com

Newsgroups

Newsgroups are electronic bulletin boards that are read by a closed community. Questions or statements are posted by one person; the other members reply. Lists of related questions are held together by a thread. Newsgroups are often used by special-interest groups; leisure interests such as theatre or gardening are typical discussion topics. Newsgroups are of interest to businesses as a means of gathering intelligence about consumer attitudes, behaviours, interests, values and beliefs.

FTP (File Transfer Protocol)

FTP is a standard for moving files across the Internet. It is available as a feature of web browsers. Typical business related applications include:

1. Uploading, or transferring HTML web pages and graphics to a website, when a site is created or modified.
2. Communicating large documents or databases, such as price lists, product catalogues and lengthy contract information to customers, particularly in business-to-business marketplaces. This data may be made available through a website as a file that can be downloaded by customers or agents as required.

Telnet

Telnet is a long-established tool that allows remote access to computer systems. It is frequently used, for instance, as a means of deploying sales-order-processing systems across a wide area network. For example, when a holiday is purchased and booked in a travel agency branch, the booking may be placed on the computer at head office using telnet to access the central computer.

GROUP DISCUSSION ACTIVITY

View the list of chat channels listed at 100.Hot.com. Each member of the group should select one on a topic that interests him, visit the chat channel and investigate what he can learn from participating in a chat room.

Compare notes using the following criteria to guide your analysis:

- Level of activity (that is, number of contributions)
- Number of different contributors
- Quality of the content
- Authority of the content
- Organiser's contribution and role and any intervention.

Figure 2.8 draws together a number of aspects of the technologies discussed earlier in this chapter by focusing on the hardware, software and other requirements for connecting to the Internet and hosting a website.

EXPLORATORY ACTIVITY

Visit the domain name registration sites and compare the coverage and services offered at the different sites.

ACCESS TECHNOLOGIES

The network infrastructure provides an important backbone but the growth of commerce in consumer markets depends upon the penetration of technologies that allow access to the Internet. Key amongst these technologies are telephone connections, PCs, television, mobile phones and kiosks. This section reviews some of the characteristics of these various access technologies that constrain the sphere of applicability of the technology.

Telephone connections

Telephone lines are the key technology that has facilitated networking to homes and offices. Telephone connections now convey both analogue and

Figure 2.8 Making it work – connecting and hosting

Connecting to the Internet is straightforward and the connection can be established from any location. The basic requirements are hardware, software and an ISP.

The **hardware** requirements are:

1. A computer to run the web browser and software to connect to the Internet. (Alternatively this can now be achieved through a mobile phone or a set-top TV box)
2. A modem to connect to the Internet (for home and small business connections) or a gateway server to the Internet (from a large organisation)
3. A digital or analogue connection to the Internet, in the form of phone lines, cable or wide-area network.

Essential **software** components are:

1. A web browser that is compatible with the operating system of the computer to view web pages
2. Communication software supporting TCP/IP that allows access to the Internet. For home users using Windows this is achieved by software known as Winsock.

Hosting a website is the term used to describe the process of creating, managing and making a website available. The configuration to support such an activity is a little more complex, although still an option for enthusiastic individuals and small businesses.

Hardware requirements include:

1. A relatively powerful server computer, such as a high specification PC or workstation
2. A gateway server to the Internet
3. A digital connection to the Internet in the form of a dedicated communications link.

Software requirements include:

1. Web server software for sending web content to web browsers when they request it
2. Tools to create content in HTML or XML, and graphics formats using scripting languages such as JavaScript
3. FTP tools to transfer the completed content to the web server
4. Tools to monitor the performance of the website by producing reports from the server log file
5. Communication software supporting TCP/IP.

In addition a host requires an ISP to provide an authorised connection to the Internet. ISPs may also provide the option to host the website; such an option acts as a filter to reduce the risk of outsiders accessing other confidential information within the organisation's databases. Finally, a domain name is necessary for the website. Domain names should be chosen to be memorable, and usually embed the organisation or brand name. Domain names need to be registered. This can be achieved through an ISP or directly with domain name services: InterNic (www.internic.net), CentralNic (www.centralnic.uk.com), and Nominet (www.nominet.org.uk).

digital data in the form of voice, data, graphics and video. One major constraint of existing consumer accessible telecommunications technology is its limited bandwidth. Broadband technologies are currently available in the United States, and are in the process of becoming available in the United Kingdom and Europe. Not only will broadband networks facilitate faster access but they will also support the delivery of a range of services, such as video on demand, music, interactive advertising, real-time online news, interactive gaming and videoconferencing.

PCs

PCs are currently the most widespread access technology to the Internet and commerce. The penetration of PCs in homes and offices is now considerable but penetration does vary between different countries, regions, and social and economic classes. For most market segments the penetration is around 20 to 50 per cent of the population, compared with approaching 100 per cent for the television. Users access the Internet using PCs from home, work or in cybercafes. In recent years there has been a significant trend towards standardisation of PCs with the standard configuration being an Intel (or Intel-like) processor, Microsoft Windows as the operating system, and Microsoft Office as the suite of applications software.

The biggest issue for both users and businesses is managing the changes in PC technology. Each new version of software requires more storage capacity and higher processor speeds. The consumer needs to make decisions about when to update her configuration. Businesses are then presented with the dilemma of which versions of hardware, software and browsers the members of their target segments are using. Applications that are only accessible to those with the latest confirgations may exploit the latest technology but they will be unavailable to a significant proportion of the target market. This is particularly a challenge in the games sector and where multimedia presentations are important.

Digital television

Television sets are available in almost all households in industrial countries. It has taken around 50 years to reach this level of penetration. Set-top boxes with digital capability link televisions to the Internet. At the present time access to the Internet via this technology is through a keypad, which restricts the user's ability to enter data and to search, but this technology does have some potential advantages over PCs. A much higher bandwidth is possible than for PC-based implementations and the screen size is larger. Running video on demand and the use of extensive video sequences are possibilities. In the current Internet, the downloading of such video sequences would take a few minutes; with set-top boxes real-time transmission will be possible. An estate agent might show a walkthrough of a home or a travel agent might offer a view of the highlights of a travel location. As more consumers access the Internet through their TV, designers will need to make their websites look good whether they are accessed through a TV or a PC.

In addition to TV Internet, shopping channels on conventional digital TV are another form of commerce. The format for presenting the product offering is quite different from that on the Internet. Instead of the viewer being able to select the items to browse and perform his own search, selected products are brought to him, in much the same way as they are in advertisements on conventional broadcasts. This tends to mean that the product range is limited and presenters are keen to promote the items on offer. The atmosphere is similar to that of a market, with special offers and persuasive salespeople. The viewer has expressed no prior interest in the item being promoted. This is very much a push channel.

There are a number of different proposals for the integration of Internet and television. These variously envisage that Internet information would be made available to television viewers and broadcast information would be available through the Internet. One model for this is WebTV (www.webtv.net) being promoted by Microsoft. This allows the simultaneous display of a television channel and web pages. WebTV uses an existing television, a telephone line, and a 'set-top box' (about the size of a VCR). Interaction is via a handset. Content designed for WebTV needs to be slightly differently coded than that for the Internet to accommodate the lower resolution of the typical television set and the use of a special WebTV browser.

Mobile phones and WAP

WAP (Wireless Access Protocol) servers have made it possible to access the Internet through mobile phones, Personal Digital Assistants (PDAs) and, also, portable computers and other devices on the move. Mobile phones have a relatively significant penetration, especially in Japan and Europe, and the rate of penetration is particularly impressive. Further, the mobile technologies marketplace is highly price-sensitive (as compared with the PC marketplace) so competition will ensure that prices stay at an accessible level. Key users are the young, business people and the consumer with larger expendable income. These are interesting segments and it is not surprising that the opportunity to provide access to the Internet through this medium is attracting considerable attention. In addition, mobile devices are viewed by the mass market to be much more intuitive for the user and to integrate well with other handset functions. Users will use this technology to execute specific tasks.

Mobile phones and other hand held devices typically have:

- CPUs with limited power
- Limited memory
- Limited power consumption constrained by battery life
- Small displays
- A variety of input devices, including phone pad, voice input and fold-up keyboard.

One of the main constraints of **m-commerce** is the display on mobile phones. This is small and lacks colour, and has limited graphics capabilities. The content of a website needs to be adapted to a format readable on a small screen. As electronic banking requires no graphics, little text and just a few numbers, banking is an ideal early application. Another challenge is the relatively limited bandwidth available to transmit data to such devices. Wireless data networks also have more latency, less connection stability and less predictable availability. Full m-commerce also requires appropriate payment methods; development is focused on smart cards, e-wallets and virtual credit cards.

WAP applications are developed using Wireless Mark-up Language (WML). WMLScript is similar to JavaScript in supporting interactivity in this environment.

EXPLORATORY ACTIVITY

By talking to friends with a WAP mobile phone or by examining the publicity from a bank, investigate the banking transactions that can be executed using a mobile phone.

Kiosks

Information kiosks, or public access kiosks, are located in public thorough-fares, shopping malls, airports, railway stations and other locations as a substitute for, or to complement customer service, through a human service agent. The latest kiosks are both a means of accessing the Internet – and thereby open up options in terms of commerce – or supporting transactions, such as placing orders through a dedicated link to a specific supplier.

Early kiosks were typically uninteresting boxes with relatively simple interfaces, designed specifically to allow customers to conduct a simple transaction, such as placing an order or locating a specific item of information like a recipe or a repayment rate for a mortgage. For example, Argos had kiosks in some of its stores through which it was possible to order items in the Argos catalogue. The Halifax Building Society had kiosks that supported the calculation of repayments on mortgages and other loans. The latest generation of kiosks represents a significant change of perspective on the role and nature of kiosks. These kiosks support multiple functions including most or all of:

- information provision,
- interaction between user and consumer to support the customisation of information,
- transactions (such as ticket purchase), and
- relationship building through loyalty schemes or other communication opportunities.

Most significantly, these kiosks exhibit a shift from task focus to customer focus in kiosk design. Instead of being designed to allow a customer to complete a single task or set of closely related tasks, the kiosks offer a range of information and services tailored to the 'customer in context'. Thus a kiosk in a shopping centre focuses on shopping-related transactions, and information, whilst a kiosk in a hotel lobby provides travel and tourist information (often with several language options) appropriate to the location of the hotel. This transition to multifunctionality and the creation of a complete support service for the 'customer in context' necessitates strategic collaboration in the provision of the information and services that can be accessed through the kiosk. Responsibility for the management of the kiosk in these instances often lies with an infomediary, who specialises in kiosks, rather than individual retailers or store groups.

Early kiosks had very simple touch screen interfaces in which customers selected options by touching one of a number of buttons and thereby navigated their way through the limited number of screens available for display. The latest kiosks offer Windows or Web type functionality that includes scroll bars, pointer, hyperlinks, data entry forms, drop-down lists and animation – which makes for a more complex interface. Also the location and physical design of the kiosk and its housing is much more eye-catching than previously. Consistency with corporate images, the use of moving images either on the screen itself (in the form of video feeds or animation), or on television screens above the kiosks all attract attention. Figure 2.9 shows how kiosk facilities have developed.

Figure 2.9 Comparing early kiosks with the latest developments

	Early Kiosks	**Kiosks 21**
Physical characteristics	Uninteresting boxes, static displays	Eye-catching housings, consistent with corporate image. Moving images
Dialog design	Menu-based access to a limited number of screens. Touch screen	Web/Windows-like interfaces, with data entry dialog boxes, dropdown lists, scroll bars, pointer and hyperlinks. Touch screen supplemented by keyboard
Location	In-store, in a corner	In public thoroughfares, entrances and centrally positioned
Philosophy	Task based	Customer service-based
Originator	Service provider or retailer	Infomediary or assembler
Transaction	Single transaction	Multiple transactions, communication and information provision
Connectivity	Stand alone or connected to one proprietary database	Internet enabled for real-time information provision and communication

EXPLORATORY ACTIVITY

When you spot a kiosk in a shopping centre, a railway station, or an airport, investigate the transactions that can be performed through the kiosk.

CHAPTER SUMMARY

This chapter has introduced some of the technology that underpins e-business. The Internet and the Web are key technologies, but other access technologies, such as PCs, digital television, kiosks , and mobile technologies may also be very significant for specific applications. The interconnectivity and ubiquitous nature of the Internet and the Web is achieved through protocols or standards such as FTP, HTTP and mark-up languages. Web browsers make it possible for users to navigate through the web. Web pages and sites are hosted either by an organisation or through an Internet Service Provider. In addition to using the Internet, organisations may use Internet protocols as the basis for intranets (within the organisation) and extranets (for wider access across their community).

KEY CONCEPTS

Internet is a collection of interlinked computer networks, or a network of networks.

Internet protocols are standards that support the open communications and inter-connected nature of the Internet.

World Wide Web (WWW) or the Web are those servers linked to the Internet using the HTTP protocol.

URL (Universal Resource Locator) is an addressing system that allows the location of any object stored on a networked computer to be uniquely identified.

Mark-up languages are standard languages used to define the text and layout of web pages.

HTTP (Hypertext Transfer Protocol) is a standard that defines the way in which information is transmitted across the Internet and thereby allows copies of target sites on remote servers to be retrieved and displayed.

continued

Web browser or **browser** is a client program that provides the user with control over the retrieval process across the Web.

Java is a programming language that permits complex applications, including graphics, to be developed for access using a web browser.

Home pages are the pages on which organisations or individuals present their information.

Websites are a collection of home pages on the same server.

Scripting languages are programming languages that are used to write scripts. Scripts support animation and interactivity, such as the generation of an acknowledgement for an order.

Plug-ins allow rich content files, such as video, radio programmes, and other multi-media content to play through browsers.

Web servers are used to store, manage and supply information on the World Wide Web.

Internet Service Providers provide home or business users with a connection to the Internet.

Application Service Providers (ASPs) are a type of ISP that delivers a more complete service package, including the management of applications and computer services from a remote data centre to multiple users via the Internet or a private network.

Intranets are communication systems internal to organisations that use Internet technology.

Extranets are extended intranets allowing access to users outside the organisation such as customers, suppliers, collaborators and sometimes competitors.

E-mail is a means of communication between two parties or from one person to a defined list of recipients.

Chat rooms offer real-time communication between two or more individuals.

Newsgroups are electronic bulletin boards whose content can only be read by a closed community.

continued

FTP (File Transfer Protocol) is a standard or Internet protocol that allows files to be moved across the Internet.

Telnet is an Internet protocol that supports remote access to computer systems.

Hosting a website is the process of creating, managing and generally making available a website.

M-commerce is electronic commerce through mobile technologies such as mobile phones and Personal Digital Assistants (PDAs).

WAP (Wireless Application Protocol) is a protocol to allow 'wireless' access to the Internet, such as is used with mobile technologies.

Information kiosks are electronic service points typically located in public thoroughfares and retail outlets, through which information, e-mail, and web pages can be accessed, and transactions can be executed.

ASSESSMENT QUESTIONS

1. Why is there a need for parallel technologies? Discuss the criteria that you might use to differentiate between the different access technologies, such as the PC, the mobile phone and digital television, when assessing these technologies for a specific application.
2. Explain the difference between the Internet and the Web. In what sense is the differentiation important?
3. What is meant by the following terms: HTML, HTTP, browser, home page and URL?
4. Using examples, discuss the structure of a URL. What factors should be considered in the design of a URL?
5. What is an Internet Service Provider? What contributions do ISPs make to e-commerce?
6. Compare the following Internet tools: chat rooms, Usenet newsgroups, FTP and e-mail.
7. Explain the components of the hardware and software configuration that is necessary to host a website.
8. WAP-enabled mobile phones and kiosks are two access technologies for users on the move. Compare these technologies and their relative usefulness to consumers in the arena of banking transactions.
9. In what ways are the latest generation of information kiosks different from earlier generations?

GROUP ASSESSMENT 1 – WEBSITE CREATION

Plan a simple website of, say, 5–10 pages for a club or organisation with which you are associated. Discuss and determine the information content and the basic structure, or information architecture, of the site.

- Register with one of the ISPs that allows you to create your own website. Using the facilities that it offers to support you with the process, implement your design for this website.

- Evaluate your website by drawing up a table of its strengths and weaknesses.

GROUP ASSESSMENT 2 – MOBILE TECHNOLOGIES

Use a search engine to locate as many sites as possible that provide information about mobile Internet technologies. For each site visited write a summary of the site. Arrange these summaries to create a guide to websites that are useful in monitoring developments in mobile Internet technologies.

REFERENCES

Chaffey, D, Mayer, R, Johnston, K and Ellis-Chadwick, F (2000) *Internet marketing*. Harlow: Pearson Education.

Cram, C M (2001) *E-commerce concepts*. Boston: Thomson Learning.

Daum, B and Scheller, M (2000) *Success with electronic business: design, architecture and technology of electronic business systems*. Boston: Addison-Wesley.

Ellsworth, J H and Ellsworth, M V (1997) *Marketing on the Internet*. 2nd edn. New York: Wiley.

Evans, P B and Wurster, T S (1999) Getting real about virtual commerce, *Harvard Business Review*, Nov-Dec, 84–94.

Gabay, J J (2000) *Successful cyberm@rketing in a week*. Abingdon: Hodder & Stoughton.

Hanson, W (2000) *Principles of Internet marketing*. Cincinnati, Ohio: South-Western College Publishing.

Hardaker, G and Graham, G (2001) *Wired marketing: energizing business for e-commerce*. Chichester: Wiley.

Kalakota, R and Robinson, M (1999) *E-business: roadmap for success*. Boston: Addison-Wesley.

Kleindl, B A (2001) *Strategic electronic marketing: managing e-business*. Cincinnati, Ohio: South Western College Publishing.

May, P (2000) *The business of ecommerce; from corporate strategy to technology*. Cambridge: Cambridge University Press.

Morath, P (2000) *Success @ e-business*. London: McGraw-Hill.

Peterson, R A (1997) Electronic marketing and the consumer. Thousand Oaks, London: Sage Publications.

Sterne, J (1999) *World Wide Web marketing*. 2nd edn. New York: Wiley.

Timmers, P (1999) *Electronic commerce: strategies and models for business-to-business trading*. Chichester: Wiley.

Turban E, Lee, J , King, D and Chung, H M (2000) *Electronic commerce: a managerial perspective*. New Jersey: Prentice Hall.

Website design and searching 3

After reading this chapter you will:

- Appreciate the importance of considering different audiences in website design
- Be able to explain the key considerations in the design of a home page
- Understand that website content needs to be both dynamic and valuable
- Be aware of the different approaches to navigation within websites
- Be able to take account of colour, shapes and type styles, graphics and forms when evaluating website design
- Be able to draft a plan to reflect the stages and processes in the creation and maintenance of a website
- Be aware of the array of search tools for locating sites and product offerings
- Be more effective in searching and navigating the Internet

INTRODUCTION

This chapter is concerned with website design, navigation and searching and, in general, the consumer response to specific features embedded in the interface between the consumer and the organisation. This interface is largely embodied in the website so much of the work in this area is concerned with the impact of various aspects of website design. Response is typically measured in terms of click through rates and, more recently, in purchases.

Much of the earlier research on the Internet and marketing was in the area of advertising because the Internet was a communication, or marketing communication, medium long before commerce and transactions were possible. In this literature there are many contributions on issues related to advertising effectiveness, such as site attractiveness, hit rates, visit rates, and click-through rates. This area is explored more fully in Chapter 4. In addition, the human–computer interaction literature has many contributions on effective website design, user attention, and search and navigation strategies. These issues are the focus of this chapter.

This chapter first introduces some principles of website design as these are understood to affect user understanding of the electronic environment and to affect their consequent behaviour. The first group of sections (pp. 48–69) focuses on individual websites. The next section then introduces some of the tools that are available to support the consumer in searching for information or products on the Web or navigating between websites. These facilities are examined at a micro level by considering the different indexing languages and search tools that they offer to consumers. The final section explores the variety of different ways in which consumers may approach the information search that is associated with the consumer-buying process. Implicit in this chapter are the assumptions that consumers do use information in purchase-decision making, and that some of them sometimes engage in a searching process. In other words, it is assumed that persuasive marketing of specific websites does not send the consumer immediately in the direction of one website armed with the URL, and that the consumer is prepared, on occasions, to consider alternatives. Chapters 4, 5 and 6 investigate other factors that affect consumer response to organisations in the virtual marketplace.

WEBSITE DESIGN

The design of the website defines the e-experience of the site visitor. Accordingly the website must have all of the features that support the functions of an e-business as summarised in Figure 1.1: content, communication, commerce and community. Small businesses that are merely seeking Web presence and a point of contact with customers may need only a simple website. However, businesses that need to provide access to a catalogue of products or a significant database of information, as well as opportunities to transact business, need to reflect on the experience that the website provides. Later chapters explore the issues of marketing communication, customer service and community building in more detail. This chapter examines some of the features and considerations in effective website design.

Website design is concerned with creating a website that:

- Is usable and takes account of recommendations from the human–computer interaction literature in the context of usability.
- Communicates appropriate marketing messages to customers, which means that matters such as brand, corporate image and relationships need to be accommodated.
- Supports an appropriate range of functions in relation to communication, customer service and transactions.

This means striking a balance between what the business wants an audience to see, hear, read, learn and do, and what the audience want to see, hear, read, learn and do. The issue of website design is crucial. The site will not attract and capture regular visitors unless it is easy to access, interesting, valuable, generally adds value from the user's perspective and offers a pleasant or even pleasurable experience.

Audience

Most organisational websites have a number of different audiences, particularly if the website is accessible through Internet, intranet and extranet. Figure 3.1 summarises some typical audiences for a website.

Websites are public access with a range of different audiences. As such there are a number of challenges with which system designers are faced. In general, public access systems exhibit challenges in respect of both the user

Figure 3.1 Audiences for an organisational website

Audience	Examples
Customers and buyers	New and existing prospects Consumers and business buyers Different market types Different locations
Staff	New and existing staff Different functions and professional expertises Sales staff involved with different markets Staff at different locations
Other stakeholders	New and existing suppliers Distributors Investors Media Students

profile and the task. (Rowley and Slack, 1998) The user profile has two aspects, which make system design more demanding:

■ Users have a wide range of different educational backgrounds and levels of experience with the system. Users range from being subject domain novices and computer novices all the way to subject experts and computer experts. The degree of knowledgeability of the computer user and the domain experience should be reflected in the design of the user-interface prompts, alerts and help facilities. Developers must also consider the needs of the system manager as user.

■ A large proportion of the population are naive and new users who need to adapt quickly to different systems. Many users are also subject novices and their system use is constrained by their inability to appreciate what the system can be expected to contain.

The task is ill defined and there is an element of uncertainty in both:

■ What the user is likely to retrieve and accept as output from the process
■ The search strategies that the user will adopt and find to be the most effective.

In the Internet environment, the remoteness between information provider and information user is especially acute. Here, for example:

■ The designer does not know who the user will be, and
■ The user often does not understand how the search engines are conducting the search process.

In addition, searchers will perform a range of different kinds of searches, including browsing and, at the other end of the spectrum, directed searching for a specific item, as discussed later in this chapter.

EXPLORATORY ACTIVITY

Visit the website of your university or college. In a few sentences describe the audiences that you think this website is designed to reach. Explain how this is achieved in terms of:

■ Messages
■ Content
■ Information structure and navigation
■ Design and graphics.

DESIGNING A HOME PAGE

The particular challenge of website design is the small screen, and this screen is even smaller for laptop PCs and mobile phones. Through the home page the organisation needs to communicate key messages about who they are and what they have to offer, as well as displaying the navigation devices that will assist users to locate the part of the website that they would find to be of value. Figure 3.2 summarises some of the typical contents of a website. It is possible to design a home page that is larger than the screen on which it will

Figure 3.2 Checklist of typical contents of a website

What's new	
What's been added since (date)	News
New products	Company and industry events
Press releases	
About the company	
History	Financial information
Contacts and key people	Employment opportunities
Current achievements, including	
annual reports	
Product information	
Product catalogue	Product information and specifications
Online sales	Product evaluations
Stock levels and delivery times	Special offers
Customer service	
Frequently asked questions	Product support
Order processing support	Help desk
Returns policy and support	
Community	
Chat rooms	Bulletin boards
Expert forums	

be displayed at the customer end, but this is generally not satisfactory because:

- The home page looks unfinished and untidy
- Users are reluctant to scroll and will often miss any information that is not displayed on the screen when the home page is first loaded.

One way to solve this dilemma is to create a scrolling window within the screen, whilst the title bar and the menu bar remain stable.

Another important feature of the home page is that it must be simple. Often businesses are so eager to make sure that all of the messages that they wish to communicate feature on the home page that it becomes overcrowded and jumbled. Portals, such as search engines eager to provide access to as many other websites as possible and to generate income from banner ads, are prone to overcrowding. Packing dense information onto an opening page is a real challenge. The quantity of information that can be communicated can be optimised with attention to the layout of a web page. It is now relatively standard practice to:

- Include a button bar at the top of the home page that will appear in a similar or identical form on every page of the site.
- Include a column on the left of the site that includes the index/contents/site guide.
- Include a menu at the bottom of the page that appears at the bottom of every page on the site.
- Include the content of the page, including any special offers or other items that the user should see, in the centre of the screen.

Since the first three features will often be carried over, possibly in a modified form, to other pages on the website, the design of the home page determines a number of aspects of the design and navigational features of the remainder of the site. This typical home-page layout also accommodates the way in which people scan web pages. Web pages are scanned in a Z-pattern. That is, the user views the top line, scans diagonally across the body of the page, and then along the bottom of the screen. Thus, the user is first orientated by the top bar, has key products or messages drawn to his attention in the middle of the screen, and discovers other menu options on the left-hand side of the screen or across the bottom of the screen. The left-hand menu is also likely to be read from bottom to top. If, instead, a right-hand column menu is used, this will be read from top to bottom.

GROUP DISCUSSION ACTIVITY

Examine the web pages in this book. Discuss the object or text that has been positioned in the middle of the screen (on the diagonal of the Z). What does this tell you about the key message that this organisation wants to communicate to its audience? Make a table showing the messages that, on the basis of your analysis, you think that the different organisations are seeking to communicate.

GROUP DISCUSSION ACTIVITY

Using Figure 3.2 as a checklist revisit the website of your university or college and tick off those components that appear on this website. Remember that in this context 'products' are often 'courses' and other activities such as research or consultancy services. Discuss:

- What is meant by the term 'customer service' in this context.
- How 'communities' might be supported through such a website.

Dynamic content

The information content of web pages is an important element in e-business. Often in this context information content and marketing messages are subtly intertwined. Both need to be dynamic and changing in order to encourage customers to return to a site. There are three types of information content that might be used by an organisation to attract customers to its site:

1. *Valuable information,* which is offered to users to entice and engage them. This might include information about the company, its products and the industry. This category of information is free. Typical examples are games or other information that is relevant to the business, or community-generated information (see Chapter 6 on online communities).

2. *More valuable information*, which may be used to engage users into a dialogue. An example might be: 'We've collected a wide variety of copyright free images. You can download them after helping us to improve our website. Please complete the following brief evaluation form.'

3. *Trading information*, which is information for which customers pay. This information is the stock-in-trade of the knowledge business. For example, publishers typically allow access to contents pages of journals and possibly abstracts of articles but charge for delivery of the full text of the article. Other businesses may offer content in, say, the form of videos, databases or unique images which are ancillary to their main business.

EXPLORATORY ACTIVITY

Visit a website of your choice and make a list of the different types of information that are made available through the website.

NAVIGATION

Provided that attention has been paid to the issues addressed above, a customer arriving at the home page of a website knows where she is. The corporate logo and the short summary of what the organisation does and stands for act as useful initial orientation. However, once a user moves away from the home page to view other pages on the site, or even the pages of associated organisations, it is easy for the user to become lost in cyberspace, unless the website provides anchors, flags and maps which assist in the navigation of the website. If a user cannot locate the area of a website that she wishes to view, whether she is concerned with information gathering, making enquiries or completing transactions, she will become frustrated with the website and is unlikely to visit again. Users need to be able to go quickly to the area of the site that is of interest to them. Whilst there is no experimental evidence that indicates how many clicks a user will tolerate, the 'three clicks' principle is a useful aid to web page design. Can a user arrive at where she wishes to go with only three clicks?

Navigation is concerned with moving between different parts of a website. It is governed by menu arrangements, site structure and the layout of individual pages. Flow is related to navigation. Hoffman and Novak (1996) suggested that **flow** describes the ease with which users find the information that they need as they move between different parts of the site. Good navigational support should enhance the smoothness of flow.

Navigation involves:

- Designing and structuring individual pages
- Choosing an appropriate site structure, and
- Offering users tools to help them to find their way around that site structure.

MIXING INFORMATION AND COMMERCE – GUARDIAN UNLIMITED

Figure 3.3 shows the Guardian Unlimited money page (www.guardian.co.uk/money). The homepage offers access to a wide range of different types of information and commercial links. For example, there are special reports on a number of financial issues, news items, information on choosing an ISA, and, through the menu at the top of the screen, access to a number of other sources of information. Various of the banner ads provide links to financial services providers. For example, clicking on the Virgin Credit Card banner ad takes the surfer to a page showing information on personal loans and other services available from Virgin Credit Card.

Figure 3.3 The Guardian Unlimited Money home page

Attention to consistency, simplicity and context will make a website easy to navigate:

- *Consistency.* The user needs to be presented with a consistent user interface across all areas of the site.
- *Simplicity.* Simplicity relates to the quantity of information and the way in which it is grouped or 'chunked'. The simplicity of a website is associated with the number of levels in a menu hierarchy – the fewer levels the better.
- *Context.* Signposts are necessary so that users understand where they are in the site.

Navigation can be supported through the following devices.

Using the title bar as a placeholder

The title bar is retained at the top of every page in the website. The user can then easily go back to the home page, or back to the entry point for one of the main sections on the site. A second bar might display the heading of the section that the user is currently viewing and possibly a menu that shows the main subsections in that section. ToysЯus (www.toysrus.co.uk) offer effective and simple navigation. The menu bar across the top provides links to pages giving general information about the company and its services. This also appears at the bottom of the screen, tying the website together. The next horizontal section presents an internal advertisement, and links to screens where customers can view products that they have already selected. The colour-coded submenu identifies the current page as being Home, and offers next level navigation.

Menus and contents pages

Menus can be offered either as a set of headings on a screen, as a drop-down list box, or as a series of graphic icons or buttons. The user clicks on an appropriate menu item. Menus are widely recognised to be helpful to novice users because the menu options provide a guide to the users in relation to system functionality. In this context, the menus give an overview of the content of a website or, in the case of a portal, the websites to which the portal provides access. Menus can be discretely embedded in a web page. Some websites prefer to make transparent this hierarchy of sections, or departments, according to which their site is organised. To do this they may use contents pages. Tesco (www.tesco.com) supplements the basic department structure with a range of other tools. Themed lists group foods that go together, Quickstart lists the most popular products, and Express Shopper is based on the shopper creating a simple shopping list. The search engine then offers a selection of products to match the items on the shopping list. Menu options may be selected by moving the pointer over them, and clicking. The pointer may change shape when it is over a menu option, or the colour of the menu option may change (known as **roll-over**).

Search tools

Search tools for navigating within a site operate in a similar way to search engines that locate specific sites, as discussed in the later section on search

Figure 3.4 ToysЯus web page

tools. The user is invited to enter a phrase, and the search tools will locate the occurrence of the phrase within the website. A list of hits should identify one or more locations in which users can find information relevant to their search phrase. Large sites and, specifically, information product sites may also have search engines that allow advanced search options, as discussed in the later section on search tools. Even within a site search engines are prone to generate false drops and users are not always able to locate the area of the site that they are seeking. Careful attention to structuring of the site and the terminology used in section headings can improve the relevance and helpfulness of search output.

Figure 3.5 An example of search help: Buyers Index

■ What information or fields can I search?

■ Why do I see listings that do not contain my search words?

■ What characters can I use in my search words?

■ Can I search for phrases?

■ What are the 'Listing Types' and their associated icons?

■ What is the difference between 'Retail' and 'Wholesale'?

■ What is meant by 'Conditional' and 'Unconditional' return policies?

■ What does the 'Include Similar Words' option do?

Help

Help can provide guidance on navigation and searching, product offerings, customer service and communities. Figure 3.5 shows the questions on which help is provided in searching Buyers Index, a service which accesses over 11 000 websites and mail order catalogues.

Links to other sites

Links to other sites are useful and users are likely to return to a site that contains helpful pointers to additional information. However, it is important that the user is aware that she is leaving one site and moving onto another site. In addition to the navigational support that users might need in moving from one site to another, there may be an issue of liability. Accordingly, it is important to indicate to the user that she is leaving a site and moving on. Boundary messages such as 'Are you sure that there isn't anything else that you would like to buy?' can remind the user that she is moving between sites. Links back to the first site on any partner sites also ensure that users are reminded of the opportunity to return.

OTHER ELEMENTS OF WEBSITES

Colours

Colour is a significant component of website design. Colour can affect readability and usability, but it can also communicate values and cultivate expectations. Different combinations of colours have different associations. Thus red, white and blue with stars and stripes triggers images of the US flag; the same colours used with triangles and diagonal lines and in a different balance may be associated with the UK flag. Certain combinations of colours are common in specific industries, and the business that does not acknowledge these colours will not be identified with its sector. Yet such colour associations are not global. For example, in the Western World and the United States, the colour blue represents trust but in Korea, pastel shades, like

Figure 3.6 Using colour

> **Dos**
> Do concentrate colour in a few, possibly large, areas
> Do use colour on company logos and as a reverse on document headings
> Do use colour with business charts and graphs
> Do use colour tinting behind graphics to bring them alive
> Do use colour to separate and provide selective emphasis
> Do use colour to organise elements of tables
> Do use colour for connection devices, such as arrows, circles etc.
> Do use colour on the website in a way that is consistent with the use of colour in other marketing communications
>
> **Don'ts**
> Do not add colour just to brighten things up or out of habit.
> Do not scatter mixed colours across the page
> Do not use tinted backgrounds behind small type
> Do not use colour for all of the text on a page or it will lose impact. Coloured text is hard to read
> Do not display coloured text over a background of a tint of the same colour
> Do not use colour for thin lines, vertical rules and small graphics

pink, are more likely to communicate trust. In the Western world the colour white represents joy and union but in many Far Eastern countries, white represents mourning. When choosing colour, website audiences need to be considered.

Colour can be used to:

1. *Add emphasis*. Red is often used in spreadsheets to indicate negative numbers.
2. *Organise*. Gradients lead the eye through content. Shades can indicate sidebars or areas of particularly pertinent or related information. Changing a colour can demarcate a clear separation between points of interest or sections.
3. *Add impact*. Colour is often used in graphics.
4. *Create emotion*. Bright colours suggest optimism, aggression and energy. Dark colours suggest wealth and conservatism. Back-to-nature colours suggest holiday and seasonal themes.

Figure 3.6 summarises some dos and don'ts in the use of colour.

Shapes and type styles

Shapes are key elements in web page design. Shapes have a subtler effect than colours. For example, using circles and rounded boxes promotes the feeling of security. Many logos use a combination of circles and rounded boxes.

Type styles also communicate the style, mood and temperament of a web page. The type style is the personality of the publication and should match the personality and values of the intended audience. Type style must be appropriate to the purpose. Above all else the type style must be legible and readable. It is usually advisable to stick with no more than two or three typefaces within a web page. Any body text should always be displayed in the same typeface. Other typefaces can be used for headings and subheadings and for areas that need emphasis.

GROUP DISCUSSION ACTIVITY

Examine the colours and typefaces used on a website of your choice, and answer the following questions:

- How many different colours are used?
- Is colour used to organise information on the page? Give examples.
- Is colour used for impact or to draw attention to an area of the screen? Give examples.
- Is colour used on text or graphics?
- Which uses of colour are the most effective?
- How many typefaces are used?
- If different typefaces are used, how are the different typefaces used?
- What personality do the typefaces lend to the page?
- What is the overall message that colour and typeface, and other features of design (without reference to the text) communicates?

Graphics

. . . a picture is worth a thousand words. But a picture takes a thousand times more data than a word. (Sterne, 1999, p. 75)

Graphics can make a page look more interesting. Software developers have a range of graphics tools at their disposal, including both static and animated graphics. They create web pages embedding graphics on fast machines with big monitors. Users, on the other hand, typically have smaller screens (and lower resolution and fewer colours). Portable PCs and mobile phones can have significantly smaller screens and much slower connections to the server. Even though technology makes ever faster connections available, Netiquette – the code of behaviour for the Internet – dictates that we all use this Internet resource economically. Graphics need to be effective for the lowest common denominator in terms of the technology. The key issue about the use of graphics is the download time. If downloading takes more than a few seconds, the user is likely to become dissatisfied with the site even before he has encountered any of its content. There are ways to shrink graphics to smaller file sizes so that they are much faster to load, and with very little deterioration in image quality. The message is that graphics should not just be used for decoration, but must have a clearly understood purpose. Another approach that can be useful is a 'Text only' button, displayed at the top of the screen, that can be selected as the page begins to load. Alternatively, pictures can be displayed as icons initially, and the user can then choose whether to display a larger graphic.

Forms

Forms are important for interacting with a website. They are a common means of collecting customer information. They are used to:

- Collect customer and user registration details
- Allow customers to formulate more complex search strategies
- Collect customer orders
- Collect customer feedback.

The checklist in Figure 3.7 summarises a number of points of good practice in relation to form design and use. Figure 3.8 shows a form used during a registration process.

EXPLORATORY ACTIVITY

Visit two websites concerned with booking boating holidays on inland water-ways. Make a list of the types of forms that each site uses. Compare these forms. What are the similarities and differences? Possible sites for evaluation are www.british-waterways.org, www.broads.co.uk, www.canalholidays.com.

EXPLORATORY ACTIVITY

Visit a website of your choice and evaluate the forms that are used on the site, using the criteria in the checklist.

EXPLORATORY ACTIVITY

1. Examine a series of websites in the insurance industry in the United Kingdom (or a country of your choice). What are the colours for this industry?
2. Take any two websites and examine their use of colour for: emphasis, organisation, impact and emotion.
3. Visit the following two sites: indigosquare.com, and Fish4.com and compare the use of graphics.

Figure 3.7   Checklist for completion of online forms

1. Information requested should be kept to a minimum. This makes the form quicker to complete, and also prevents balking arising from customer sensitivity about offering too much information.

2. Make it clear why information is being collected. Customers will offer more information if they can have a greater insight into the way in which the information will be used. They feel that the company values their participation.

3. Observe good form layout conventions, and try to place the data entry boxes in a 'logical' order for the task that the customer is completing.

4. Use clear prompts and labels on the form.

5. Indicate mandatory fields, and don't leave it to an error message at the end of the form completion to direct customer's back to uncompleted mandatory fields.

6. Information should be validated when the customer has completed the entry of data. The user should be clearly prompted with what information is missing and why.

7. Provide opt-out. Check boxes should be made available so that the user can indicate if they do not wish to receive further marketing communications from the merchant.

8. Provide prompt confirmation. As soon as an organisation has received a form it should confirm that receipt, and indicate what action the customer can expect next. Standard e-mail can acknowledge receipt, and, for example provide information about delivery arrangements.

Figure 3.8   An example of a registration form

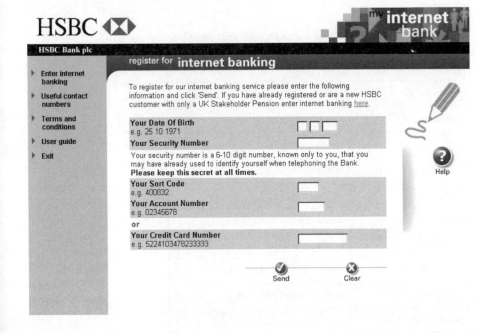

GROUP DISCUSSION ACTIVITY

Table 3.9 shows the websites visited in a survey conducted by Systems Concepts Ltd to measure the user friendliness of UK Premier League Football Club websites. Evaluators tried to carry out two common tasks on each site:

■ To find out the team's next fixture
■ To buy a home kit for a ten year old.

The websites of these large organisations exhibited a number of problems. These include:

■ Search function only working on part of the site
■ No fixtures list on home page
■ Small font with too many options on home page
■ No kit ordering option
■ Difficult to read text buttons
■ Registration to make purchases causes database error
■ Frequent pop-up adverts encourage visitors to exit to another site
■ Site availability intermittent.

Your activity is to visit some of these sites, to conduct the trial searches and to investigate whether any of these sites still exhibit these limitations.

Figure 3.9   Web addresses of some Premiership websites

Team	Web address
Tottenham	www.spurs.co.uk
Manchester City	www.mcfc.co.uk
Ipswich	www.itfc.co.uk
Leicester	www.lcfc.co.uk
Derby	www.dcfc.co.uk
Aston Villa	www.astonvilla-fc.co.uk
Bradford	www.bradfordcityfc.co.uk
Sunderland	www.sunderland-afc.com
Liverpool	www.liverpoolfc.net
Manchester United	www.manutd.com

Databases

Forms collect data to be entered into databases. XML is the basis for this link. Databases have an increasingly important role in websites, both in providing the data that is displayed on the website and in collecting data that is entered through the website. All of the large database systems suppliers, such as Oracle, Sybase and Microsoft, offer applications that support web-to-database integration. Databases are used in:

Content management. In complex and dynamically changing websites, the format of the website is separated from the content. Typically the content of the website is created and stored in a database, and then this is dynamically uploaded into a preformatted template to create the web pages. As the content and format are separate they can be changed independently. This makes it possible to instil greater consistency in formatting of web pages, but also allows content creators to focus on the content and its quality, without being distracted by formatting considerations. Content may be derived from both internal and external sources.

Customer service. Product catalogues, frequently asked questions (FAQs) and many other items of information that the customer needs to access are stored in databases.

Customer relationship management. Customer details are entered into the customer database on registration. Further details can be recorded with each transaction, and these can be used as the basis for customisation and relationship management as discussed in later chapters.

Multimedia components

Developing and converging technologies, coupled with broadband networks, will gradually fuel the development of more sophisticated websites that include real-time audio, real-time video and internet videoconferencing. News sites, such as ABN, are using real-time video streaming to broadcast news through their website. Realnetworks (www.real.com) are broadcasting live sports, music, news and entertainment. NetMeeting offers free videoconferencing products. Internet conferencing allows users to share data through text messaging, whiteboard, audio and video in real time.

EXPLORATORY ACTIVITY

Visit the sites of Open Market (www.shopsite.com) and Mercante (www.mercante.com) and explore the features of Shopsite and SoftCart, respectively. This software offers a quick route to the creation of a transaction- or e-commerce-based website.

CREATING AND MAINTAINING A WEBSITE

Developing a website is an integral part of the development of an e-business presence. This is discussed in more detail from a strategic perspective in Chapter 8. This section identifies the stages in the process of creating and managing a website and discusses some of the tools that are available to assist in this process. Figure 3.10 summarises the key stages in this process. These stages proceed in roughly the order that they are listed in Figure 3.10, but the development process is iterative and there may be many cycles through some of the stages. Further, promotion does not start after publication, but must be planned as the site is being developed. In addition, many businesses with sites review and develop those sites and may at any time review any of the decisions made in earlier design projects. We discuss these stages below.

Initiate the project

A project to create a website will emerge from a strategic planning process that acknowledges the need for a website, and sets the broad objectives of the website. There may then need to be a process that develops these objectives more fully, identifies the resources (IT, staff and budgets) necessary to execute the project, and agrees a project plan and timescale. The project plan should include all of the stages discussed below.

Figure 3.10 Stages in website development

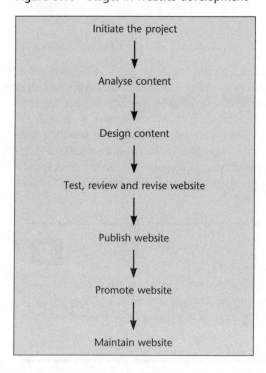

Other preliminary issues to be considered include domain name registration and selecting the Internet service provider, as discussed in the previous chapter.

No project will get started without some people to execute it. Like many information systems projects, website design is a team activity. Typical members of this team are:

1. *Site sponsors* – the managers who set the objectives for the site and provide the financial and other resource base to support the project.
2. *Site owner* – the site owner is the person who has responsibility for the website within the organisation. Typically this will be the marketing manager.
3. *Project manager* – the project manager is responsible for planning and coordinating the website project. It is her responsibility to ensure that the project delivers to plan and within budget, and generally meets objectives. In small organisations the project manager might also be the site owner.
4. *Site designer* – the site designer designs the site, including its layout and structure.
5. *Content developer* – the content developer writes the copy for the site, and converts it into a form suitable for the site.
6. *Web master* – the web master is responsible for the technical aspects of the site, such as availability, speed, working links between pages and connections to company databases. In small organisations, the web master may take on the roles of graphic designer and content developer.
7. *Stakeholders* are typically the users of the site and others whose working practices are affected by the presence of the site as a communication medium.

The multiplicity and diversity of these different roles reflects the complexity of website design.

Analyse the content

Analysis of the content starts with the objectives of the website. These will include:

- The e-business functions that are to be facilitated through the website
- The support necessary at different stages in the consumer decision making and buying process
- The audience, including their knowledge of the organisation's products (there may be significant differences between business-to-business and business-to-consumer marketplaces in this context), their experience with e-shopping or e-acquisition
- The messages that the organisation wishes to communicate to the intended audience
- Any technical constraints that might, for example, affect the extent and nature of the use of graphics
- Any constraints imposed by the need to integrate the website with other business processes.

Customer needs and feedback can be gathered through the usual marketing research channels. Initial opinions need to be gathered from service and sales and marketing staff with customer contact. Business-to-business applications can collect useful information through interviews or questionnaires with representatives from partner organisations. Ideas for solutions can be gathered from competitors' websites. An awareness of the characteristics of such sites is important for benchmarking and positioning, as discussed in Chapter 8.

Design content

Design of the content of the website is concerned with:

- Collecting and creating the necessary content, as specified by the analysis stage
- Designing the structure of the content with reference to issues associated with navigation and information architecture
- Designing the website interface and particularly any template elements that will feature on several or all pages
- Designing the site navigation features, such as menus, and embedding search tools
- Graphic design of the website, including how graphics are used but also the overall 'look and feel' of the website and consistency with corporate identity as used in other marketing communications.

This book does not attempt to introduce readers to the details of website development. Due to the volatility of the area, and the continuing development of new tools it is more appropriate to consult websites that offer guidance in these areas.

Test, review and revise

The key to successful website design is communication with users. Testing of the website should be conducted by its producer, both during the design process to inform the original design and subsequent to the design process, in order to gain user feedback that will influence the design of upgrades and subsequent versions of the website. In general, the objective of evaluation is to find out what the users want and what problems they experience, with a view to improving website design.

There are a number of approaches to the evaluation of interfaces and dialogues that can be employed in website evaluation:

- *Observing and monitoring users' interaction*, in either a laboratory setting, or the environment in which a search would normally be performed. The most popular approaches are those that involve some kind of indirect observation. Examples of such approaches are those in which a video recording of the user is made, or where the keystrokes that the user performs are logged through data logging or transaction logging.

■ *Eliciting users opinions*, which can offer a greater insight into why users perform particular actions or pursue specific search strategies and can identify the problems that users might have with a system. Approaches which may be helpful in this context include individual interviews, focus groups (group interviews), questionnaires and surveys.

■ *Experiments or benchmark tests*, in which the experimenter seeks to control some of the variables, whilst examining the effect of varying others. Typically such tests are conducted in a laboratory environment and work focuses on usability objectives and measures. Typical usability objectives might be suitability for the task, learnability and error tolerance.

■ *Prototyping*, in which the user and the designer work together to evolve the system. This may be performed in a laboratory setting or in a real life setting. The designer creates a prototype; the user tests the prototype and identifies any weaknesses; the designer produces a further prototype, and so on until the designer is satisfied that the prototype meets the user's requirements.

■ *Predictive evaluation*, is concerned with predicting the usability of a product without direct feedback on users' opinions. Prediction is typically based on expert reviews and usage simulations. These simulations may be more or less structured. One way of structuring such simulations is to use walkthroughs. Walkthroughs require experts to simulate the actions that a user might take in using the system. Experts are asked to report on their experience with the system.

In addition to usability testing with users, other basic testing needs to ensure that the website works. This involves testing the website features listed in Figure 3.11.

Figure 3.11   Checklist for features of a website needing basic testing

■ The operation and performance of all code

■ Operation on different browsers

■ Plug-ins

■ Interactive facilities, especially interfaces with organisational databases, such as inventory databases and order databases

■ Spelling and grammar, and generally proof reading

■ Consistency with corporate image

■ Validity of links to external sites

■ Timeliness and accessibility

■ Security and firewalls

■ Load tests to ensure that the system can handle several times the maximum anticipated hit rate per hour.

Publish website

Testing typically takes place in a test environment. Once all testing has been undertaken, and appropriate revisions have been made and tested, the website will be transferred to its live environment and made publicly available.

Promote website

Website promotion and, conversely, the role of the website in marketing communications is discussed at length in the next chapter. This stage is included here to emphasise that website publishing is not the end of the process but rather the beginning.

Maintain website

a website is always a work in progress. (Sterne, 1999, p. 34)

In addition to promotion, the other ongoing process associated with the website is maintenance. Maintenance is necessary because website content needs to change to reflect changes in the business and also, and most importantly, to keep the site live and fresh in order to encourage return visits. Maintenance as discussed here is primarily concerned with the maintenance of the content. Content needs to be updated on differing schedules, depending upon the type of content. For example, some sites may display daily or weekly industry news, which needs updating at these intervals. Product information and other corporate information need to be updated on the Web at the same time that it is updated in other communication media.

The key steps in the maintenance of website content reflect those in the creation of the website content. They are:

1. *Write copy*, including, as necessary, layout design and selection or creation of any associated images.
2. *Review, check and revise copy.* Reviewing and checking is best performed by someone other than the writer.
3. *Load copy to Web environment in a test situation*. Check and test copy in this environment.
4. *Publish* copy to live environment.

In a small organisation with a compact website this process might be quite straightforward. In a large organisation, in which the web content may originate from different parts of the organisation possibly located in different countries, the process associated with maintaining the website is much more complex. Sterne (1999) suggests that it is important to understand where the responsibilities for the different dimensions of website maintenance lie. These dimension are: the process, the content, the format and the technology. The process needs to be designed and controlled in order that those responsible for the other three areas can function. Content often derives from knowledge owners in different parts of the organisation. Content-owners need guidelines as to the area of content for which they are responsible and the format. The format, in terms of the design and layout of the site, must be centrally controlled. This control is most effectively exercised if content-providers only submit text and graphics for inclusion into a standard format. Finally, the IT department needs to take responsibility for the technology, especially if the website needs to be integrated with other IT capability within the organisation.

WAL-MART

Wal-Mart's store is an online superstore, which has been designed as an electronic duplicate of the bricks-and-mortar store. Visitors are presented with a diagrammatic floor plan that replicates the layout of a typical Wal-Mart store. The directions say 'This electronic floor plan of the Wal-Mart store makes it easy for you to find the department you want.' Using the diagram shoppers can navigate quickly through the store and visit departments of interest. A prime principle of retailing has been translated to e-tailing – making the store familiar so that customers feel at home and revisit in the future.

SEARCH TOOLS

With the vast array of databases and other services available via the Internet, it has been important to design interfaces that help users to search the information sources and services available on the Internet. Retrieval is recognised to be a significant problem on the Internet, with databases in a wide variety of different formats and a wide range of different services. Numerous different search and retrieval software packages mounted on different computers provide access via different interfaces to subsets of the databases.

Most e-business applications operate within the context of the Web. This means that there are two approaches to searching: those offered by browsers, which exploit hyperlinks between documents or sites, and search engines, which perform searches on the basis of words or phrases, through the use of a large index of Web resources. Browsers have been discussed in Chapter 2. There are also specialised tools such as shopping bots that can be used to assist in the location of specific items.

A **search engine** is a retrieval mechanism that performs the basic retrieval task, the acceptance of a query, a comparison of the query with each of the records in a database and the production of a retrieval set as output. The primary application of such search engines is to provide access to the resources that are available on the WWW, and stored on many different servers. Most search services are free, with their financial support coming from advertising revenue and through sales of the underlying technology. Indeed, the advertisements embedded in these search engines are one avenue for drawing attention to an organisation's products. Search engines can be located on a remote server on the Web, or located on a home PC or internal network. Increasingly search engines are becoming more than a Web index, and are adding content to their sites, in the form of additional services (see Figure 3.12).

Figure 3.12 Services available from Yahoo!

Yahoo! Astrology
get personalized horoscopes

LOSE 10lbs by December 25th   FREE Profile CLICK HERE eDiets

Yahoo! Personals
find the one for you

[Search] advanced search

Autos - 2002 Car Guide, **Sell Your Car**, Blue Book Pricing, Classifieds, Auctions, Consumer Reports

Shop Auctions · **Autos** · Classifieds · Shopping · Travel · Yellow Pgs · Maps **Media** Finance/Quotes · News · Sports · Weather
Connect Careers · Chat · Clubs · GeoCities · Greetings · **Mail** · Members · Messenger · Mobile · **Personals** · People Search · Photos
Personal Addr Book · Briefcase · Calendar · My Yahoo! · **PayDirect** **Fun** Games · Kids · Movies · Music · Radio · TV **more...**

Yahoo! Shopping
Thousands of stores. Millions of products.

Departments	Stores	Features
· Apparel	· Jewelry	· Barnes&Noble	· Holiday Gifts
· Computers	· Sports	· Wal-Mart	· Harry Potter
· DVDs	· Toys	· PhotoAlley	· Xbox Exclusive
· Electronics	· Video Games	· Sportmart	· Free Shipping
· Flowers	· more depts.	· more stores	· Toys by Age

QVC - Gifts and more delivered to your door

In the News
- U.S. Marines enter combat near Kandahar
- Taliban vow to defend stronghold
- U.S. envoys in Mideast for talks
- 3 charged in school bomb plot
- New breast cancer treatment may be effective with single dose
more...

Arts & Humanities
Literature, Photography...

News & Media
Full Coverage, Newspapers, TV...

Business & Economy
B2B, Finance, Shopping, Jobs...

Recreation & Sports
Sports, Travel, Autos, Outdoors...

Computers & Internet
Internet, WWW, Software, Games...

Reference
Libraries, Dictionaries, Quotations...

Education
College and University, K-12...

Regional
Countries, Regions, US States...

Entertainment
Cool Links, Movies, Humor, Music...

Science
Animals, Astronomy, Engineering...

Government
Elections, Military, Law, Taxes...

Social Science
Archaeology, Economics, Languages...

Health
Medicine, Diseases, Drugs, Fitness...

Society & Culture
People, Environment, Religion...

powered by COMPAQ

Marketplace
- Sony VAIO® Notebook only $1999 - buy now and receive a free Epson color printer
- Yahoo! Post-Thanksgiving Sale
- Buy a camera, share photos, print photos, personalize gifts
- Y! Auctions - bid on Christmas decorations

Broadcast Events
- 7pm ET Illinois vs. Maryland
- 9pm Duke vs. Iowa
more...

Inside Yahoo!
- Network for Good - make a donation, volunteer your time.
- Movies - Harry Potter, Monsters, Inc., Spy Game, Black Knight
- Y! Photos - share your holiday pix online
- Y! Games - pool, spades, canasta, chess, dominoes, euchre

Local Yahoo!s
Europe : Denmark - France - Germany - Italy - Norway - Spain - Sweden - UK & Ireland
Asia Pacific : Asia - Australia & NZ - China - HK - India - Japan - Korea - Singapore - Taiwan
Americas : Argentina - Brazil - Canada - Chinese - Mexico - Spanish
U.S. Cities : Atlanta - Boston - Chicago - Dallas/FW - LA - NYC - SF Bay - Wash DC - **more...**

More Yahoo!s
Guides : Buzz Index - **Education** - Health - Outdoors - Pets - Real Estate - Yahooligans!
Entertainment : Astrology - Broadcast - Events - Games - Movies - Music - Radio - Tickets - TV - more
Finance : Banking - Bill Pay - Funds Transfer - Insurance - Loans - Taxes - FinanceVision - more
Local : Autos - **Careers** - Classifieds - Events - Lodging - Maps - Restaurants - Yellow Pages - more
News : Top Stories - Business - Entertainment - Lottery - Politics - Sports - Technology - Weather
Publishing : Briefcase - Clubs - Experts - Invites - Photos - Home Pages - Message Boards
Small Business : Biz Marketplace - **Domain Registration** - Small Biz Center - Store Building - Web Hosting
Access Yahoo! via : Pagers, PDAs, Web-enabled Phones and Voice (1-800-My-Yahoo)

Make Yahoo! your home page

How to Suggest a Site - Company Info - Copyright Policy - Terms of Service - Contributors - Jobs - Advertising

Copyright © 2001 Yahoo! Inc. All rights reserved.
Privacy Policy

Since search engines need to provide access to a large and distributed collection of documents the retrieval process must be efficient: this is achieved by the search engine using **metadata** to represent websites. Typical metadata include URL, titles, headers, words, first lines. Some search engines also use abstracts and full text. We return to the importance of this metadata for organisations in the next chapter.

Each of the records contained in the database maintained by a global Web-search service is created automatically by a program called a spider, robot, Web wanderer or Web crawler. Each time a spider is run, it is initially issued with the URLs of a small seed set of target Web pages. It retrieves and downloads copies of the targets of those links and then activates every link contained in those pages, and so on, until it has downloaded copies of every single page that it can find. Typical target web pages are server lists, What's new pages and the most popular sites. Retailers may adopt specific strategies in order to ensure that their pages are visited by such spiders, and that they can be accessed via a search engine. Hidden comments and irrelevant meta tags are a hazard; since these are at the discretion of the message sender, some providers of goods and services massage metadata to draw attention to the products (Laursen, 1998).

The content of each page is stored in a record which also comprises other fields containing basic metadata such as the title of the document, the date on which it was last modified, its size in megabytes and its URL. The values of these attributes are determined automatically from the document. Searching on these records is facilitated by the creation of an inverted index. The inverted index is stored using compression techniques that reduce to a significant extent the storage capacity that it requires.

The **user interface** supports the interaction between the user and the system. For query formulation, the web page presented to the user of a Web search engine typically contains a 'form' made up of a text entry box in which the user is invited to enter search terms. Check boxes or menu boxes to allow field limitations or the use of operators may also be featured on the form. Once the query has been formulated, the depression of a button labelled 'Search' or some related term triggers a standard HTTP request to GET a document of a particular URL from the search service's Web server. The data entered by the user is appended to the URL in the form of a string of characters representing certain parameters and their values, together with a specification of the search program which is to be run, and to which those values should be passed, before the GET request is fulfilled. Figure 3.13 summarises some of the search facilities available in three well known search engines (based on Blakeman, 1998). Effective use of these facilities in the formulation of search strategies requires a reliable, sophisticated awareness of search facilities and their application in searching. The majority of searchers are unlikely to make full use of these facilities.

Most Web search services use a best-match search process and present search output in order ranked by relevance. Relevance is calculated by the search engine and is based on:

- How many of the search terms were found in the document
- How often the search terms were found in the document

Figure 3.13 Search facilities available in search engines

Facility	Yahoo!	Altavista	Lycos
Case sensitive	Sometimes	Yes	No
Wildcard/truncation	*	*	No
Phrases	"......"	"......"	"......"
Must include word	+	+	+
Exclude (NOT)	−	−	−
Default search options	Any of your words	Any of your words	Any of your words
Word in URL	u:word	url:word	Lycos pro
Word in title	t:word	Title:word	Lycos pro
Links to specified URL	No	Link:url	No
Specify part of domain	No	Domain:	No
Specify website	No	Host:	No
Limit by date	Yes – via Options	Yes, Advanced	No
Limit by language	No	Yes	Lycos pro
Limit by geography	Yes (Country Yahoo)	Yes e.g. +domain:uk	Yes in country versions
Search operators	AND, OR	AND (&), OR ( ), AND NOT (!), NEAR (~)	AND, OR, NOT, ADJ, NEAR, FAR, BEFORE
Refine search	No	Yes	Yes

- Where in the document the search terms were found (for example, URL, meta tags etc.)
- Proximity of the terms to one another
- Rarity of the terms.

Different search engines give different weightings to each of the above elements. The assumption here is that the more similar a record is to a query, the more likely the document that it represents will be relevant to the user's information need. It is not unusual to find a very large number of hits; if this is the case, a rule of thumb is to scan the first fifty hits and, if these do not provide useful information, to consider redesigning the search strategy. On occasions it is possible with some search engines to get a completely different set of results on the basis of the same search strategy. This idiosyncrasy arises because some search engines allocate a set amount of time to each search, and with complex or long searches the results displayed are those found before time has run out and are not a complete set.

Once the search has been run, the Web server responds to the GET request by sending to the user a Web page for display in place of the original search form, whose content includes the output of the search program. The display of the retrieval set typically takes the form of a list of Web pages representing the records retrieved, ranked in order of their potential relevance to the query and presented a certain number, say 10, at a time; each of these incorporates a hypertext link to the source document presented by the record and clicking on it will call up the source document This may be accompanied by a statement of how often each of the search terms were found in the whole database.

Not only are the search facilities available through the search engines relatively complex for the novice user, but there is significant variability between the different search engines. Search engines vary in coverage of sites, search facilities and process, and the presentation of the outcomes or results. It is also important to remember that some search engines are available in different versions for use in different countries.

Types of search engines

There are a number of different types of search engines. These include directories, subject gateways, meta search tools, and search bots and intelligent agents.

- **Directories**, such as Yahoo!, add value through human intervention in the assignment of subject headings to records in databases. In addition, all sites are evaluated prior to inclusion. Website creators may submit their page for consideration, but inclusion is subject to an evaluation process. Searching is via menus of the added subject headings or through keyword searching. The maintenance of such directories is a labour-intensive process, which means that the search service is selective in the sites that are included. However, selection reduces the amount of garbage that can often present real problems in searching the Internet. Experiments are under way in the areas of semantic knowledge bases and the use of thesauri to improve search effectiveness. In addition, the user's ability to assess the relevance of a document depends critically upon the metadata that is displayed about the document in the displays of the retrieved set.

- **Subject gateways** are similar to directories except that they have a specific subject focus. All resources are evaluated prior to inclusion. Subject gateways are often created and maintained by academic or public libraries or other bodies interested in offering structured access to information and advice.

- **Meta search** and **all-in-one tools** search for words and phrases across a number of search engines at the same time. They then amalgamate results, remove duplicate entries and present a single listing. They are a quick way of searching across several search tools, although they may not support some of the more sophisticated search facilities.

- **Search bots** act like meta search tools and search many Internet search engines in parallel. They differ from meta search tools in that they are

Figure 3.14 Search engine output

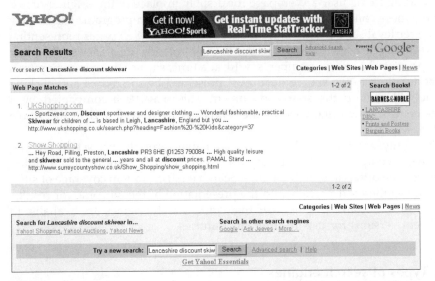

Reproduced with permission of Yahoo! Inc. © 2000 by Yahoo! Inc. YAHOO! and the YAHOO! logo
are trademarks of Yahoo! Inc.

loaded on the local workstation, rather than operating in client server
mode. **Intelligent agents** can be used to collect relevant items on the basis
of a search profile. Once a search has been performed, the user needs to
assign relevance rankings to the items retrieved. The intelligent agent uses
this information to modify its search process in its next iteration. Such tools
are particularly useful in current awareness searching and other contexts
in which the same search needs to be re-run.

■ **Search engines for specific sites**. Businesses with large online catalogues
of products need a search engine to support users in finding their way
through their product range. This is typically likely to be the case for
retailers involved in selling books, CD-ROMs and music. A good example
is Amazon.com. Figure 3.14 shows the search form for Amazon.com. Even
searching using such a tool is not straightforward and in fact carries all of
the complexity of searching other bibliographic databases, compounded by
considerable inaccuracies in the underlying database. It is not difficult to
find errors in the database, which lead to non-retrieval, and there are
strange idiosyncrasies associated with the effect of selecting, for example
'Exact Start of Title', 'Title Words', and 'Start(s) of Title Word(s)'.
Helpfully, Amazon.com offer the searcher several pages of search tips;
the necessity for these also serves to illustrate the complexity of searching
for books, music and associated information products.

EXPLORATORY ACTIVITY

Visit the website of Search enginewatch (www.searchenginewatch.com). Choose
two search engines, and examine any comments on those two search engines.

Shopping bots

Shopping bots are specialised search bots that are designed to locate and compare products. They take a query, visit shops that may have the product sought, bring back the results and present them in a consolidated and compact format that allows comparison shopping at a glance. Many also provide access to an order form. Most shopping bots claim to eliminate the searching necessary to identify the right product at the best price. Searching is on the basis of full text and/or product categories. Coverage varies both with respect to product range, sites and virtual retailers or catalogues covered, and frequency of update to data accessed. Bots use a variety of algorithms to perform searches with keywords. Some also offer product comparisons, reviews and pricing services. Others can use a range of indicators to perform a personal lifestyle analysis and use this as a basis for recommending specific products. MySimon is an intelligent bot, which can imitate human navigational behaviour and can be taught to shop at thousands of merchants in hundreds of product categories. Tete-a-tete is a project within MIT Media Lab's Agent-mediated Electronic Commerce initiative. It engages consumer-owned shopping agents and merchant-owned sales agents in integrative negotiations over the full value of each product offering to maximise its owner's individual needs.

Wal-mart, a retail giant with a very significant product range, offers an in-site comparison service, called Click and Compare. Users pick a product type, choose up to three competing items and then receive a comparison on dimensions appropriate to the product category. For a VHS-C camcorder this included price, format, AC/DC inputs, type of zoom lens, battery life, type of display and type of stabilisation. Future generations of bots that undertake comparisons that are less price dominated may be more useful to the consumer in comparing value and making purchase decisions.

EXPLORATORY ACTIVITY

Visit the website for BotSpot (Http://botspot.com) or SmartBots.com (www.smartbots.com). Choose one of the shopping bots listed on this site. Visit the website of this shopping bot and use it to try to identify merchants for the purchase of a book of your choice. Comment on the experience and the output from this process.

SEARCHING AND NAVIGATING THE INTERNET

Using a search engine, a shopping bot or the site of an individual merchant that is of a significant size and has a significant product catalogue requires consumers to make use of the search facilities that are available to them. All sites have information architecture. The **information architecture** describes the way in which a site or other information resource is structured. Typically users are offered:

- Hierarchical categorisation
- Keywords
- Special search facilities
- Advanced search facilities
- Browsing and directed searching

Hierarchical categorisation

The structure of menus is typically hierarchical with a set of more general categories and a series of lower level terms, linked in a tree like structure. Users make choices at each step as they move through submenus. Some terms can appear in more than one branch of the hierarchy, although this might be more confusing than helpful. Generally between 5 and 7 is the maximum number of menu options that should be included. On the other hand, more than three levels of menu leads to many click-throughs and complex navigation. These two principles conflict with one another and pose interesting challenges for organising information on websites! It is, however, possible to design a site with 20 000 products with only four menu levels. Interface designers have been concerned to allow users to move backwards and forwards between menu options (hence, for example, the Back and Forward buttons on most Web browsers). Figure 3.15 shows one such hierarchy, or search tree. This hierarchical structure is the information architecture of a website.

One of the main benefits of menus is that they identify and declare preferred terms and forms of terms so, for example, the user can be sure that all material on aubergines and eggplants is gathered under the menu option: aubergines. In addition they provide a structured map of an area of knowledge, or an information architecture, that shows the relationship between the concepts. The key disadvantage lies with the need for users to learn and understand the terms and, for instance, to make the correct selection close to the top of the menu hierarchy in order to arrive at the most appropriate destination. The system designer needs to employ techniques to

Figure 3.15 Information architecture: part of the hierarchical organisation of the BBC website

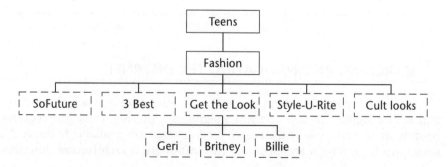

elicit the terms that are most appropriate for this purpose. The other key disadvantage is the resource that must be devoted to organising the knowledge base, in advance of its use and without knowledge of the way in which it might be used. In a web-based environment, in particular, the system designer has no idea of the profile of the potential users of the tool that she is constructing. For example, there are several different versions of English in common use and whilst I, with my UK background might use the term 'trousers', searchers from the United States use the term 'pants', and my mother might use the term 'slacks'. In addition, most areas have both a popular and a technical language. The health professional might use the term 'Rubella', whereas the mother seeking a remedy for her child might use the term 'German Measles'.

GROUP DISCUSSION ACTIVITY

Visit the BBC website and locate the series of links that are represented in the hierarchy in Figure 3.15. Taking a large sheet of paper, explore further links and sketch out an expanded version of the hierarchy.

Keywords

Search terms, or keywords can be entered. The search engine will locate these within the database and, using a best match search as described above will display product records or website pages. Some search engines offer a range of more sophisticated search options as illustrated in Figure 3.13. The process of entering a keyword is deceptively simple. Difficulties may arise from:

1. potential variations on word form (plurals and singular),
2. different terms for the same concept (for example, autos or cars), and
3. searching for multiple word terms (for example, credit cards).

Searchers may also need to hit the correct level of specificity and specification. Specification is concerned with providing sufficient – but not too much – information to retrieve sites. For example, although a searcher may be able to specify both the title and author of a book, the item may not be retrieved if the form in which these are specified does not match those in the database. A lower level of specification based, say, only on the author's name might be more successful in locating the book. Specificity is concerned with being precise about the product that is being sought. Large databases will generate hundreds, if not thousands, of hits in response to an imprecise search. Brand names can be a useful search term in this context. Keyword searching is particularly useful in searching for products with unique names.

Typically, consumers have the opportunity to search using both of these tools. A good searcher might narrow a search by choosing a product category, and then use keywords to specify the exact product for which they are searching. With tools, such as search engines and shopping bots that search across several sources, slightly different search strategies are likely to result in different recommendation sets.

▌ Special search facilities

Some product categories merit more specialised search facilities. These include:

Author, title, and ISBN searching for books. Sites such as Amazon.com, or other merchants with significant catalogues of books, CDs or other recordings, offer searching by either author or title or both. Search terms, such as author names or title fragments can be searched as keywords or, for a more precise search, an exact match can be forced by enclosing the terms in quotes and inviting a phrase search. The ISBN can also be a useful means of identifying a known book, if the user is, say, concerned with comparing prices for an item from several different merchants.

Parametric searching allows the searcher to be more specific. Customers specify a range of choices by checking off boxes or selecting options in drop-down boxes (as in Figure 3.16). When the customer clicks on the search button, the search is executed. Typically the parameters or characteristics to be specified are product specific. Parametric searching for products with complex technical specifications (such as digital cameras or air flights) assumes that the customers have product knowledge.

Figure 3.16 A form for specifying the parameters for identifying a property to purchase

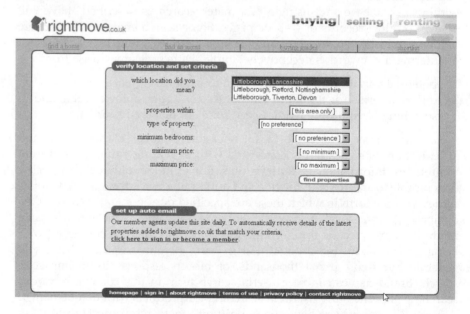

▌ Advanced search facilities

Search engines generally offer advanced search facilities that allow searchers to be specific in the way that they search and to develop a search strategy.

Such facilities typically include: Boolean operators, phrase searching, specifying search sections, truncation and hypermedia links.

Most search engines allow the user to enter a search phrase such as *'Purchasing Books on the Internet'*. This phrase is then deconstructed into the key words in the phrase and the search engine looks for the occurrence of each of these terms. In other words, the search engine performs an implicit OR search, for example, *'Purchasing* OR *Books* OR *Internet'*. Searchers have the option of formulating their own search strategy using the Boolean logic operators AND, OR, and NOT to combine terms:

■ AND reduces the number of items retrieved, and can therefore be used to narrow a search when too many hits have been retrieved or are anticipated.

  Children AND *Parents* retrieves items in which both terms occur

■ OR increases the number of items retrieved, and can therefore be used to broaden a search when a first attempt has been unsuccessful.

  Children OR *Parents* retrieves items in which either term occurs

■ NOT subtracts the second term from the first, and can therefore be used to eliminate some items from the results list.

  Children NOT *Parents* retrieves items in which only the first term occurs

It is common to use more than one operator in a search statement as in for instance:

  Children AND *Parents* AND *Conflict* OR *Discord.*

With these more complex statements it is important to understand the way in which terms will be grouped for searching. This statement could be searched as:

  (*Children* AND *Parents* AND *Conflict*) OR *Discord*

or as:

  Children AND *Parents* AND (*Conflict* OR *Discord*)

Different search engines have different ways of interpreting these statements. Brackets can be used as indicated to specify a preferred grouping of terms. This use of brackets in formulating a search statement is often known as nesting. Nesting offers a clearer search specification.

Other ways of improving the specification of a search include:

■ *Phrase searching*. In most search engines enclosing a phrase in quotes, for example, *'panic attacks'*, will cause the search engine to look for these two words adjacent to one another and in the specified order. On the other hand, this would exclude items with the phrase *'panic disorder'* which is a common alternative term. The alternative search strategy of *Panic* OR *Attacks*, would also retreive items containing the phrase *Panic Disorder*.

■ *Specifying sections* of documents to be searched – for example, a good way to narrow a search is to specify that the search should look only at the words in the web page's title, the text that appears in a browser's title bar.

- *Truncation* supports searching on character strings. For example if the user asks for a search on *COUNTR** this would retrieve records including words such as *Country, Countries, Countryside* and *Countrywide*. Common use of truncation is to cover plurals, so, for example, *Book** would retrieve pages with the words *Book* and *Books*.
- *Links*. Hypermedia links embedded in web pages can be used to move to associated pages. Many of these links, such as those in the form of banner ads, are inserted for commercial purposes and may or may not support the user in effective navigation. Information based sites, such as those of government departments, libraries and other document, advice and information providers, are more likely to have embedded links that can assist in finding other relevant sites or documents. The browser button is important in recording the search path that a user has taken through a series of linked sites.

Figure 3.17 lists quick tips for success in searching on the Web.

Figure 3.17 Quick tips for successful Web searching

1. Check your spelling.
2. Always type in lower case – the search will return both upper and lower case matches. This avoids problems with search engines that are case sensitive, and only look for upper case matches if the search term is entered in upper case.
3. Bookmark results. When you next select the bookmark, the search updates automatically.
4. If you are looking for a specific website, start by guessing its URL, before using a search engine. Try the name followed by .co.uk or.com for companies, gov.uk for government departments, and .org.uk for charities.
5. If the results are not relevant, or not sufficiently comprehensive, try another search engine. No search engine covers more than about 10–15% of the sites on the Web, so different search engines give different results.
6. Use meta search engines, such as www.dogpile.com or www.mamma.com that search other engines for results. They are slower, but can be faster than checking each search engine yourself, and are useful when you require a comprehensive search.

EXPLORATORY ACTIVITY

Visit two of the major search engines, such as Yahoo!, Google or Ask Jeeves. Explore their advanced search options. Use their help systems to provide additional information if this is available and useful. Draw up a table to compare the advanced search features offered by two of these search engines.

Browsing and directed searching

Systems need to be able to accommodate the spectrum of different search strategies that might be adopted by a consumer. The spectrum ranges from a search strategy designed to locate a specific item of information (sometimes called directed or purposeful searching) through to the almost aimless or general browsing over the Web and through other sources (such as magazines) for 'something interesting'. Many searches can be placed at some point in the middle of this spectrum. Often the user is refining not only the search strategy but also his information requirements as the search proceeds, so that a search that may start with browsing may eventually have a very focused intended outcome. Alternatively, the Web search that starts with a very targeted objective may open up other experiences, access to other sources and suggest other lines of investigation or action that had not occurred to the user at the start of the search. Breitenbach and Van Doren (1998) identify five categories of Web visitors: directed information seekers, undirected information seekers (browsers), bargain hunters (browsers of a type), entertainment seekers, and directed buyers or directed searchers with a buying intent.

CHAPTER SUMMARY

Website design, navigation and searching are important in defining the interface between the customer and the organisation. Website design is concerned with the creation of a website that is usable, and that communicates appropriate marketing messages. A key consideration in website design is the audience; many websites have multiple audiences, including customers, staff and other stakeholder groups. The design of the home page establishes a corporate style and page structure that should be carried through to other pages on the website. Content on a website needs to be dynamic and to invite further visits to the website. Navigation within websites is achieved through the information architecture of the website, as defined by its menu structure, and through keywords and search engines. Other elements of websites that require attention include colour, shapes and type styles, graphics and forms. The website development process includes the stages of project initiation, content analysis, content design, testing and revision, publication, promotion and maintenance. Search engines, including directories, subject gateways and search bots, are important in locating relevant websites. Search approaches rely upon subject hierarchies and keywords, and associated advanced search facilities. Users may use these facilities to support both browsing and directed searching.

KEY CONCEPTS

Website design is concerned with the creation of a website that is usable, that communicates appropriate marketing messages and that has any necessary functionality.

Audiences for an organisational website include customers and buyers, staff and other stakeholders.

Dynamic content of a web page needs to be ever-changing in order to add value and encourage customers to return to a website.

continued

Navigation is the process by which the user moves between different parts of a website.

Flow describes the ease with which users find the information that they need as they move around a website.

Website development is the process by which websites are created. The process includes the following stages: initiating the project, analysis of content, design of content, testing, publishing, promoting and maintaining the website.

Search engines are searching tools that perform the basic retrieval task of the acceptance of a query, the comparison of the query with each of the records in the database, and the production of a retrieved set as output.

Metadata are used to represent websites, and as the basis for search engine visits to websites. Typical metadata include URL, titles, headers, words and first lines.

User interface supports the interaction between the user and the system. For query formulation, this is typically a form, made up of a text entry box in which the user is invited to enter search terms.

Directories are a type of search engine that add value to the search process through human intervention in the evaluation and indexing of the sites that they cover.

Subject gateways are directories with a specific subject focus.

Search bots or **intelligent agents** search many Internet search engines in parallel.

Shopping bots are specialised search bots that are designed to locate and compare products.

Information architecture describes the way in which a site or other information resource is structured. The information architecture of a website has a significant impact on the way in which users can navigate a site.

Boolean operators are logic operators that are used to combine terms in search strategies. The three common operators are AND, OR and NOT.

ASSESSMENT QUESTIONS

1. What is unique about the audience for websites in an Internet environment?

2. Identify some key considerations in the design of a home page.

3. List the contents that you would expect to find on a company website. Discuss why each of these items is included.

4. Why is dynamic content important? Explain the concept of value in the context of website content.

5. What does navigation within a website involve? What devices can be used to assist users with navigation within a website?

6. Discuss the use of colour on a website.

7. Is graphics important on a website? How might graphics be used to enhance communication with audiences? Give examples.

8. How are online forms used on websites? Offer some suggestions relating to the effective use of forms on websites. Give examples.

9. Explain the stages in a website development project.

10. Why is website maintenance important? What are the key steps in website maintenance? Make some proposals for the management of this process in a large organisation.

11. What is the difference between a browser and a search engine? Illustrate your answer with reference to the way in which an e-shopper might use these different navigation tools.

12. Explain what is meant by the following terms: directory, subject gateway, search bots.

13. Evaluate the devices offered by search engines to support searching and navigating the Internet. Why is such a wide range of facilities necessary?

14. Explain the difference between browsing and directed searching. Discuss how each of these might be used in:

   ■ Locating information for an essay
   ■ Locating a book for purchase on the Amazon.com website.

GROUP ASSESSMENT 1 – WEBSITE CONTENT

Mapping sites offer an interesting kind of content. Visit four mapping sites and compare and evaluate the content. You will need to develop your own detailed criteria for this evaluation, but the following pointers should act as a basis:

■ Scope of maps available (for example, United Kingdom, World)
■ Nature of maps available (for example, street maps, walking maps, road maps, demographic and geological maps, scales)
■ What is available digitally, as opposed to ordering in print form
■ What is free and what needs to be paid for.

Also create a number of typical scenarios for which either a traveller, or a geography student might need a map, and use these to inform your assessment of the websites. Good sites to visit are: www.multimap.com, www.ordnancesurvey.co.uk, www.mapquest.co.uk and www.maps.com, but you should also be able to find others.

GROUP ASSESSMENT 2 – WEBSITE DEVELOPMENT

Write and act out a mini-play of the first meeting of a website development team. The team members are the site owner, the project manager, the site designer and the content developer. The team has just received the following terms of reference as a guide to its remit:

■ Design a website for an Internet-based flower delivery business
■ Propose a strategy for the maintenance of the website.

The objective of this meeting is to plan the stages in the project and to develop a project schedule (with timing attached). This schedule is also an output for this assessment and should be accompanied by a statement of any assumptions that are embedded in the project plan. Also write the minutes of this first meeting and include them in the assessment output.

GROUP ASSESSMENT 3 – NAVIGATION

Agree a checklist that can be used as a basis for the evaluation of the navigation facilities offered by search engines. Visit one search engine each, and perform a comparative analysis based on the group's results. Here is a list of possible search engines to evaluate: Altavista (www.altavista.com), Excite (www.excite.com), Hotbot (www.hotbot.com), Infoseek (www.infoseek.com), Lycos (www.lycos.com), Yahoo! (www.yahoo.com), Ask Jeeves (www.askjeeves.com), Google (www.google.com), Northern Light (www.northern-light.com).

REFERENCES

Adobe Creative Team (1999) *Official Adobe Publishing Guide.* Adobe Press

Andres, C (1999) *Great web architecture.* IDG Books Worldwide

Black, R and Elder, S (1997) *Websites that work.* Adobe Press.

Blakeman, K (1997) Intelligent search agents: search tools of the future?, *Business Information Searcher,* **7**(1), 16-18.

Blakeman, K (1998) *Search strategies for the internet: how to identify essential resources more effectively.* Caversham: RBA Information Services.

Bradshaw, R (1997) Introducing ADAM: a gateway to Internet resources in Art, Design, Architecture and Media, *Program,* **31**(3), July, 251–67.

Breitenbach, C S and Van Doren, D C (1998) Value added marketing in the digital domain: enhancing the utility of the Internet, *Journal of Consumer Marketing,* **15**(6), 558–75.

Carroll, J M (1997) Human computer interaction: psychology as a science of design, *International Journal of Human Computer Studies,* **46**(4), 501–22.

Chowdhury, G G (1999) The Internet and information retrieval research: a brief review, *Journal of Documentation,* **55**(2), 209–25.

Clarke, S J and Willett, P (1997) Estimating the recall performance of Web search engines, *Aslib Proceedings,* **49**(7), 184–9.

Cohen, L (1999) *Design essential.* Adobe Press.

Czerwinski, M P and Larson, K (1998) Trends in future web designs: what's next for the MCI professional?, *Interactions,* **5**(6), 9–15.

Dong, X and Su, L T (1997) Search engines on the world wide web and information retrieval from the Internet: a review and evaluation, *On-line and CD-ROM Review,* **21**(2), 67–81.

Ellis, D, Ford, N and Furner, J (1998) In search of the unknown user: indexing, hypertext and the World Wide Web, *Journal of Documentation,* **54**(1), 28–47.

Elofson, G and Robinson, W N (1998) Creating a custom mass-production channel on the Internet, *Communications of the ACM*, **41**(3), 56–62.

Flanders, V and Willis, M (1998) *Web pages that suck: learn good design by looking at bad design.* Sybex.

Fleming, J and Koman, R (1998) *Web navigation: designing the user experience.* O'Reilly and Associates.

Fodness, D and Murray, B (1999) A model of tourist information search behaviour, *Journal of Travel Research*, **37**(3), 220–30.

Hairong, (1999) Psychographics of consumers in electronic commerce, *Journal of Computer Mediated Communication*, **5**(2). Available at http//www.ascusc.org/jcmc/vol5/issue2/hairong.

Heleander, M G , Landauer, T K, Prabhu, P (eds) (1997) *The handbook of human computer interaction.* Oxford: Elsevier Science.

Honeywill, P (1999) *Visual language for the World Wide Web.* Intellect.

Jasco, P (1998) Shopbots: shopping for electronic commerce, *Online*, Jul/Aug, **22**(4), 14–20.

Johnston, K (2001) Why e-business must evolve beyond market orientation: applying human interaction models to computer-mediated corporate communications, *Internet Research*, **11**(3), 213–25.

Kim, J, and Moon, J Y (1998) Designing towards emotional usability in customer interfaces – trustworthiness of cyberbanking system interfaces, *Interacting with Computers*, **10**(1), 1–29.

Kirakowski, J, Claridge, N and Whitehand, R (1998) Human centred measures of success in website design. Human Factors & the Web Conferences (4th Conference) Available at www.research.att.com/conf/hfweb/proceedings/scholtz/index.htm.

Krisof, R and Satran, A (1995) *Interactivity by design: creating and communicating with new media.* Hayden Books.

Laursen, J V (1998) Somebody wants to get in touch with you: search engine persuasion, *Database*, **21**(1), 42–6.

Liu, S, Turban, E, Lee, M K O (2000) Software agents for environmental scanning in electronic commerce, *Information Systems Frontiers*, **2**(1), 85–98.

Mediamatic (1999) *Website graphics now.* Thames & Hudson.

Miller, D (1998) Seven deadly sins of information design. Available at http://devedge.netscape.com/docs/articles/inforch/sins-vz.html.

Millon, M (1999) *Creating content for the Web.* Intellect.

Palmer, J W and Griffith, D A (1998) An emerging model of website design for marketing, *Communications of the ACM*, **41**(3), 44–51.

Pen, C (2000) *Design through digital interaction.* Intellect

Poulter, A (1997) The design of the World Wide Web search engines: a critical review, *Program*, **31**(2), 131–45.

Reda, S (1997) Improved search function seen as key to Internet shopping, *Stores*, **79**(8), 60–7.

Rowley, J and Slack, F (1998) *Designing public access systems.* Aldershot: Gower.

Sano, D (1996) *Designing large-scale websites: a visual design methodology.* Wiley.

Schneiderman, B (1992) *Designing the user interface – strategies for effective human-computer interaction*, 2nd edn. Reading, MA: Addison Wesley.

Siegel, D (1997) *Creating killer websites*, 2nd edn. Hayden Books.

Sonnemans, J (1998) Strategies of search, *Journal of Economic Behaviour and Organisation*, **35**(3), 309–32.

Spiteri, L F (2000) Access to electronic commerce sites on the World Wide Web: an analysis of the effectiveness of six Internet search engines, *Journal of Information Science*, **26**(3), 173–83.

Sterne, J (1999) *World Wide Web marketing*, 2nd edn. New York: Wiley.

Williams, R and Tollet, J (1997) *The non-designer's web book: an easy guide to creating, designing, and posting your own website.* Peachpitt Press.

4 Creating an e-presence

LEARNING OUTCOMES

After reading this chapter you will:

- Appreciate the embedded nature of marketing communications in e-business
- Be able to discuss promotional objectives in e-business
- Be able to explain the role of banner advertisements in the creation of e-presence
- Understand key aspects of the role of brands and domain names
- Be able to evaluate the role of search engines and portals in marketing communication
- Be aware of other promotional options for e-commerce
- Be able to adopt a critical approach in relation to measurements of Internet marketing communication performance and metrics

INTRODUCTION

Traditionally, the focus in marketing communications has been on promotion and on the transmission of messages. Media available for communication, such as television, radio, newspapers, magazines, newsletters and direct marketing through telephone sales encourage this 'push' approach. Such media are linear, following a scripted flow, and often follow a one-to-many communication model in which a single promotion, such as a print advertisement, is sent by one source and seen by many without the opportunity for immediate feedback. The Web allows non-linear communication in which there is free flow and exchange of information, and there is potential for two-way communication between a business and its audiences in different contexts on a one-to-one basis, and a many-to-many basis. The many-to-many model involves communication between customers (Hoffman and Novak, 1995). The Web is a meeting place where anyone can communicate with anyone else. Promotional activities of specific organisations take place against this backdrop. Hoffman and Novak (1995) and Timmers (2000) argue that there are a number of characteristics of the Internet that make an important impact on marketing communications. These are listed in Figure 4.1.

Figure 4.1 Important Internet characteristics that impact on marketing communications

- 24 hours online
- Interactive
- Multimedia
- One-to-one and/or micromarketing
- Ubiquity
- Integration
- Global availability

EXPLORATORY ACTIVITY

Take two traditional advertising media, such as radio and billboards, and grade them using the criteria in Figure 4.1.

Figure 4.2 summarises the differences between advertising online and through more traditional media. Notice the shift in power from the business to the customer as customer time becomes an asset that both parties need to learn to value – and customer needs are paramount. In this context, information, and not image, is the main currency.

Figure 4.2 Comparing online advertising with advertising in traditional mass media

	Traditional Media	**Online**
Space	Expensive commodity	Cheap, unlimited
Time	Expensive commodity for marketers	Expensive commodity for users
Image creation	Image is everything Information is secondary	Information is everything Image is secondary
Communication	Push, one-way	Pull, interactive
Call to action	Incentives	Information (incentives)
Audience	Mass	Targeted
Links to further information	Indirect	Direct/embedded
Investment in design	High	Low, allows change
Interactivity	Low	Range across a spectrum from low to two-way dialogue

Source: Developed from D Janal (1998) *Online marketing handbook: how to promote, advertise and sell your products and services on the Internet.* Van Nostrand Reinhold.

Although Internet promotion is attracting much attention, it is important to remember that it is still a new and minority medium. For most consumer and retail businesses, advertising spends for this medium are only a fraction of spend on traditional media. The main factors that affect advertising spend are the size and composition of the audience and the effectiveness of the medium for advertising. The size of the audience and number of different groups with a significant representation in the Internet audience is increasing rapidly. This is a good basis for projecting further growth in Internet advertising activity. In addition, there is evidence to suggest that Internet advertisements can be as memorable as television advertisements. Further, Internet use is reducing exposure to television advertising because Internet users watch less television (Nielsen, 1999; Parry, 1998). Advertisers need to follow audiences to new media. This is a further reason to believe that expenditure on Internet advertising has not yet peaked.

EMBEDDED MARKETING COMMUNICATIONS

Customer relationships are at the core of e-business. Using the simple model in Figure 4.3, two-way information exchange takes place in any e-commerce transaction. The customer learns about the suppliers from the information offered on a website and any interactions in which they engage through the

Figure 4.3 Two-way marketing communications

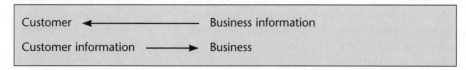

website. This embeds the brand, communicates marketing and cultural messages, and identifies the product offering and other aspects of the organisation's positioning in the marketplace. Amongst the factors that may influence customer perceptions are the catalogue of products, delivery arrangement, special offers, added value features, such as information and advice, extent of product details and the quality of the interaction with any personal service agents, such as help desk personnel. The customer uses this information to formulate an impression of the 'personality' of the organisation and makes a decision concerning the basis upon which they are prepared to do business. Reciprocally, when a customer enters into a transaction, such as placing an order, he tenders whatever customer information is requested on the order form. This must include his name (which gives a contact for subsequent communications), an address (for both shipment and ordering) and details of the items ordered, and may include telephone number, e-mail and fax, where he saw the advertisement and credit card number. This information is a sufficient basis upon which to construct customer profiles that support targeted marketing communication. No longer does the marketer need to speculate about customer needs and to market on the basis of demographic or psychographic variables; she actually knows the customer purchasing profiles and the only speculation relates to new products or changes in customer status or lifestyle. In such a business process model, it becomes difficult to differentiate between marketing communications and businesses operations, and marketing communications becomes embedded in business processes.

There are a number of important consequences of this simple observation:

1. The communication or, more appropriately, the exposure is two-way. This represents a good basis for a relationship, and the issues and nature of relationships and communities in e-commerce is an important aspect of marketing communication. This also emphasises the long-term perspective on marketing communication that can be lost in discussions of individual promotional activities and approaches, such as those covered in the remainder of this chapter. The issue of relationships and communities is explored at greater length in Chapter 6.
2. Organisations need integrated marketing communications that drive consistent marketing messages and relationships through the way in which business processes and the service delivery impact on customers. This, for example, includes the effectiveness of customer service and delivery (discussed in Chapter 5). Put another way, communication is not only about what the business says, but rather about what its does: *actions speak louder than words*.

Not all organisations are engaged in commerce, and some maintain a Web presence to provide information or to promote their services. For these organisations and organisations that have yet to establish a presence, loyal or repeat customers, or a community, the creation of a Web presence through effective marketing communications and promotion meets their e-business objectives. Marketing communication also continues to be important to established e-commerce players, as they seek to attract new customers and communicate effectively with existing customers.

This chapter focuses on the consumer marketplace. Marketing communication, as exhibited through promotion, tends to lean towards the consumer marketplace. Strategies such as customer service, relationships and communities that are explored in subsequent chapters are much more significant for business-to-business contexts.

OBJECTIVES OF WEB PRESENCE

As a marketing communications medium there are a number of ways in which the Web is different from other communications media. In particular, approaches for grabbing attention that have served well in traditional media, such as advertisements in a magazine or on a billboard, need to be re-interpreted in an environment in which the customer only views what is on a small screen, and only if something attracts his attention on that screen, or if he is purposively searching for something, is he likely to move on to another screen. The challenge for e-marketers is to take control of that first screen or, failing that, to ensure either that their messages are displayed to the customer on that screen or to be sure that their screen will be readily located or encountered through some other route. As with all media, acquiring traffic is expensive, retaining traffic is profitable and developing traffic requires value (Hanson, 2000). In order to establish a Web presence, an e-merchant needs to undertake a **traffic-building campaign**. Once there is a significant level of visits to the site there are opportunities for the achievement of other website presence objectives.

Effective promotion of a website is necessary in order to ensure visibility. Although a website has many of the characteristics of an advertisement, in that it can be used to inform, persuade and remind customers about a company or its products, its impact will be minimal unless other strategies are adopted to draw traffic to the website. Building a website is not sufficient of itself to create a Web presence. **Promotional activities** associated with a website are designed to attract traffic and thereby to achieve a satisfactory marketing outcome. The objectives that can be achieved by a Web presence vary in accordance with the stage of development of e-commerce. Leong *et al.* (1998) collated business managers' views on the areas in which web presence makes an impact. They found that the most important objective was to promote corporate image, followed by brand/product awareness, customer service and finally online sales. McNaughton (2001) identified three types of website based on the objectives, image building, sales assistance and integrated, and found that most were sales assistance sites. Berthan *et al.*

(1996) propose other objectives for websites. Consolidating these contributions a web presence is effective for:

- Creating brand, product and corporate awareness and image, and continually bringing these to the customers' attention
- Providing product and other information and, in general, delivering content, such as information or an offer
- Generating qualified leads
- Customer service including handling customer complaints, queries and suggestions, and establishing two-way dialogues
- Allowing customers access to the extranet and thereby forging B2B relationships
- Facilitating transactions and sales.

Web presence of the brochureware type is less effective for changing and maintaining attitudes. The later stages of e-commerce that encourage interaction, and offer the opportunity for a two-way relationship might have more potential for impacting upon attitudes (Ghose and Dou, 1998). This interactive model of e-commerce is reflected in the five-step model for web advertising and marketing proposed by Kiani (1998) which identifies the following five stages: consumer awareness, attraction, website visit and contact, purchase and repurchase.

Berthan *et al*. (1996) also emphasise that many organisations have yet to formulate promotional objectives for their web presence. They do not know what to expect of the media, and a key objective is to learn about the media. A non-interactive website is a relatively inexpensive venture from which it is easy to retract rapidly. On the other hand, organisations will not achieve a holistic appreciation of business and marketing communications in this context without engaging in Stage 4-type activity. Such activity requires a complete e-business model, including mechanisms for delivery, return and financial transactions, and investment in this scale of operation is less easy to 'write off'. At this relatively early stage in e-commerce and with limited knowledge of the character of consumer response, organisations have grounds for being cautious in setting promotional objectives. Nevertheless, until expectations of outcomes from web presence are clarified, the e-venture will be a 'ship without a rudder'. Ultimately, evaluation cannot proceed in the absence of specified objectives.

BANNER ADVERTISING

Banner advertisements are placed on web pages other than the organisation's home site, such as those of the search engines. They are called banner ads because they are usually displayed across the top of the web page as a 'banner'. Banner ads usually offer links through to other web pages. They may be static or animated. Companies place banner ads in pursuit of two desired outcomes:

1. That visitors will see the advertisement and note it consciously or subconsciously; this viewing helps to create and reinforce brand image.

2. That visitors will click on the banner ad, and thereby **click through** to their website. **Click-through rate**, which is an important measure of the impact of banner advertisements, is the proportion of visitors who click on the banner ad and visit the organisation's site.

Placing banner ads

Banner ads are typically placed on websites that already have established traffic. This increases the likelihood that the banner ad will be seen. There are three different types of sites that attract banner advertising:

1. *Portals*, which provide access to a large but relatively undifferentiated audience. It is also usually possible to place adverts whose display is triggered by keywords that a user enters when performing a search. Thus, a user searching for 'Flights to Spain' might be presented with a banner ad about flights and hotels in Barcelona.
2. *Generalised news services*, such as the *Sunday Times* website (www. sundaytimes.co.uk). These sites still provide access to a general audience, but the audience is bounded in a similar way to the audience for the print equivalent.
3. *Special interest sites*, such as the sites of men's magazines, for example, www.playboy.com and www.golf.co.uk, women's lifestyle magazines, for example, Femail (www.femail.com), and vertical portals, such as those associated with the online computing trade press.

A banner advertisement campaign usually involves placements on several sites. This is normally achieved with the aid of traditional advertising agencies or advertising networks, such as Doubleclick (www.doubleclick.net). **Advertising networks** are collections of organisations, each of which has an arrangement with an advertising broker to place advertisement banners. Under this arrangement, businesses do not deal directly with the businesses that wish to place an advertisement on their site.

EXPLORATORY ACTIVITY

Examine the websites of two generalised news services such as the *Sunday Times* website (www.sundaytimes.co.uk). Make a list of the banner advertisements shown on these services. Compare the products that are being advertised on the two different sites. (*Note:* you may have to click through from the banner ad to the associated website to check what products or services are being advertised.)

Payment for banner advertising

An **ad impression** occurs when a person views an advertisement placed on the web page. Banner advertising is typically paid for on the basis of **CPM** or **cost per thousand ad impressions.** Prices are typically of the order of £20 to £100 per 1000, although the rate depends on the site and its attractiveness.

When payment is according to the number of viewers of a site it is important that the number of viewers is measured reliably and can be agreed. **Website auditors** measure the usage of different sites in terms of the number of ad impressions and click-through rate. The main auditing bodies are:

- BPA (www.bpai.com)
- Audit Bureau of Circulation, ABC (www.abc.org.uk)
- Internet Advertising Bureau, IAB (www.iab.net)

EXPLORATORY ACTIVITY

Choose one of the website auditors mentioned above. Visit this website and write some notes on the activities in which they engage.

There is some growth in other payment methods and, in particular, in combined methods that use CPM in conjunction with one or more of:

- Per exposure – measured through ad impressions or possibly through the length of time that the user views an advertisement
- Per response – based on the number of click throughs
- Per action – payment according to a marketing action, such as a purchase or a registration.

Figure 4.4   Checklist for successful banner ads

1. **Click Here** banners elicit greater response rate than those without this
2. **Banners that stay** – choose banners in frames that stay on the screen as the user moves between pages
3. **Banner burn-out** – avoid over-exposure to the same surfer by changing banners
4. Keep to the **seven word limit** – banners are small so they cannot hold much text
5. Keep **file size small** to ensure fast loading
6. Use **bright colours** for impact
7. Use **animation**, but avoid intrusive animation
8. Offer **interactivity**, such as data entry boxes or voting buttons
9. Use **text to identify graphics**; this text displays whilst the banner is loading
10. Choose sites for **placement of ads** carefully, with the aid of an agency
11. Consider **banner design** carefully and test with different audiences
12. Offer **incentives** to enhance click-through rates
13. Consider **timing of placement** of ad carefully
14. Seek click-through **quality**, not just quantity. Click through must be to a product that the customer might be persuaded to buy
15. Check that the **infrastructure** on the site can cater for the click throughs. Is there a mechanism for responding to e-mails? What other customer service features are available?

▌ Ad blocking

Finally, customers may exercise their right to receive an advertisement or not, through filters that undertake ad blocking. These filters look at the HTML code and check files and file types against a filter list to block ads, interstitials or animated banners. Ad blocking is often performed inside organisations in order to improve network speed and performance.

GROUP DISCUSSION ACTIVITY

Visit any website that carries banner ads. Evaluate each of the banner ads on this site in terms of the following points in Figure 4.4: 1, 2, 4, 5, 6, 7, 8, 9 and 12.

▌ Reciprocal placement of banner ads

A healthy range of reciprocal arrangements for mutually useful placing of banner advertisements exists between strategic partners. Dholakhia and Rego (1998) suggest that the number of links to other web pages is a crucial factor in popularity.

Affiliate networks are established by portals or large online retailers in order to build traffic to their site. The networks are based on the placing of banner ads. Amazon.com is a prime exponent of this approach. Amazon has over 300 000 affiliates; these affiliates display small Amazon banner ads on their sites. Each affiliate partner earns a commission every time that a customer clicks on the advertisement and then makes a transaction at Amazon. Amazon claims that nearly a quarter of its revenue is generated through affiliates. In this model, payment is only made to the advertiser when the banner display results in a transaction.

Bcentral from Microsoft (www.bcentral.com) is a free advertising network that supports the exchange of banner advertisements. For every two advertisements that appear on a company's site that company's advertisement is displayed on another site free of charge. The network links thousands of sites in 32 languages.

EXPLORATORY ACTIVITY

Visit the Amazon.com website and find out how to become an affiliate to Amazon.com. What are the benefits associated with affiliate status? Should your college or university website carry banner ads for Amazon.com? Evaluate the pros and cons of this proposition.

DOMAIN NAMES AND BRANDS

Both the domain name and brand need to be memorable to the customer. The use of established brand names in a domain name significantly increases the chances of a customer being able to use existing brand knowledge to locate a website. Organisations need to acquire the domain names that might be associated with any established brand names, either with the intention of using them or to prevent their use by other people. Whether or not specific brand names are used in domain names depends on whether customers are to be encouraged to access through individual brand names, or whether the organisation seeks to direct all traffic through the main corporate page. So, for example, Nestlé own domain names corresponding to their key brands as indicated in Figure 4.5, but apart from Nestle.com, none of the other brands are active.

Promoting a domain name or URL in real world promotion, such as on billboards and television advertisements, is an important means of heightening awareness of the website. As discussed previously, in such promotion the organisation needs to consider carefully the website address that it chooses to give. This depends on the objective, which may be:

1. *To promote the corporate website* – use the corporate domain name
2. *To promote a specific product or brand* – use the brand or product domain name
3. *To entice customers with a special offer* – use a special domain name for the special offer, so that the users can go directly to what they want.

On the other hand, simpler domain names are more memorable and their promotion is likely to have a more lasting impact. This is particularly important because viewers do not sit watching television or drive past a billboard with a pencil in their hands or a keyboard at their fingertips.

Pure play Internet companies have invested significantly in promotion of their existence in other media. For such organisations, in the promotional campaign the domain name is at the centre of the marketing message. For example, Letsbuyit.com (www.letsbuyit.com) and Ask Jeeves (www.askjeeves. com), commissioned significant television advertising to bring their URL to public attention. Early use of URLs in advertisements for bricks-and-mortar retailers did little more than announce the URL. Now that websites often

Figure 4.5 Nestlé brands and domain names

Type of brand	Brand Name	Domain name
Corporate brand	Nestlé	Nestle.com (owned and active)
Range brand	Carnation	Carnation.com (owned, not active)
Product line brand	Carnation Instant breakfast	Instantbreakfast.com (owned, not active)

have more to offer customers, and are a more central component of business strategy, advertisements are more proactive in seeking to entice customers to websites through special offers, intriguing information and other draws. The use of website addresses in other media provides a link between media, which is a basis for translating relationships across media.

GROUP DISCUSSION ACTIVITY

Each group member is asked to examine the advertisements in:

■ A magazine
■ A period of television watching

And then:

1. Make a note of the percentage of the advertisements that use URLs or domain names.
2. Categorise these domain names on the basis of whether they are: corporate, brand or product, or other.
3. Make a note of any special offers that are associated with the URL.

Consolidate the results and discuss them as a group.

OTHER CONSIDERATIONS FOR BRANDS

Brands help customers identify the products they want and influence their choices when they are unsure. (Dibb *et al.*, 1994, p. 215)

Brands have a wider role than that of label or address as discussed above. Traditionally, brands have been viewed as a set of values or verbal and physical cues which an organisation has been successful in encouraging the consumer to attach to the brand. The organisation may then use this association by attaching it to a number of products (Sharp, 1993; Martinson, 1995). Loyalty or lack of loyalty is the consumer's response to the brand.

The purpose of branding is to facilitate the organisation's task of getting and maintaining a loyal customer base in a cost-effective manner to achieve the highest possible return on investment. (De Chernatony and McDonald, 1998, p. 17)

However, the concept of brand may have multiple meanings as indicated in Figure 4.6 (De Chernatony and Dall'Olmo Riley, 1998). The brand construct is complex and consumers may adjust their concept of brand for different product categories. Thus, in car purchase, 'Mercedes Benz' might be perceived as a shorthand, whilst in purchasing a financial services product, such as a savings account, the brand 'Halifax' may signify 'risk reducer'. Further, different customers may place differing emphasis on the different interpretations of the concept brand even in the context of the same brand, as is consistent with the concept of the evolving brand (Goodyear, 1996).

Figure 4.6 Alternative definitions of the brand construct

Brand definition	Brief explanation
Legal instrument	Mark of ownership as in trademark, name or logo
Logo	Recognised name, term, design, symbol
Company	Recognisable corporate name and image
Shorthand	Represents characteristics or values which are associated with the brand
Risk reducer	Brand as a contract with the consumer
Identity system	Holistic, consistent, integrated vision
Image	Image in consumers' minds is the brand reality
Value system	Brand values to match relevant consumer values
Personality	Brands as symbolic devices with personalities that users value beyond their functional utility
Relationship	Extension of brand personality. Brand is an expression of the relationship between the consumer and product
Added value	Added value differentiates brands. Added value represents the non-functional benefits that are offered in addition to functional benefits. Consumers imbue brand with subjective meaning that they value sufficiently to buy
Evolving entity	Brand concept changes by stage of development

Source: Summarised from De Chernatony and Dall'Olmo Riley (1998).

GROUP DISCUSSION ACTIVITY

Individually note down the values (in words or phrases) that you associate with the following Internet and non-Internet brands. Discuss your results, and identify the extent of agreement amongst the group:

Dell, Amazon, Microsoft, IBM, Google, Tesco, Sainsbury's, Asda, Iceland, Wal-Mart, Ford, Toyota, Mercedes Benz, Morgan, Daewoo.

A key definition is that of **brand** as an expression of a relationship between the consumer and the product. Indeed many of the other definitions of a brand could be viewed as supporting the relationship between the brand and the customer. Thus logo and company are concerned with the first stage of relationship building – awareness and recognition. Shorthand, identity and image are perhaps characteristic of the courting phase in a relationship where a brand needs to make the first move. Risk reducer is concerned with facilitation of the early stages of a relationship, possibly associated with cognition. A two-way dynamic is introduced in the concepts, identity system, image, value system, personality, relationship, and adding value. In these concepts the consumer contributes to the nature and concept of the brand, and the brand is consumer-centred. The customer has some ownership of the brand and identifies with it. At this stage brand managers will be seeking to generate an affective orientation or an affinity towards the brand. Different types of relationships may be signified by different brand definitions. Goodyear (1996) proposes that brands evolve through these different definitions over time.

A company has number of options when they launch or relaunch a website in respect of brand strategy. These choices may apply to individual brands or to the entire corporate entity. A key factor influencing choice between these options is the strength and identity of the existing brands, and the extent to which they are perceived to be appropriate for the Internet world.

Migrate established brand online   Companies that are well established can build on their brand by duplicating it online. Sites from companies such as FedEx, Virgin and Disney have all translated their traditional brand identity into a virtual-world environment. This approach clearly marks the online channel as just another channel, offering flexibility for access to the company and its products. Risk is associated with the potential for the Internet offering to damage the existing brand.

Extend traditional brand   Brand extension typically involves applying an existing brand to a new product range, or marketplace. Such extension normally impacts on the ranges of products with which the brand is associated and therefore affects the underlying brand identity. This approach allows the business to capitalise on an existing brand and to add new values that might be more appropriate in the Internet environment.

Partner with an existing digital brand, such as Yahoo!, Amazon or Microsoft. This approach uses the established Internet brand as a portal, as discussed further in the section on portals and search engines.

Create a new digital brand   This may be necessary if the existing brand is not seen as suitable for the new medium, or if the business is seeking an opportunity to evolve from its existing brand, perhaps because it has a history that it wishes customers to forget. A number of the banks have chosen new brands. Prudential's Internet bank has been launched under the brand name, Egg, the Cooperative Bank has spawned the Internet brand, Smile, and somewhat surprisingly the Halifax's Internet offering glories under the brand, IF. In this arena, in which trust is a big issue, customers often look for the underlying company brand and are reluctant to accept the new brand on its own merit ('Egg from the Prudential').

GROUP DISCUSSION ACTIVITY

1. Examine the web addresses of the football clubs in Figure 3.9 (p. 62). Have they used their brand name in their domain name?
2. Visit the Smile.co.uk website and also the Coop.co.uk website. Note the design and messages on both sites. Draw up a table of the similarities and the differences.

PORTALS AND SEARCH ENGINES

Portals aim to be the entry points of preference to the Web and to provide direction to other sites. Portals aggregate a large audience and then segment it, in much the same way as supermarkets and department stores (MacMillan, 1998). Because portals offer value-added services such as directories, searching, information, news, e-shopping and links to related websites, users are attracted to the portal and may use the portal as a means of access to the Internet. Portals have a role in structuring the way in which customers, users, citizens, members and other groups access the Internet, and have had, and continue to have, a significant role in generating traffic on the Internet. The concept is consistent with the dictionary definition of the term portal as: 'a door, gate or entrance, especially one of imposing appearance, as in a palace'. As with all entrances, users must be attracted to the building; then they must be able to locate the door. Once inside the building they need to be able to find their way around. Different users will want different rooms in the building and even users who are visiting the same room may take different routes to get to the same place.

Portals offer a range of value-added services to encourage users to visit. Major Internet portals have partnerships with information or content providers, so that they can provide various categories of information. Typically, information and access to other websites that is available via the portal is organised through an index, so that users can find the information that is of potential interest to them. Also many portals offer communication facilities, such as e-mail, message boards, chat lines, forums, news groups and so on. Since e-mail is one of the biggest uses for the Internet, providing e-mail facilities encourages repeat visits and creates a community associated with the portal. For commercial portals to be sustainable they need to encourage commercial transactions, such as e-shopping. Such facilities can be extremely valuable to the user, but portals are also powerful in directing consumers to specific products and selected sites.

In addition to intranet and extranet portals designed to support the activities of an organisation, there are a number of other types of portal. These include:

1. *Search engines*, such as Yahoo!, Excite and AltaVista. These portals provide value-added services such as directories, searching, information news and links to related websites.

2. The *home pages of Internet service providers*, such as Tesco and AOL.
3. *Vertical portals* or *niche portals* designed for specific user groups. The leading sport site is ESPN (www.espn.com) which is targeted at males aged 18–34. Ivillage (www.ivillage.com) is a portal targeted for women. Some, such as those of Amazon.com and travel.com, are the home pages of significant e-tailers, whilst other portals are mounted by publishers or online search service providers. Some vertical portals are designed to offer business users in specific industries or trades a one-stop shop for information and supply. VerticalNet (www.verticalnet.com) is a portal site linking other niche vertical portal sites. These sites cover technology, communications, food service, health care, and other.
4. *Subject gateways*, which are a type of vertical or niche portal. Many of these are 'public service' portals funded through public finance to support, for example, academic, research or professional communities.
5. The *sites of intelligent agents*, or 'bots'. For example, the shopping bot acts as a portal to the sites of the e-merchants that it visits on the consumer's behalf.

Organisations can achieve visibility through portals, with banner ads, hyperlinks and registration, so that the portal's search engine includes the site in any search for a related topic. Achieving sufficient visibility through a portal requires careful attention to web page content and registration. The problem with search engines is that their response to a typical keyword search is to create an extensive list of output. Searchers want to see the item that they are seeking in the top ten hits and shown on the first screen, and businesses would also like their page to appear in this set where it is likely to capture the interest of the searcher. Achieving good positions in search listings has become a specialist job. This is because:

1. The site needs to be registered with each of several main search engines. www.mediametrix.com lists the search engines that attract the most users and calculates a digital media reach percentage.
2. Search engines have different search technologies and use different criteria to order the list of results. www.searchenginewatch.com and Northern Web (northernwebs.com/set/) explain how search engines work and offer tips on achieving good rankings.
3. Search technology and ranking criteria change, thus necessitating a new registration.
4. Search engines index large numbers of sites. The competition for top positions in listings is severe.

Optimising site presence through search engines can be a time-consuming and demanding task, and businesses often outsource this task to organisations that specialise in **traffic-generating** or **visibility campaigns.** The website addresses of some such companies are listed in the Activity below. Factors affecting site listing and ranking are presented in Figure 4.7.

Figure 4.7 Checklist of factors that affect site listing and ranking by search engines

1. **Registration**. A site must be registered with a range of search engines. Even the larger search engines do not have a reach in excess of 20% of the potential e-audience, so it is important to register with all major search engines. Directories such as Yahoo!, are more selective in the web pages that they list and all web pages listed are evaluated before being included. This means that it is more difficult to be listed in a directory but the tool is more selective, and therefore often favoured by searchers.

2. The **keywords in the title of a web page** that appears at the top of a browser window, as indicated in the HTML code by the <TITLE></TITLE> keyword, have more impact on listings than keywords in the body of the page. The title appears at the top of the browser window in the actual browser header bar. There will be titles on the home page and on other pages. Titles should therefore include the name of the company and a descriptor of the product or service offered.

3. The **number of occurrences of keywords** in the text of the web page affects the listing, so this text needs to be designed from an indexing perspective (as well as taking into account readability and impact perspectives). In addition, the proximity of search terms may affect the ranking. Thus, the term 'running shoes' will rate a higher ranking than 'shoes that can be used for running'. Similarly searchers may use alternative terms, such as shoes, footwear, trainers, pumps and running boots, as search terms; consideration needs to be given to including possible alternative search terms as keywords.

4. **Meta tags** are used by some engines to determine rankings. They are also used to specify the first line of text displayed in connection with the web address in the listing. The description can also be used for this purpose. This text is used as the basis for user relevance judgements and is important in determining whether users will click on the entry to visit the site.

5. The **popularity of the site** is used by some sites to influence the ranking of a site (see www.google.com).

6. **Frames and graphics** are not indexed. Website designs that make heavy use of these need to remember to include text. Hidden text can be used with graphics, which is indexed, but not visible to the user.

7. Information generated **'on the fly'** from a database associated with a website is not indexed by the search engine. Appropriate information in a database should be mirrored on a server where it can be indexed.

EXPLORATORY ACTIVITY

Visit two of the following websites of companies offering traffic-generating campaigns, and explore what such organisations have to offer:

- Sitelynx (www.sitelynx.co.uk)
- XXist (www.xxist.com)
- Web Marketing (www.web-marketing.co.uk)

OTHER PROMOTIONAL STRATEGIES

Paid advertising

Paid advertising in other media, including the press, billboards, television and radio, is becoming more prevalent. Some of this advertising simply emphasises the URL and invites the audience to visit the website (see Figure 4.8). Whereas in other advertisements, other marketing messages about the product or the brand may be to the fore, the URL is given as a contact or follow-up address (Pardun and Lamb, 1999). The website address is often used in magazine and television advertising to offer a direct response opportunity from these media (Philport and Arbitter, 1997).

Figure 4.8 Checklist of corporate literature in which a URL might appear

Letterhead	All stationery	Business cards
Flyers	Fax cover sheets	Brochures
Press packs	Press releases	Notebooks
Folders	Report covers	Mouse pads
Pens, and other give-aways	Internal and external newsletters	Bulk mailing items

Source: Based on J Elsworth and M Elsworth (1997) *Marketing on the Internet*, 2nd edn (New York: Wiley).

Publicity and word of mouth

The Web is rich in opportunities for users to communicate with one another. These include e-mail, Usenet groups, e-mail listservs, portal discussion areas, consumer forums and information promulgated by those who view themselves as opinion leaders. As always, this word of mouth (touch of keyboard) communication can be positive and negative, and is subject to gentle manipulation. The difference is that it is much easier for disgruntled customers to get their voices heard in this forum and their reach may be global. Whilst e-business remains only a small fraction of a business's total activity, the threat from this source may be limited, but, in the longer term, businesses need to be aware of the potential of word of mouth (Buttle, 1998; Bayus, 1985).

Co-branding and sponsorship

A further means of traffic building is to create hyperlinks to other sites. The first step is to audit existing links to the site. This can be achieved through a log file analysis (using a log file analyser program) or through the use of the 'link:' facility that is available from search engines such as AltaVista and Infoseek. The user types 'link:', followed by the URL to generate a list of the websites linked to the site with the specified URL. This list is a useful resource from which it is possible to:

1. Develop an understanding of the types of sites that might refer to an organisation's site, seek out additional sites and suggest links from those sites. This is particularly likely to involve connections with industry, trade and local sites.
2. Place paid banner advertising on significant referring sites to strengthen presence on that site.
3. Establish a co-branding arrangement. **Co-branding** is an arrangement by which two or more organisations jointly display each other's content and conduct joint promotions using brand logos or banner advertisements.
4. Sponsorship can take the form of a promoter sponsoring a site, and can also make use of special events and individuals in sponsorship. Often such sponsorship arrangements will embrace both real and virtual media.

E-mail

E-mail is an important communication device in the virtual world, perhaps ranking with speech in the real world. As such its use is ubiquitous. We discuss the use of e-mails in customer service and the personalisation of e-mails in Chapter 5. Here the focus is on e-mails for 'mass' communication. One option is advertisements within an e-mail newsletter. Such newsletters have many of the benefits of print newsletters in that they are targeted and the advertisement is embedded in the newsletter. Another option is to sponsor such a newsletter.

Web casting is a push technology that delivers personalised information to the individual's computer. For effective personalisation, web casting needs to build a profile of the user's interests. Approaches, such as cookies, are discussed in Chapter 5.

Web exhibitions

Web exhibitions can appear to be an attractive option because they may reach many more visitors than a 'stand-and-stare' exhibition, especially in these days when, instead of collecting information at the exhibition, many visitors will be directed to visit the website after the exhibition. The development of web exhibitions is dependent on the capability to create an exhibition experience with opportunities for interaction, examination of products and enjoyment. Innovative applications of VRML are likely to lead to further experimentation with this format.

On-site promotion

Chapter 3 explored website design. An organisation's website is a promotional event in its own right. Just as in traditional consumer environments, the waiting experience is loaded with first impressions. Speedy downloading of the website is essential; visitors may zap a site that takes too long to load and move on. The longer the individual must wait for a site to download, the more negatively the individual rates the website (Mosley-Matchett, 1998). An easy-to-use site with a good search interface is a priority if, once customers arrive at a website, they are to be able to locate the information that they are seeking and to complete their transaction. Raman and Leckenby (1998) suggest that utilitarianism affects the duration of a visit to a greater extent than the hedonistic aspects of the site. As discussed in Chapter 3, most websites of any size and complexity need both a search engine that allows searching by keyword and a set of categories. For example, a number of shopping sites simulate departments, or shelf isles, by grouping products into categories that customers have been accustomed to seeing grouped together.

Other authors have commented on other features of website design. For example, Watson *et al.* (1998) have examined the strategies for creating an attractor site, which they define as a site with the potential to attract and interact with a relatively large number of visitors from a target group. They look at types of attractor, such as the entertainment park, the club, and the customer service. All of these models create a different ambience which the visitor has the opportunity to identify with or to reject. Ovans (1999) notes that salespeople change their demeanour and tone of voice in response to cues from customers. Interactive websites need to be able to respond in a similar way. People are more likely to make purchases from a computer that presents a personality similar to their own. Yet, on the other hand, Ovans (1999) also cites evidence that blatant personalisation of the computer response, that the customer can see is based on information that was not directly volunteered by them, made them less likely to make purchases. Marketing communication needs to embed a great deal of sensitivity as to what are acceptable messages and behaviour in the customer relationship.

Cultivating return visits

Although many sites are in the innovation stage of their lifecycle and there is considerable emphasis on new visitors, there is an increasing recognition that Web consumers are expensive to attract. Retention is therefore a key agenda. The site must exhibit features that encourage return visits. Visitors are likely to return to a site if they had a successful experience with the site on a previous visit, but only if they think that the site has something new to offer. Thus, it will be important that the site creates a sense of a dynamic environment. Content needs to change, as do links to other websites and the content of these other websites. Information content may change, as with news, stock market information and weather, or offers may change, with special limited period discounts, late availability offers and seasonal products. Sponsorship of an event, or a sport personality or team, as discussed above may serve to create news and prompt return visits to a visit. Sales promotions, quizzes, treasure hunts, and prize draws may also add interest. Other approaches to creating relationships are explored in the next two chapters.

EVALUATING SUCCESS

Measuring the success of marketing communications with traditional media was never straightforward. Measurements such as audience size or journal circulation only hint at potential viewers or readers and do not yield actual exposure figures, let alone any data on the impact of those exposures. In Internet communication the inherent one-to-one communication would appear to offer opportunities for monitoring the effect of website presence, specific pages within the website, and specific features such as customer service or banner advertisements. The inherent measurability of many sources of traffic and the ease of recording whether transactions take place suggest that there is an opportunity to gather more detailed information about consumer behaviour than was possible in other environments. On the other hand, these measures are less easy to collect and interpret than they might first appear (Leckenby and Hong, 1998; McKim, 1999; Nicholas *et al.*, 2001). Dreze and Zufryden (1998) suggest that standardised measures are a necessary prerequisite if the effectiveness of exposure in e-media is to be compared with that in traditional media. Nevertheless, measurement is essential in assessing whether a website and its associated e-business activity achieve their objectives.

There are a number of different types of performance measures or metrics that may be used to assess the effectiveness of a website. The appropriateness of any one of these depends upon the objectives that were established in the e-business strategy and related strategies. Typically these objectives will be at three levels:

1. Corporate objectives
2. Marketing objectives
3. Marketing communication objectives

Figure 4.9 summarises some of the different metrics that might be used at the various levels. It should be noted that such metrics must be articulated more precisely for use within a specific organisation. In addition they need further interpretation. Many of these measures would also be applicable to traditional business operations and environments. We discuss those that are specific to the Internet environment in more detail below.

SERVER LOG FILE METRICS

Online metrics are measures that can be collected automatically by software on the web server. This software records data in the log server file when someone visits a web page. Such software is then useful for recording details of the web traffic. These visits are described as '**hits**'. For each hit it is possible to store the date and time of the hit, the pages in the site that are visited, the country of location of the visitor and the browser that she is using.

Hits give an indication of **traffic**, but it is important to remember that there is a gulf between traffic and use, which means that any measures of traffic need to be interpreted very carefully if they are to offer insights into user behaviour (Zawitz, 1998; Meyer, 2000). A hit is recorded for each graphic or

Figure 4.9 Website and e-business performance metrics

Level of objectives	Examples of typical metrics
Corporate objectives	Contribution to revenue
	Profitability of e-business and website activities
	Return on investment
	Cost savings in service delivery
	Quality enhancement
Marketing objectives	Customer acquisition, new leads generated
	Sales generated, whether directly or indirectly though the website
	Customer satisfaction
	Customer retention rate
	Enhanced customer loyalty
	Enhanced corporate and brand presence, image and value
	Cost of acquiring a new customer
	Cost of relationship maintenance
Marketing communication objectives	Awareness efficiency – target web users/all web users
	Locatability/ attraction efficiency – number of individual visits/number of seeks
	Contact efficiency – number of active visitors/number of visits
	Conversion efficiency – number of purchases/number of active visits
	Retention efficiency – number of repurchases/number of purchases.
	Source: Berthon *et al.*, 1998.

block of text requested from a web server. Complex web pages may comprise several graphics and blocks of text. For example, a home page may have a main graphic image, a logo, a list of five items with different graphic bullets next to each one and a menu bar at the bottom. One person visiting this home page will notch up nine hits – one for the home page plus eight for the image files. A further problem with number of hits as a metric is that it does not provide any indication of the nature of the activity that was conducted when a hit was generated.

A more important measure of exposure and use is that of **page impressions**. A page impression corresponds to one person viewing one page. To convert hits to page impressions, it is necessary to factor in the number of components on a given web page.

Another widely used metric is that of **site visits**. A site visit occurs when a visitor visits a website. If the user is interested in the website he may view several pages during one site visit and linger on the site for a while. Visit duration is another measure that has attracted some attention. Longer visits potentially mean more exposure and perhaps a higher level of interest. But, unless we know what the visitor is doing while he is connected, this may be an invalid assumption. Longer visits may mean that the visitor is having a cup of coffee or is otherwise distracted while online. Longer visits may be a sign that users cannot locate the page that they want on a site, or that it takes a longer time to load pages or complete transactions. Longer visits are not necessarily a positive measure.

Web server log file analysis software can be used to analyse log server files, and to create a number of different measures of page impressions. Examples are WebTrends (www.webtrends.com), Superstats (www.superstats.com) and I/PRO site audit (www.ipro.com). Such software report on page impressions, offering for example the following measures:

- Page impressions for different pages in the site
- Page impressions broken down by different time intervals
- Page impressions by domain (for example, by country)
- Page impressions by browser types
- Referring sites, the site that a user visited immediately before the visit to this site
- Exit pages, or the pages from which the visitor exits the site
- Document trails, which summarise the most frequent routes through the site
- Average length of visit.

GROUP DISCUSSION ACTIVITY

Examine each of the measures above and explain how they might inform future site design.

Page caching is the process by which each individual's browser caches pages onto the local client computer, so that the user can revisit that page without calling it from the Internet. This reduces Internet traffic and makes it quicker to go back to a page that a user has already viewed. It may have a serious impact on the accuracy and validity of measures of hits or page impressions, and will cause traffic to be undercounted. Page caching occurs at both institutional and personal levels. There is no way of knowing how frequently an individual has viewed a specific page. The user may also print pages and read the page content 'offline' so that online measurement of use or length of time spent with the content of a website is not possible.

Institutional caching introduces even more complexity. If employees within an organisation are making frequent use of a specific web page, such as the home page of British Airways, the user organisation will store a copy of the BA page on the local server. Viewing the home page can be achieved at the local server; it is only when the user clicks onto something on the home page that a link is made to the Internet server. Now, under standard caching procedures, every page that is viewed from the organisation gets cached until the disk space for caching runs out. Then the organisational server starts to delete the oldest pages and any visits to those pages will provoke a link to the server. Thus many of the page views are to locally-cached versions of pages. This makes it impossible for BA to measure how many pages have been viewed by the employees of any specific organisation. This model is replicated across many institutional servers, so that the number of hits bears little relationship to the level of use of the web page.

MEASURING INDIVIDUALS

Ultimately, analysing anonymous hits on a server has a number of imperfections as a basis for understanding even such factors as audience reach, and goes no way towards understanding the kind of engagement that the user has with the website. One of the big advantages of transaction-based sites is that transactions require individuals to identify themselves. Once individuals have identified themselves through some kind of registration it is possible to measure their activity on a number of different dimensions. Chapter 5 explores a number of approaches that may generate data that can be analysed to profile the behaviour of the customer group as a whole. These include personal profiles, cookies and feedback in the context of the delivery of customer service. This might yield data relating to measures such as:

■ *Access* – an analysis of hits, hosts and sessions, and the identification of sites that refer the most traffic.
■ *Activity* – an analysis for what visitors are doing and what actions are taken.
■ *Community activity* – mailing list signings, traffic and volume of such lists, community participation levels.
■ *Sales transactions* – analysis of which items people are purchasing and the level of sales of these items.

OTHER DATA COLLECTION METHODS

Many of the metrics summarised in Figure 4.9 cannot be collected through analysis of traffic or transactions data online. There are two reasons for this:

■ Some require specific direct dialogue with customers in order to be able to formulate metrics and identify issues for quality enhancement
■ It is often difficult to differentiate between the effect of online and offline channels in, for example, assessing impacts on customer retention, brand enhancement and conversion rates (converting interest to a transaction).

GROUP DISCUSSION ACTIVITY

Which of the metrics in Figure 4.9 might be collected through analysis of traffic or transactions data online?

Dialogue with customers can be achieved using many of the methods that have been tried and tested in marketing research. These methods support the collection of data about customers' attitudes, preferences, and actual and anticipated buying behaviour. Many of these can be executed online or through other channels, such as in person or by post. Online surveys and dialogues are most appropriate when it is necessary to target a group of active web users. Approaches include:

- Individual interviews
- Focus groups
- Questionnaires and surveys
- Observation.

Individual interviews

Interviews are useful for gathering facts and opinions; the data collected is generally qualitative in nature. The two-way communication that is a feature of interviews should provide a more multidimensional analysis of the situation, yielding qualitative data concerning not only what a user does, but also why they do it. Interviews can be conducted in person, over the telephone or possibly through an e-mail dialogue.

There are two main types of one-to-one interview: **structured interviews** and **unstructured** or **flexible interviews**, sometimes called **in-depth interviews**. Structured interviews are guided by a set of predetermined questions often recorded on an interview checklist. Structured interviews are easier to analyse and comparing the comments made by different people is more straightforward. Flexible interviews are guided only by a list of set topics; the interviewer allows the interview to develop in response to the interviewee's comments. Such interviews are useful for 'discovering the unknown' and identifying facts or attitudes that might not have been predicted to be an issue. The main disadvantages of this type of interview are that it is time consuming, needs to be conducted by a trained interviewer and, consequently, can be very expensive. **Semi-structured interviews** are guided by a list of topics, but the way in which this list of topics is used depends upon the interviewees' responses; accordingly, the interview may progress along different routes.

Focus groups

Focus groups are group discussions with, say, 8 to 10 specially selected people in accordance with a set of predetermined criteria. The members of the groups exchange attitudes, experiences and beliefs about the particular topic. The advantages of focus groups are:

1. Respondents experience a sense of safety in numbers and therefore greater willingness to express insights and greater spontaneity

2. The process highlights the possible range of different attitudes and behaviours in a relatively short time
3. The group can be observed with the aim of yielding data on reactions, vocabulary and perceptions
4. Group discussion triggers counter responses which might not surface in individual discussion.

Online focus groups often follow a bulletin board or discussion-group form where different members of the focus group respond to prompts from the focus group leaders. Such groups eliminate the need to bring customers together, which may be difficult if they are geographically scattered.

Questionnaires and surveys

Questionnaires can either be used to conduct a wider survey than might be possible with other methods or to collect subjective data, such as user attitudes that customers might not be prepared to discuss in a person-to-person situation. If users are scattered and it is impossible to conduct interviews, a questionnaire may elicit a quick response from a large number of people. Questionnaires may also be used to identify 'key' individuals, so that interviews can be focused on these individuals. Questionnaires provide quantitative data. This means that analysis is likely to involve at least some basic statistical processing. The nature of these analyses must be determined at the questionnaire design stage, and not after the data has been collected.

A number of sites use onscreen forms to ask questions about the site. Such questionnaires are often in a feedback section of the site. Many of these questionnaires use closed questions, which do not ask the respondent to do more than check an option.

Once questionnaires have been completed and returned to the researcher, any rating scales are converted to numerical values and appropriate statistical analyses are performed. Typically this may involve the calculation of descriptive statistics such as means and standard deviations, and cross tabulations. More sophisticated analysis, possibly using multivariate analysis, will be necessary for surveys including members from a number of different market segments, and where one proposed outcome is a profile of the differences between such segments.

GROUP DISCUSSION ACTIVITY

Make a list of the limitations of e-mail questionnaires in collecting opinions on the information content of a website, with a view to informing the future development of the website.

Observation

Observation of particular individuals or groups, such as customers, potential customers or children, is undertaken by trained observers. The objective is to gather information on some aspect of consumer behaviour and reaction. Observation is not as straightforward as it may seem because observers bring a host of preconceptions to the observation process. Cross checking analysis based on observation is important, and can be performed by using other research methods or by other observers conducting parallel observations. Also, a subject who is aware that she is being watched may modify her behaviour.

Direct observation is where users are observed in specific environments, possibly fulfilling specific tasks. They may be offered a new type of online service to investigate or they may be asked to use a new piece of electronic equipment, such as a kiosk or a mobile phone. Cognitive information such as attitudes, beliefs and motivation or perceptions cannot be observed. One way of gathering this information is **active observation**, where the subject is asked about their actions after the observation episode. Such discussions are also an option with **indirect observation**, in which a video recording of the subject is made, and the subject and the observer then discuss the video recording. These approaches have been used in usability testing of new interface designs, such as web pages, and are useful in testing the acceptability of the design of new information products.

Experiments

Experiments are normally conducted in laboratory environments in which it is possible to manipulate some of the variables and hold others constant, and determine the effect of changing aspects of a design for promotion purposes, or aspects of a product. An experiment might, for example be used to investigate how a group of students make use of a subject information portal. Because well-designed experiments involve careful control of most variables so that other variables can be isolated, most experiments have a very narrow scope and are of limited applicability. **Walk throughs** are a type of field experiment which are useful for assessing service experiences, whether they be real or virtual. In designing a walk through an expert determines the exact task, context and important characteristics of the user population. The evaluator then 'walks through' the necessary action or tasks that take users towards their likely goals with a view to identifying the problems likely to be encountered and strategies used to solve the problems.

CHAPTER SUMMARY

Creating an e-presence starts with a focus on marketing communication. In e-business marketing communication takes on a more strategic role than previously because communication and information exchange become tightly coupled with transactions and other business operations. Organisations need integrated marketing communications that drive consistent marketing messages and relationships through the way in which business processes and service delivery impact on customers. Yet e-businesses, in an unknown marketplace, have been slow to formulate either marketing or promotional objectives for their Web presence. There are a number of key strands to marketing communication in e-business. For example, businesses need to manage their banner advertising campaign, thinking carefully about the design and placement of banner ads. Brands are important for recognition and website location, but the significance of brand extends beyond this role to communication of personality, values and images. Businesses need to choose whether to translate existing brands online or to launch new digital brands. Portals and search engines are points of entry to the Web. Visibility through portals in the form of banner ads and search engine coverage and listings play a role in generating traffic. Other promotional aspects that need to be considered include paid advertising, publicity by word of mouth, co-branding and sponsorship, e-mail and on-site promotion. Measuring the success of marketing communications is never easy. The inherent measurability of many sources of traffic and the ease of recording whether transactions take place suggest an opportunity to gather more detailed information about consumer behaviour. Yet server log file metrics, such as hits, traffic and site visits, are difficult to interpret. Cookies can be useful for tracking individual consumer behaviour, but these need to be supplemented by individual interviews, focus groups, questionnaires and surveys, observations and experiments.

KEY CONCEPTS

Traffic-building campaigns are undertaken to direct traffic to a website. Typically such a campaign will involve an integrated approach including attention to the placement of banner ads, registration with portals and search engines, and exposure of the URL in other offline media.

Promotional objectives are a statement of what an organisation seeks to achieve through its promotional activities.

Banner advertisements are small ads placed on websites other than the organisation's home site. Typically they are displayed across the top of the page as a 'banner' and offer links through to the placing organisation's website.

continued

Click through occurs when a user clicks on a banner ad and is thus directed to the website of the organisation that has placed the banner ad. Click-through rate is the proportion of visitors who click on a banner ad.

Advertising networks are collections of organisations, each of which has an arrangement with an advertising broker to place banner advertisements.

Ad impressions occur when an advertisement is viewed.

Website auditors measure the usage of different sites in terms of the number of ad impressions and click-through rate.

Affiliate networks are established by portals or large online retailers in order to build site traffic. Affiliates place the parent organisation's banner ad on their site in exchange for commission every time click through occurs.

Digital brand is a brand created specifically for use in the Internet context.

Portals are entry points to the Web that provide direction to other sites. Consumers are attracted to use portals through their value-added services, such as directories and search engines, information, news and e-shopping opportunities.

Co-branding is an arrangement between two or more organisations in which they jointly display each other's content and conduct joint promotions.

Server log file metrics are the metrics that represent traffic to a website. Such data includes hit rate and characteristics of site visits, such as the length of visits.

Page caching is when a local workstation stores a recently visited web page to make it easy for the user to return to that page, without actually revisiting the remote server. Page caching can be conducted at individual and institutional level.

ASSESSMENT QUESTIONS

1. Explain how the role of marketing communication is being transformed in the Internet environment.

2. Compare the Internet as an advertising medium with other more traditional media, such as television and newspapers.

3. What is meant by a traffic-building campaign? What might be the objectives of such a campaign?

4. Explain some of the factors that organisations need to consider when designing their plans for banner advertising.

5. What is the difference between a portal and a search engine? Why are portals important in marketing communication?

6. Write a critical account of the factors that influence site listing and ranking in the search output from search engines.

7. Evaluate the role of domain names in marketing communications.

8. What does the concept of 'brand' mean? Offer some suggestions that might guide an organisation in the development of its branding strategy into the online marketplace.

9. Why is word of mouth particularly important in marketing communication in the Internet context?

10. Explain and illustrate with examples the following concepts: co-branding, web casting, affiliate networks and server log metrics.

11. Discuss the different levels at which it is possible to evaluate the performance of a website and its associated e-business. Give examples of some of the metrics that might be applied at each level.

12. Critically discuss the significance of the interrelationships between the following terms, in the context of the evaluation of marketing communication: hits, page impressions, caching, web server log file analysis software.

13. Discuss when you might use:

    (a) focus groups
    (b) questionnaires

    to collect information about customer response to an online retailing operation. What might the strengths and weaknesses of these two approaches be?

 ## GROUP ASSESSMENT 1 – A TRAFFIC-BUILDING CAMPAIGN

You have been commissioned by a small business that sells Scottish salmon and wants to capitalise on all of the opportunities that e-commerce has to offer in order to extend its reputation and customer base, and to encourage return customers. Write a consultant's report that describes how you would go about building traffic to this site. In order to prepare this report you will need to surf the Web for other providers of the same product, both to learn from their approaches to visibility but also as the basis of some of the strategies that you propose. In addition, visit some of the sites quoted in this chapter to learn more about approaches to traffic building. Do not forget to start by proposing some objectives for the traffic-building campaign.

 ## GROUP ASSESSMENT 2 – BANNER ADS

Using as many of the criteria in Figure 4.4 as are appropriate evaluate the banner ads on the home pages of four major portals or search engines. You will proably need to try the evaluation on one or two ads first so that you are sure about how to interpret the criteria.

GROUP ASSESSMENT 3 – WEBSITE EVALUATION

Conduct an evaluation of your university's or college's website, using focus groups. Your primary objective is to identify the nature of the use of the website amongst present students. Refine this objective and then design a set of questions for the focus group. Analyse your results and report on any insights that you have gathered. Comment on whether these insights could be supplemented by any server log metrics. Present your findings as a fifteen-minute verbal presentation.

REFERENCES

Aijo, T (1996) The theoretical and philosophical underpinnings of relationship marketing, *European Journal of Marketing*, **30**(2), 8–18.

Bayus, B L (1985) Word of mouth: the indirect effect of marketing effort, *Journal of Advertising Research*, **25**(3), 31–59.

Bellizzi, A (2000) Drawing prospects to e-commerce websites, *Journal of Advertising Research*, **40**(1 and 2), 43-54.

Berthon, P, Hulbert, J M and Pitt, L F (1999) Brand management prognostications, *Sloan Management Review*, **40**(2), 53–65.

Berthon, P, Pitt, L F, and Watson, R T (1996) The World Wide Web as an advertising medium: toward an understanding of conversion efficiency, *Journal of Advertising Research*, **36**(1) 43–55.

Berthon, B, Pitt, L and Watson, R (1998) The World Wide Web as an industrial marketing communication tool: models for the identification and assessment of opportunities, *Journal of Marketing Management*, **14**, 691–704.

Bradley, N (1999) Sampling for Internet surveys: an examination of respondent selection for Internet research, *Journal of the Marketing Research Society*, **41**(4).

Brassington, F and Pettitt, S (1997) *Principles of marketing*. London: Pitman

Breitenbach, C S and Van Doren, D C (1998) Value added marketing in the digital domain: enhancing the utility of the Internet, *Journal of Consumer Marketing*, **15**(6), 558–75.

Buttle, F (1996) *Relationship marketing: theory and practice*. London: Paul Chapman.

Buttle, F A (1998) Word-of-mouth: understanding and managing referral marketing, *Journal of Strategic Marketing*, **6**, 241–54.

Christopher, M, Payne, A and Ballantyne, D (1991) *Relationship marketing: bringing customer service and marketing together*. Oxford: Butterworth-Heinemann.

Coffey, S (2001) Internet audience measurement: a practitioner's view, *Journal of Interactive Advertising*, **1**(2).

Dahlan, M and Bergendahl, J (2001) Informing and transforming on the web: an empirical study of response to banner ads for functional and expressive products, *International Journal of Advertising*, **20**(2).

Day, A (1997) A model for monitoring Website effectiveness, *Internet Research*, **7**(2), 109–206.

De Chernatony, L and Dall'Olmo Riley, F (1998) Defining a 'brand': beyond the literature with experts' interpretations, *Journal of Marketing Management*, **14**(5), 417–43.

De Chernatony, L and McDonald, M (1998*) Creating powerful brands in consumer, service and industrial markets*, 2nd edn. Oxford: Butterworth-Heinemann.

Dekimpe M, Steenkamp J-B, Mellens M and Abeele P (1997) Decline and variability in brand loyalty, *International Journal of Research in Marketing*, **14**(5), 405–20.

Dholakhia, U M and Rego, L L (1998) What makes commercial Web pages popular?, *European Journal of Marketing*, **32**(7/8), 724–37.

Dibb, S, Simkin, L, Pride, W M and Ferrell, O C (1994) *Marketing concepts and strategies*, 2nd European edn. Boston, London: Houghton Mifflin.

Dreze, X. and Zufryden, (1998) Is Internet advertising ready for the prime time?, *Journal of Advertising Research*, May/June, 7–19.

Ducoffe, R H (1996) Advertising value and advertising on the Web, *Journal of Advertising Research*, Sept/Oct.

Dutta, S and Segev, A (1999) Business transformation on the Internet, *European Management Journal*, 17 (5) 466–77.

Galkoff, R (2000) The big picture (movie marketing), *Marketing Business*, **85**, 14–16.

Ghose, S and Dou, W (1998) Interactive functions and their impacts on the appeal of Internet presence sites, *Journal of Advertising Research*, March/April.

Goodwin, T (1999) Measuring the effectiveness of online marketing, *Journal of the Market Research Society*, **41**(4), 403–6.

Goodyear, M (1996) Divided by a common language, *Journal of the Market Research Society*, **38**(2), 105–22.

Hanson, W (2000) *Principles of Internet Marketing*. Cincinnati, Ohio: South-Western College Publishing.

Hallowell R (1996) The relationship of customer satisfaction, customer loyalty and profitability: an empirical study, *International Journal of Service Industries Management*, **7**(4), 27–42.

Hoffman, D L and Novak, T (1995) Commercial scenarios for the web: opportunities and challenges, *Journal of Computer-Mediated Communication*, **1**(3), Dec.

Hoffman, D L and Novak, T P (2000) How to acquire customers on the web, *Harvard Business Review*, **78**(3), 179–90.

Kannan, P K, Chung, A and Whinston, A B (1998) Marketing information on the I-way, *Communications of the ACM*, **41**(3), 36–43.

Kiani, G R (1998) Marketing opportunities in the digital world, *Internet research*, **8**(2), 185–95.

Langeard, E, Bateson, J, Lovelock, C and Eiglier, P (1981) *Marketing of services: new insights from consumers and managers*. Cambridge, MA: Marketing Sciences Institute.

Leckenby, J D and Hong, J (1998) Using Reach/Frequency for Web media planning, *Journal of Advertising Research*, January/February, **38**(1) 7–21.

Leong, E K F, Huang, X and Stanners, J P (1998) Comparing the effectiveness of the web site with traditional media, *Journal of Advertising Research*, Sept/Oct, **68**(2).

Lockett, A and Blackman, I (2001) Strategies for building a customer base on the Internet: symbiotic marketing, *Journal of Strategic Marketing*, **9**(1).

Loebbecke, C, Powell, P and Trilling, S (1998) Investigating the worth of Internet advertising, *International Journal of Information Management*, **18**(3), 181–94.

Lombard, M and Snyder-Duch, J (2001) Interactive advertising and presence: a framework, *Journal of Interactive Advertising*, **1**(2).

MacMillan, G (1998) Portals: web advertising's holy grail, *Campaign (UK)*, 2 Oct, 30–1.

Martinson, R (1995) The role of brands in European marketing, *Journal of Brand Management*, **2**(4).

McKim, R (1999) Monitoring website visitors: a case study of IBM's SurfAid, *Journal of Database Marketing*, **6**(4).

McNaughton, R B (2001) A typology of website objectives in high technology business markets, *Marketing Intelligence & Planning*, **19**(2), 82–7.

Meyer, E (2000) Web metrics: too much data, too little analysis, in D Nicholas and I Rowlands (eds) *Impact and evaluation of the Internet*. Proceedings of a conference held at Windsor Great Park, 1999. London: Aslib.

Morgan, R M and Hunt, S D (1994) The commitment-trust theory of relationship marketing, *Journal of Marketing*, **58**, 20–38.

Mosley-Matchett, J D (1999) The effects of presentation latency on proficient and nonproficient users of internet-based marketing presentations. Proceedings of the 1998 AMA Winter Educator's Conference. Chicago, Ill.: American Marketing Association, 399–400.

Nicholas, D, Huntington, P, Lievesley, N and Wasti, A (2001) Evaluating consumer website logs: a case study of *The Times/Sunday Times* website, *Journal of Information Science*, **26**(6), 399–411.

Novak, T and Hoffman, D (1996) New metrics for new media: towards the development of web measurement standards, *World Wide Web Journal*, Winter, **2**(1), 213–46.

Ovans, A (1999) Is your website socially savvy?, *Harvard Business Review*, **77**(3), 20.

Palmer, J W and Eriksen, L B (2000) Digital news: content, delivery, and value propositions for an intangible product, *Journal of End User Computing*, **12**(2), 11–20.

Pardun, C J and Lamb, L (1999) Corporate Websites in traditional print advertisements, *Internet Research*, **9**(2), 93–100.

Peterson, R A (1997) *Electronic marketing and the consumer*. London: Sage.

Philport, J C and Arbitter, J (1997) Advertising: brand communication styles in established media and the Internet, *Journal of Advertising Research*, **37**(2), 68–77.

Raman, N V and Leckenby, J D (1998) Factors affecting consumers' Webad visits, *European Journal of Marketing*, **32**(7/8), 737–49.

Ranchhod, A, and Gurau, C (2000) On-line messages: developing an integrated communications model for biotechnology companies. Proceedings of the British Academy of Management.

Rowley, J (2001) Remodelling marketing communications in an Internet environment, *Internet Research*, **11**(3), 203–12.

Rowley, J E and Dawes, J (1998) Enhancing the customer experience: contributions from information technology, *Management Decision*, **36**(5), 350–7.

Rowley, J E and Slack, F (1998) *Public access interface design*. Aldershot: Gower.

Sharp, B M (1993) Managing brand extension, *Journal of Consumer Marketing*, **10**(3).

Sterne, J (1999) *World Wide Web marketing*, 2nd edn. New York: Wiley.

Stout, R (1997) *Website stats: tracking hits, and analysing traffic*. McGraw Hill.

Strader, T J, and Shaw, M J (1999) Consumer cost differences for traditional Internet markets, *Internet Research*, **9**(2), 82–93.

Storbacka, K (1997) Segmentation based on customer profitability – retrospective analysis of retail bank customers, *Journal of Marketing Management*, **13**, 479–92.

Thelan, S (2001) The Internet as a channel for market research: avenues for future research, *Quarterly Journal of Electronic Commerce*, **2**(3).

Timmers, P (2000) *Electronic commerce: strategies and models for business-to-business trading*. Chichester: Wiley.

Van Doren, D C, Fechner, D L and Green-Adelsberger, K (2000) Promotional strategies on the World Wide Web, *Journal of Marketing Communications*, **6**(1), 21–36.

Watson, R T, Akelsen, S and Pitt, L F (1998) Attractors: building mountains in the flat landscape of the World Wide Web, *California Management Review*, **40**(2), 36–57.

Yang, C C (1997) An exploratory study of the effectiveness of interactive advertisements on the Internet, *Journal of Marketing Communication*, **3**.

Zawitz, M (1998) Web statisitics – measuring user activity. Available at www.ojp.usdoj.gov/bjs/pub/ascii/wsmua.txt.

Zufryden, F (2000) New film Web site promotion and box-office performance, *Journal of Advertising Research*, **40**(1 and 2), 55–65.

5 Serving customers

Your website is a two-way street, not a one-way broadcast
(Sterne, 1999)

LEARNING OUTCOMES

After reading this chapter you will:

- Be able to discuss the unique features of the web service experience
- Be able to evaluate critically the consumer shopping experience
- Be able to compare and contrast the different elements of customer support and service in e-business
- Understand the different approaches to customisation and personalisation

INTRODUCTION

Websites are far more than publicity and order-taking – they are for helping customers to solve problems. The nature of the service experience in e-commerce can be discussed at two different levels. E-commerce focuses on two main categories of business: retailing and service industries. In traditional marketplaces both of these categories of business have been concerned to manage the service experience and its delivery. The quality of the service experience is seen as an important competitive contribution, and integrally associated with customer satisfaction. It is important in determining when and where consumers will engage in e-commerce. Further, the enhancement of customer value through customer support and quality improvement provide two of the strongest justifications for developing Web-based applications. In e-commerce many characteristics of the service environment and context are defined through the interaction that is possible with the customer at a distance, through the screen and keyboard, and other supplementary channels, such as the telephone or post.

THE ONLINE SERVICE EXPERIENCE

First and foremost, any Web interface that is used for customer interaction and service delivery is 'critical' to the service experience and needs to be reliable and consistent in the delivery of an appropriate service, and to lead to customer satisfaction.

As discussed later in this chapter, the service experience delivered through an IT-based channel is often supplemented by human interaction, either in person as, for example, with an in-store kiosk, or via telephone or e-mail communication as is common with Web applications. Figure 5.1 shows a number of different models for the embedding of IT in the service experience. These are:

1. *The customer interacts with the service agent*, who uses IT on the customer's behalf to support the delivery of the service experience
2. *The customer interacts with the computer*, but may access a service agent through the IT interface (as in e-mail or placing an order)
3. *The customer accesses both the service agent and IT in parallel*, as when the service agent and the customer jointly pursue airline seat-availability data, prior to making an online booking
4. *The customer has only the IT channel to use and no human support*. This would be the case with a public access kiosk and websites with a low level of interactivity
5. *The customer has a choice of two different routes or channels* to effect transactions or to locate the information that she seeks.

The embedding of technology in the service experience is taking place against a backdrop of increasing technological sophistication, global marketplaces and communities, and an ever-increasing significance of service products in national and international economies. The nature of the service experience is also being shaped by some of these factors.

Figure 5.1 Roles for IT in service delivery in retailing

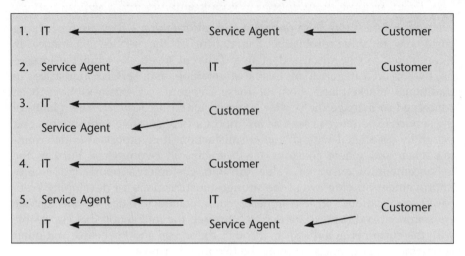

When consumers acquire or engage with a service, they undergo an experience that centres on the simultaneous delivery and receipt of the service. Services are viewed as being distinct from goods due to their inherent characteristics of intangibility, inseparability (of production and consumption), perishability and heterogeneity (Dibb *et al.*, 1994). During this interaction the employee or service provider and the customer are physically and psychologically drawn together (Solomon *et al.*, 1985). Consumers are involved in the production process and can take responsibility for the service, which they receive (Hoffman and Bateson, 1997). Further advantage can be accrued by increasing the participation of customers in the service experience so that costs of service delivery can be lowered because the consumer engages in self service. IT-based service delivery makes it possible for customers to be very active indeed in all parts of the production process so that they are not passive recipients but active **co-producers** (Storbacka, 1997). Involvement of the customer in service delivery to the extent that they are co-producers of the service experience demands revision of the roles that the customer and the service agent are expected to play (Hoffman and Bateson, 1997). The new script and any associated expectations about customer behaviour and roles need to be communicated to customers in this new environment. Typically, customers may be expected to play the role of a partial employee and enter their own personal and order details. One view suggests that customers will be drawn ever closer into the production process to the point of ultimate integration.

When considering the service experience in e-commerce transactions it is useful to remember the seven basic stages in an e-shopping service event, as shown in Figure 5.2 (Rowley, 1996), and to understand that the experience of the total service event is the accumulation of the customer's experience in each of these stages. Different aspects of the interface are typically more or less important at each of the different stages. Thus, for example, in the Search/Browse phase, website design and search facilities are crucial. In the View/Select stage, detailed product information is key. In the Ordering stage,

- The transaction, such as making a booking, can be structured by the technology, so that the experience is more standardised and rules for, say, discounts are more consistently applied.
- Where a human service agent is used as a backup, the service agent is likely to deal with less routine transactions and, therefore, needs to be more highly skilled. Further the service agent is empowered to take decisions on the basis of customer information, such as creditworthiness or loyalty, without reference to more senior or experienced staff.
- Where the service agent accesses the system on behalf of the client, the service agent will often be accessing relatively complex databases and will, again, need enhanced skills.
- In do-it-yourself applications, the customer needs to learn how to use the system and will benefit from simple and carefully designed interfaces.

This is an impressive list of advantages but there are also a number of challenges associated with the use of IT in service delivery. These include:

- The need for both staff and customer training and learning
- Customers must be persuaded that they are comfortable with IT-based service delivery
- The effect that the different configurations of IT in service delivery have on customer attraction and retention
- Whether IT-based service interactions can cultivate customer loyalty and evoke appropriate emotional responses that might lead to repeat and additional purchases requires further exploration.

GROUP DISCUSSION ACTIVITY

There are now many different ways of booking a flight to Paris and overnight accommodation for three nights. These include package deals and options where the traveller can book flights and accommodation separately. Either packages or components can be booked through a travel agent or through the Web. Which option would you use and why?

GROUP DISCUSSION ACTIVITY

Reflect on your last visit to a doctor's surgery. How could IT be used to support the service delivery in this context? For which aspects of the service delivery do you feel that it is essential to retain a human service agent? In answering these questions think about the booking, checking into the surgery, consultation, record-keeping, prescription and treatment, and the collection of drugs for treatment.

■ THE CONSUMER SHOPPING EXPERIENCE

One context in which the service experience has been much explored is in the context of the consumer shopping experience. Shopping has becomes 'a cultural phenomena within contemporary 'post modern' society' (Falk and Campbell, 1997, p. 1), and has therefore attracted much debate and attention. Shopping can be viewed simply as purchasing a commodity or service (Miller, 1997). The cognitive perspective on consumer decision-making takes an information-processing perspective. The online environment is rich in information and ideally suited to support information collection and analysis. However, in traditional retail environments there has been much discussion of the shopping experience, in which the focus is on affective factors such as entertainment and pleasure. This section explores both of these perspectives. By way of context, Figure 5.3 summarises some of the differences between traditional bricks-and-mortar and online stores, and thereby emphasises the very different contexts for the shopping experience in these environments.

Figure 5.3   Comparing a bricks-and-mortar store with an online store

Bricks and Mortar Store	Online Store
Sales assistant	Product descriptions, information pages, gift services, search options, customer service through e-mail and telephone
In-store promotion	Special offers, online games and lotteries, links to other sites of interest, appetiser information
Store display windows	Home page
Store atmosphere	Interface consistency, store organisation, interface and graphics quality
End of aisle displays	Features products on hierarchical levels within the menu system for the store
Store layout	Screen depth, browse and search function, indexes, image maps
Number of floors in the store	Hierarchical levels in the store
Number of store entrances and store outlets or branches	Number of links to a particular online retail store
Checkout person	Online shopping basket and order form
Look and touch of the merchandise	Image quality and description
Number of people entering the store	Number of unique visits to the online store
Sales per period	Sales per period

Source: Based on Lohse and Spiller (1999).

In the information-processing perceptive (Rogers, 1962), the consumer is viewed as the problem solver engaged in the goal-directed activities of searching for information, with a view to arriving at carefully considered evaluations (Punj and Staelin,1983; Kotler and Armstrong, 1994).

A simple and often-quoted model of the decision-making process associated with consumer buying is that discussed by Brassington and Pettit (1997). The rational decision-making model identifies the stages in Figure 5.4 and shows the processes of information search and information evaluation as key preparatory stages to a decision, which leads to a purchase. Subsequent to problem recognition the consumer seeks a solution to the problem. The questions to be answered include, 'What kind of purchase will solve the problem?', 'Where and how can it be obtained?', 'What information is needed to arrive at a decision?' and 'Where is that information available?'. Sometimes consumers will actively seek out information with a view to using it immediately to make a decision (directed or purposeful searching). On other occasions users browse or graze through information sources gathering information that they may use immediately or later.

In this rational decision-making model, the information available to the consumer is important and the utility of a communication channel can be judged on its attributes of quantity, quality and recentness of information. These factors determine the utility of a communication channel to meet consumer's information needs for decision-making. The function of the distribution channel is to facilitate the payment and transfer of the ownership of a product. The key attributes of a channel are pre-purchase inspection of products, security of payment, prompt access to goods bought, easy exchange and return, and other post-purchase services.

The ability to collect product information and make comparisons between the different product offerings from different providers, possibly across national and currency boundaries, is often viewed as one of the main competitive challenges of e-shopping and is therefore a key aspect of the online shopping experience.

Figure 5.4 The consumer decision-making experience

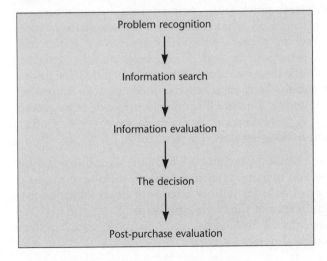

It is important to remember that consumers are not restricted to the virtual world for their information gathering. Other potential sources of information are:

- Their own previous experience with a product or brand
- Recommendations (word-of-mouth) from family, friends and colleagues
- Previous imprinting as a result of promotion, usually in association with specific brands
- Visits to bricks-and-mortar stores to experience the product
- Consumer magazines, trade press and marketing websites and literature.

Marketers need to be wary of creating information overload. There is a fine balance between providing sufficient information for the consumer to make a decision and too much information, that provokes **information overload**. In other words, consumers need just sufficient information to be able to conduct the information-evaluation stage. This stage is concerned with matching the features of the product against the consumers' criteria (or what the consumers feel that they want). This evaluation should narrow the number of potential products and, where only one product matches the criteria, lead automatically to the decision stage.

GROUP DISCUSSION ACTIVITY

Draw up a table that describes the differences between bricks-and-mortar shopping and Internet shopping in relation to the different stages in the consumer decision-making process as identified in Figure 5.4. Remember that this model of the process is most appropriate for extensive decision-making situations. Discuss how the two types of experience would differ for routine purchases, such as supermarket food shopping.

Whilst the rational decision-making model is useful for emphasising the role of information and information seeking in consumer decision making, the situation is in actuality very much more complex. This is mainly because there are all sorts of influences on what consumers think that they want. Indeed, the information seeking process, which may involve a complex mix of interpersonal sources, print sources and the Internet, may be iterative. Consumers may start with one understanding of their needs and refine this as they gather more information. Marketers will be concerned to control as much of this process as possible, whether through electronic or other media channels. Nevertheless, it is important not to overlook the myriad of other influences on the decision-making process. These include:

- The nature of the buying situation, including whether it is routine response behaviour, limited decision making, extensive decision making or impulse buying; the significance of risks (as with purchases of financial products); and the perceived significance of the buying problem
- Situational and environmental influences, such as those which reflect fashion and current cultural trends

- Individual influences, such as personality, perceptions, motivation for the purchase and attitudes
- Group influences, such as those associated with belonging to or identifying with a social class, culture or subculture, or reference groups, such as family and other social groups
- Shopping orientation of the individual consumer. Shopping orientation is conceptualised as a dimension of lifestyle. There are a number of different frameworks for shopping orientation. For example, one taxonomy identified four kinds of shopping orientations: economic, personalising, ethical and apathetic. Another taxonomy has the following three groups: inactive shopper, active out-shopper and thrifty innovator.

Shopping is often not simply a process in which consumers make decisions about purchases; they also value the shopping expedition as an experience and, sometimes, a leisure or pleasure experience (Holbrook and Hirschman, 1982). Tauber (1972) noted that consumers often shop out of personal motives (role playing, diversion from the routine of daily life, self-satisfaction, learning about new trends, physical activity and sensory stimulation) and social motives (social experiences outside the home, communication with others having a similar interest, peer group attraction, status and authority, and pleasure of bargaining). Jansen-Verbeke (1997) suggests that women view non-food shopping as a leisure experience, which includes eating, drinking in cafés and bars, sightseeing and simply walking around. Whilst some shopping trips are undertaken in order to find a specific item, many shopping trips are performed just to socialise and catch up with friends, or to have time alone. Accordingly, if a purchase is not made the quality of the activity is not lessened in any way (Campbell, 1997). Browsing is part of this process. Browsing has been described as a screening activity that is independent of any specific purchase needs or decision. Underhill (1999) argues that the function of browsing is to experience the items for sale, using senses of sight, touch, smell, taste and hearing. Sight conjures up emotions and images that are strengthened by the sensory processes of touching the item and trying on (Underhill, 1999). Further affirmation (or disconfirmation) is provided by the approval of others, such as comments made by a friend or by other shoppers to shop assistants. Browsing is gratifying in itself (Douglas, 1997).

GROUP DISCUSSION ACTIVITY

Each group member is asked to think of a 'critical incident' in the form of a recent memorable shopping trip to a bricks-and-mortar store. Share experiences in turn, and support the raconteurs in their attempts to identify what they were seeking from the experience.

It is difficult to replicate the richness of the real-world shopping experience in an online shop. Instead Internet shoppers perform the activity alone, in front of a terminal and keyboard in an environment such as the home or the office. Smith (1998) reports that many websites are functional rather than enjoyable. *Economist* (2000) notes the poverty of websites in relation to the creation of a social experience, and for browsing and generating serendipity and impulse purchases. Online shopping can be viewed as purchase driven and is seen to be suitable for those with a matching shopping orientation. Miller (1998) argues that the convenience associated with online shopping is attractive to men, but since online shopping cannot replicate the multi-dimensional shopping experience of traditional shops is likely to have limited appeal for women.

A number of authors have commented on the importance of interfaces and effective navigation in online stores (Baty and Lee, 1995; Hoffman *et al.*, 1995; Jarvenpaa and Todd, 1997; Lohse and Spiller, 1998, 1999; Hunt, 2000). Lohse and Spiller (1999) assessed navigation in terms of the amount of effort (that is, time, number of steps) required to browse and navigate the online retail store. Navigation features noted included:

- the number of hyperlinks into each store
- the number of hyperlinks between products
- the number of products on the end product pages
- the number of buttons used to browse the store
- the type of checkout and order process
- the average number of scroll list items.

These measures offer a useful perspective on navigation within the store, but it is important to recognise that shoppers need to locate a specific store before they can utilise these devices, and complexity in the search process arises from the need to locate and explore more than one store.

EXPLORATORY ACTIVITY

Choose a newly released CD. Visit the HMV (www.hmv.co.uk) website, locate the item and explore how you might purchase the item. Draw up a table to compare this experience with the experience of purchasing a CD in a normal shop.

EXPLORATORY ACTIVITY

Select two online stores and compare the checkout and order processes in terms of:

- Sequencing of stages
- Ease of deletion
- Number of items that can be purchased
- Payment processes and options.

Which store do you prefer and why?

CUSTOMER SUPPORT AND SERVICE

Customer service is concerned with giving customers the opportunity to talk to the organisation and to receive personalised responses. Contents, or customer information and advice, should be presented in such a way that customers identify with them, and they feel that their needs can be met. This is also an important component in the total experience because these activities allow customers to 'own the web merchant'. With this sense of ownership comes a sense of belonging and community (as discussed in the next chapter).

Customer support and service embraces the strategies that e-merchants use to increase the customer experience. The objective of customer support and service is to enhance the value of the interaction to the customer and thereby to improve customer satisfaction. Customers must be made to feel special. The service experience is defined by:

1. The design of the interface, including ease of use and goodness of fit between the tasks that the customer wants to complete and those available through the interface. This has been discussed in Chapter 3.
2. Opportunities for dialogue between the customer and the service agent through a variety of different channels. This aspect is developed further in this section.
3. Delivery of, and customer satisfaction with, the product or service that the customer has purchased from the e-merchant. Logistics and supply are explored in Chapter 7.

An effective service experience requires attention to detail. In an online environment, this is usually somewhat more formulaic than in some other service contexts. Figure 5.4 summarises useful operational details, and suggests some of the ways in which customer service can be offered.

Web-based customer support can lead to:

■ Lower customer support costs, or
■ Improved customer support quality, or
■ A combination of these two.

Lower customer support costs increase margins and lend scope for price competitiveness. Improved quality should lead to enhanced customer satisfaction, which should be reflected in customer acquisition and retention rates. Whatever balance of cost and quality benefits are provided through customer service, it is essential to understand where the added value of the service lies for the business and the customer. Some examples of approaches to cost savings and reduction in the resources used to offer customer service and quality enhancements are listed below.

Potential avenues for **cost savings** are:

1. Online publishing of, for example, product manuals. This has been used in the automobile industry to support ordering of spare parts.
2. Electronic distribution of software, including software upgrades, patches and new releases.
3. Virtual problem solving of customer problems. The computer industry has extensive help lines and telephone help is expensive to support.

Online help can be much more cost effective. Options that require little service intervention include FAQs, customer discussion lists, customer links to online resources and customer chat rooms. In addition, special site features can assist users to diagnose their own problems. For example, Dell offers a personalised interface (support.euro.dell.com).

4. Scalability and flexibility of online support. Traditional methods of customer support need one-to-one exchanges in real time (whenever the customer needs support). Online support can be many-to-many and 24/7.

Quality can be enhanced through all of the four stages of the development of the relationship with the customer: product design, sales activity, after sales, and understanding of the company.

There are a number of different avenues through which customer service and support can be delivered:

- E-mail
- Newsgroups, chat rooms and message boards
- FAQs
- Customer service information
- Feedback forms
- Help lines
- Other customer service information
- Co-production

E-mail

> According to Internet research firm Jupiter Communications, up to 42% of top-ranked Web sites took longer than five days to respond to a customer inquiry. (Lord, 2000 p. 44)

E-mail is used extensively as an avenue for dialogue between the customer and a service agent. From the customer's perspective, the use of e-mail may eliminate the need to explain a question to several service agents as a query is passed down the line to the department or agent with the expertise to answer the question. Furthermore, whilst customers may not get an immediate response, there is no need to queue. Most help desks suggest that they try to give a response within 24 hours. From the service agent's point of view, e-mails appear one at a time (rather than in a queue) and can be dealt with in sequence. E-mails can easily be forwarded to another service agent, a supervisor or expert if additional information is required. With more complex queries, the response will be recorded in the system and can be used to answer subsequent enquiries on the same topic. If handled effectively, the customer is satisfied by the e-mail exchange and the customer service department learns more about the types of difficulties that customers have with its products or services and evolves solutions to those problems. The checklist in Figure 5.5 summarises some useful tips relating to effective e-mail communication.

E-mail help-desk services can be expensive to operate due to the personalised nature of the response. Some e-merchants declare that they are unable to offer this facility. Others are gaining reputations for not responding at all or responding very slowly to e-mail requests from

Figure 5.5 Checklist for using e-mail to talk to customers

1. **Relevant and targeted**. Junk mail is likely to be resented and has nuisance value! Profiles of previous purchases can be used to select a targeted segment with whom to communicate about a specific new product or special offer.

2. Make contact **timely and infrequent**. E-mails should only be sent when there is something to announce and not on a routine basis.

3. **Personalise**. Give name, telephone number and e-mail address of a named contact, so that there is a personal link to whom the customer can respond and not just an anonymous face.

4. Use **auto responders** or 'mail bots' to provide automatic response where appropriate, but be careful about depersonalisation. For example, a mailbox can be used to respond to an e-mail to a customer service department, to acknowledge receipt and to indicate that the query is being dealt with, and by whom. Personal contact may then follow.

5. Provide easy **opt-out** from receiving further messages.

6. **Train** customer service agents to formulate e-mails that offer a considered and effective response. Impress on them that e-mail is a formal channel of communication and e-mails are legal documents.

7. **Respond quickly**. Give a deadline by which customers can expect a response.

customers. One way of reducing the cost of e-mail responses is to use smart e-mail, in which the system tries to produce an answer from its databank automatically. If an appropriate answer is not forthcoming the system tries to predict the best service agent to deal with the query. Over time, the system learns from the agent's response because the response is incorporated into the knowledge base. The success of this technology is dependent upon the quality of the match between standard responses received by customers and their queries. There is some evidence to suggest that customers react negatively to such standard responses, partly because their query is not really answered but also because they resent the absence of the human touch.

In addition to the use of e-mail to solve individual consumer problems, it is often also used as an avenue through which customer feedback is gathered and as a channel for marketing communication.

Newsgroups, chat rooms and message boards
These services allow customers to communicate with one another. In addition to their value in building community, they allow customers to offer each other support and to share their expertise. For example, in the computer industry a common problem is getting one piece of equipment or software to work with another. Vendors do not have the resources to check out compatibility in respect of every possible combination of equipment and software from other vendors. Individuals who share their experiences through newsgroups may well have these answers. Newsgroups are also forums through which customers can share positive and negative comments about the organisation's products and services. By monitoring these newsgroups organisations can garner a rich view of complaints and criticisms about their products, often articulated by those with some expertise. This is a valuable stream of data that can inform product development. Participation

in newsgroups can also steer discussions, and limit the escalation of unjustified criticism. **Expert forums** present opportunities for customers to collect advice from experts, often in a live chat format.

FAQs

FAQs (frequently asked questions) are common customer-service resources. They are the most common questions posed by customers, which are collected, together with their answers, and can be viewed online. From a customer perspective FAQs are immediately available 24 hours a day. They can be useful both in customer support and for 'prospects'. An e-merchant can track which FAQs customers are reading and learn about the weaknesses in other marketing communications. This information can be used in the review and revision of the FAQs and other information that is made available to customers.

GROUP DISCUSSION ACTIVITY

Visit one website each. Note the issues that FAQs cover. Discuss the coverage of FAQs on different sites. Is there a standard set of issues that most FAQ lists cover?

Customer service information

The information that needs to be provided depends upon the merchant's product range. For example, for computer systems, customers want product specifications, compatibility charts, product release schedules and pricing. If a merchant is selling theatre tickets, customers want performance schedules, ticket pricing, seating charts and location details.

Feedback forms

These are forms through which customers can complain or provide positive comments about the service and the products provided by the web merchant. Web merchants need to make an undertaking to respond to each comment and to specify the period within which the customer can expect a response. This period should be of the order of 24 hours, or two to three days at most. Most importantly, organisations should not set targets in this area and, thereby, create expectations that they cannot meet.

Help lines

Help lines can be accessed, preferably both via e-mail or telephone contact. A further option is live chat text. 24-hour/7-day-a-week lines are rapidly becoming the norm.

Other customer service information

Other information that might be available as part of customer service includes:

■ Information and transactions relating to loyalty schemes
■ Product recall information
■ A returns policy and associated details about refunds
■ Guidelines (that explain how to use the site, policies, etc.)
■ A what's new e-mail announcement service
■ An opportunity to request a print catalogue.

Co-production

Co-production develops when customer support informs and educates customers. A better informed customer base brings with it a number of benefits for both the customer and the company. Customers benefit because they:

■ Learn more about the product
■ Improve their skills in using the product
■ Learn to solve problems.

The customer is no longer the passive recipient of a product and some support material and advice. The customer is a partner who will help to solve problems and share information. Customer support can be based on previous involvement and alliances can develop. Moon and Frei (2000), however, warn that co-production should not be seen as a burden on the customer; customers like choice, but not too much choice. The theme of relationships between customers and organisations is explored more fully in the next chapter.

EXPLORATORY ACTIVITY

Visit a website of your choice. Which of the features listed in Figure 5.6 are included on the website? Would the addition of any of the other features enhance the website?

Figure 5.6   Questions to inform effective online customer service

1. Does the website greet visitors who have been there before?
2. Are there a range of different channels for customer service ranging from online ordering to advice, to telephone based help lines, and chat rooms?
3. Is there a prominent returns policy that is honoured?
4. Does customer service support the entire transaction cycle, including decision support, ordering, delivery, and returns, and the customer needs for information at each of these stages?
5. Do customers have access to FAQs?
6. Are orders confirmed by e-mail very soon after they are placed?
7. Are customers notified of any delays in processing an order?
8. Can customers track their own orders themselves?
9. Are customers invited to offer feedback on the service?
10. Are all customer e-mails guaranteed a response within 24 hours?
11. Does the system track the customer's activities to ensure that they are receiving the correct level of service?
12. Do customer service representatives have an appropriate knowledge base to support information provision?
13. Is a smart cart system in operation? Does the cart offer extra services such as gift wrapping?

CUSTOMISATION AND PERSONALISATION

> Personalisation is a special form of product differentiation – it transforms a standard product or service into a specialised solution for an individual (Hanson, 2000, p. 186)

The ultimate aim of customer service is to meet the individual needs of each and every customer. One of the oft-cited advantages of e-commerce is the opportunity for personalisation or customisation, although in a service sense some might argue that it would be difficult to replace the personalisation embedded in a one-to-one relationship or transaction between a human service agent and a customer.

Customisation through the use of IT offers value when the alternative would be a mass-market response. Customisation is attractive to customers because it reduces search costs and presents customers with products that have a higher degree of relevance. For organisations, customisation has potential to generate increased revenue, increased loyalty and reduced costs in customer acquisition and retention. The potential for customisation depends on the products and services that organisations are seeking to deliver through the Internet. Customisation is likely to be particularly significant in information intensive products and aspects of service delivery and marketing communication. In relation to products, customisation has considerable potential for music, software, publishing and education.

Prahalad and Ramaswamy (2000) differentiate between customisation and personalisation thus:

Customisation occurs when the manufacturer designs a product to suit a customer's needs. Customers can customise a host of products, such as business cards, computers, greetings cards, mortgages and flowers, by choosing from a menu of features.

Personalisation occurs when the customer is a co-creator of the content of their experiences. For an online florist, for example, this means customers could specify and design the type, quantity and arrangement of flowers, vases and colours that they desired. Customisation would allow customers to select from a range of predesigned arrangements. With personalisation, the customer would also be able to discuss his ideas with in-house experts and possibly other customers.

GROUP DISCUSSION ACTIVITY

Make a table that summarises and compares the advantages and disadvantages of personalisation and customisation. Give examples of products for which each might be appropriate.

Creating customer profiles

Whether the merchant is aiming for a customised web page, or a completely individualised product or service as the outcome of the Web-based interaction, the merchant needs to collect information about the customer in order to engage in personalisation. The sources of such information are one or more of the following:

- *The customer provides information in response to a request for the information* as feedback on customer service or as part of a Web-based or other survey.
- *The customer provides information as a by-product of a transaction.* The merchant can store the customer's name, address, e-mail address, credit card details and any other details that the customer provides during a purchase or registration transaction. AOL, for example, knows who their customers are because they have all registered. The transactions performed by a customer, in addition to the websites that they have visited, can be recorded and analysed and used to strengthen the profile of the customer. Every time a customer tells the e-merchant something in pursuit of a purchase, such as 'my skin is dry' or 'I do not garage my car', this can be added to the profile.
- *The merchant uses cookies to keep track of the customer's actions.* **Cookies** are used by server-side connections to store and retrieve information on the client side of the connection. Web browsers set aside a small amount of space on a client hard drive in which to store a server-side user identification number, the date of the user's last visit plus other useful information, such as preferences. Each time the client connects through to the server, the server looks for the cookie on the hard drive and through this cookie is able to identify the client. By this process, the server can gradually gather a profile of the client machine's Web-based activity. Cookies can be used to personalise web pages; names can be stored for subsequent use by the server application. There are however, some drawbacks to cookies:

1. Since cookies are plain text files on the client, they can easily be modified or deleted by the user.
2. Cookies are browser specific. If a customer uses both Netscape and Internet Explorer, she will have a different cookie for each software package and it is impossible to build an integrated profile of her activity.
3. Cookies are machine specific. This is a considerable handicap in trying to analyse data from cookies in order to create profiles of individuals. If a customer uses more than one machine (at home, on the move, at a kiosk, in the office), a new cookie (with no link with other cookies) will be created on each of these machines. Further, if other people also use these machines, their activities will be recorded on the same cookie.
4. There is some user resistance to cookies based on the lack of disclosure and the sense that an unknown party is placing data on the user's machine.

Cookies are used with shopping carts on e-commerce sites to store the items that the user wishes to order, until all purchases have been selected. When the transaction is completed, the server reads the cookie file and initiates a transaction based on the details in the cookie file. Cookies can also be used to link to a server database; this database may include names, addresses, credit card details, and the past purchasing history of the customer.

Types of customisation

Gilmore and Pine (1997) distinguish between two distinct types of customisation:

1. Representation, or how the product or service is portrayed to the customer. Customisation through representation can include:

   ■ Customisation of the content of marketing messages such as e-mail messages and the website seen by specific customers
   ■ Customisation of the targeting of marketing messages, as in permission marketing

2. Product attributes in which customisation can create unique functionality, targeting specific preferences of behaviour of an individual. For example, Lands' End will monogram items, and alter trousers to fit the customer's leg length. Some financial services providers design an investment portfolio to match individual needs.

Gilmore and Pine summarise these approaches in a two-by-two matrix, as shown in Figure 5.7, with marketing representation as one dimension for customisation and product definition as the other. Each dimension in Figure 5.7 shows two points along the spectrum of customisation. An organisation may supply one product to a mass market or offer a unique product to each customer or find one or more middle positions in which it tailors products to match what it perceives to be the needs of a market niche or group of customers.

Figure 5.7 Dimensions of customisation

| | | Representation | |
		No change	Change
Product	Change	Transparent	Collaborative
	No Change	Adaptive	Cosmetic

The different types of customisation in Figure 5.7 illustrate some of the options available to online businesses:

Adaptive customisation occurs without change to either the representation or the product. Instead the customisation is based on the design of filters that assist the user to locate the best product for his purpose. Filters that support customer choice are important. This approach is suitable for mass markets in which it is not possible, or even desirable, to tailor either products or their representations. In such a context the primary support offered to customers is **choice assistance** through agents that seek to determine an individual's tastes and needs and make a recommendation that simplifies the choice process. There are a number of different approaches that can be used to aid in this choice process. **Electronic recommendation agents** or **shopping bots**, as discussed in Chapter 3, typically draw together a number of products from different suppliers and make recommendations on the basis of price. A higher level of customisation can be achieved if recommendations are based on personal preferences. Current agents depend on collaborative filtering. **Collaborative filtering algorithms** take preference data from an individual, through a questionnaire or by mapping their previous choices (either in terms of websites visited or purchases), and seek other individuals in their database with similar preference patterns; product recommendations are made on the basis of the choices of these other consumers. This approach is based entirely on preference data. There are no insights into reasons for preferences, and products can only be recommended if preference data is already available.

COLLABORATIVE FILTERING: AMAZON.COM

CASE
CAMEO

When customers place an order for a book with Amazon.com, they are invited to identify a category of books that interests them most. Customers specify a category, an author or a title. Amazon.com sends them an e-mail when a newly published book meets the criteria. Through this mechanism, Amazon is able to predict sales of new books. The company knows how many people want information about the new book and how many copies of an author's last book were purchased. This is a good basis for predicting sales and appropriate stock levels.

Cosmetic customisation presents a standard product differently, through packaging, presentation and small changes, such as a school's name on t-shirts, that tie the product to a specific group. Other merchants may delay the final steps of product design and manufacturing until individual choice, taste and behaviour can be reflected in the product. For example, British Airways allows the customer to tailor her own flight experience through options in the selection of meals, seating and magazines. Cosmetic customisation of web pages and other electronic information can be achieved through modularisation, in which straightforward modifications are made to some parts of the web page, whilst using a standard format and content for the remainder of the page.

Consumer preference underlies the concept described by Godin (1998) as *permission marketing*, and by others as *consensual surveillance*. **Permission marketing** envisions every customer controlling the customisation of the targeting and marketing communications behaviour of marketers. Consumers provide infomediaries with information about their interests who then match them with advertisers; consumers agree that they will receive e-mails or banner ads related to their interest. Permission marketing is seen as reducing clutter for the consumer, lowering search costs and increasing the targeting precision of marketers. Permission marketing goes beyond relationship marketing by seeking the customer's permission before initiating the relationship. It could be viewed as a type of **co-creation marketing**, in which marketers and consumers participate in shaping the marketing mix. Research on permission marketing shows that individuals sign up for more categories if the transaction costs for entering/modifying the opt-in scheme are low, the transaction costs of processing a single e-mail are low and the incentives received from reading each e-mail are high. Privacy costs do not have an impact on the number of categories. Individuals will modify their opt-in scheme if the transactional cost of doing so is lower than the increment in benefit. If firms provide a steady stream of messages, individuals will not alter their opt-in scheme. In general, customer participation depends on the balance between expected benefit and expected costs. Difficulties often arise with encouraging consumers to add new categories, and to up-date their profiles. In addition, for effective operation, active customer feedback on the relevance and usefulness of marketing communications are necessary. The checklist in Figure 5.8 identifies the defining characteristics of permission marketing.

Figure 5.8 The rules and tests of permission marketing

The four rules of permission marketing

■ Permission must be granted and cannot be presumed. Customers must be explicitly asked for their permission.

■ Permission is selfish – permission is only granted when people expect to benefit.

■ Permission can be revoked as easily as it is granted. On the other hand, in a satisfactory relationship, permission may also deepen over time.

■ Permission cannot be transferred. Permission opens the gate to forming a relationship but permission has been selectively granted.

The four tests of permission marketing

■ Does every single marketing effort you create encourage a learning relationship with your customers?

■ Do you have a permission database?

■ If consumers gave you permission to talk to them, would you have anything to say?

■ Once someone becomes a customer, do you work to deepen your permission to communicate with that person?

Source: Based on Godin (1998).

Transparent customisation is achieved when unique products and services are delivered to customers without the customer being alerted and told of any product changes. Based on the collection of data and information about the customers, the product is automatically changed to reflect what is estimated to be the customers' needs. This is relatively straightforward for information products – training materials might, for example, be modified to suit the perceived training needs of different individuals or groups. Transparent customisation has to achieve customisation without customers' overt permission. The system must be able to recognise opportunities and patterns within customers' choices and behaviour.

Collaborative customisation or **collaborative participation** occurs when an organisation conducts a dialogue with individual customers to help them to articulate their needs, to identify the precise offering that fulfils those needs and to make customised products for them. This is an important process in the context of business-to-business exchanges associated with product development. Extranets to link businesses to suppliers and customers, online focus groups and other forms of communication can be used for extensive consultation during product development. Such **co-production** of products can be coupled with the co-production in service delivery discussed above, to form a basis for relationships.

Drawbacks of customisation

Customisation is not always a good thing. First and foremost to be effective customisation needs to make customers feel special and not excluded or invaded. Specifically:

1. People are sensitive to intrusion into their private affairs. Too much customisation implicitly suggests that the organisation knows too much about an individual. People want time to 'get to know' and do business with an organisation before they want that organisation to know too much about their private business.
2. Pigeonholing of customers into very small segments or niches may reduce opportunities for browsing and fail to accommodate changes in interests adequately.
3. There is a danger of alienating customers who are not receiving special treatment. Customers may want to know why they are not 'gold' or 'preferred' customers.
4. Excessive customisation is cumbersome, confusing and wasteful of consumer time.
5. Customisation can reduce the sense of community between customers as each has a different experience. Without a common base of product experiences or information and news, it becomes more difficult to share, debate and discuss.

CUSTOMISATION OF WEBSITE CONTENT – BOOTS CONSULTANT

Boots Consultant offers information on a number of topics, such as 'Looking after your complexion'. The customer is presented with an onscreen form into which they enter personal details such as age, sensitivity to skin care products, facial skin type, proneness to spots and blemishes, presence of dark circles under the eyes. Product recommendations take into account the data entered into this form. In the longer term, Boots aims to store this data and to use it to inform the recommendations, announcements and offers that it makes to individual customers. This is likely to be embedded in the planned Personal Page for each customer. This Personal Page will include a diary of important personal events, selected and saved articles (a customer's own reference library), a record of previous purchase history and personal results of any Boots Consultant tools that the customer has used. All of this information will be available to both the customer and to Boots. In making this page open and transparent, the customer knows what information Boots is storing about her, and it is reasonable to expect that she will have some control of this information. This is an important element in the relationship between the customer and Boots.

GROUP DISCUSSION ACTIVITY

In what ways might you find it beneficial to have a Boots Personal Page? Which types of information that might be shared on such a page would trigger concerns about security and privacy?

CHAPTER SUMMARY

Websites are for helping customers to solve problems. Customer service and support and, in general, the customer service experience are important contributors to customer satisfaction with e-business. The online service experience delivered through, or with the aid of, IT is more standardised, consistent, structured and widely accessible than some of the human service alternatives, but the customer needs to learn how to interact effectively and efficiently with this new mode of service delivery. From the perspective of the online shopping experience, online interaction may support rational decision making effectively, but cannot easily replicate a number of the experiential dimensions of the bricks-and-mortar shopping experience. Customer service is concerned with giving customers the opportunity to talk to the organisation and to receive personalised responses. This can be achieved through e-mail, newsgroups, chat rooms and message boards, FAQs, customer service information, feedback forms and help lines. Customisation depends upon the development of customer profiles. Information for these profiles may be gathered as a by-product of a transaction when the customer offers information and through cookies. Customisation can relate to representation or marketing communication, or to product attributes and on this basis it is possible to identify four different categories of customisation: transparent, collaborative, adaptive and cosmetic.

Co-production occurs when customers engage with the supplying organisation and make a contribution based on their unique competence in product or service delivery.

Rational decision making is a model which assumes that the decision maker engages in an analytical process whose outcome depends upon the information available to the decision maker.

Information overload occurs when a decision maker has access to more information than he can use effectively in a decision-making process. This makes it difficult for the decision maker to select the most useful information and may lead to him overlooking some significant factors.

Shopping experience is a term that recognises that shopping is not only about rational decision making and purchases, but also involves social and experiential elements.

Bricks-and-mortar store is a term used to describe a traditional retail outlet, when comparing these outlets with online stores.

Customer support and service embraces the strategies that e-merchants use to enhance the customer experience.

Expert forums are live chat forums in which consumers can question experts and receive answers online.

FAQs or **frequently asked questions** are the most common questions posed by customers which are collected together, with their answers, and can be viewed online.

Feedback forms are forms through which customers can complain or provide positive comments about the service and products supplied by the web merchant.

Help lines are e-mail and telephone lines that will respond to customer queries, usually on a 24-hour/7-day-a-week basis.

Customisation occurs when the manufacturer designs a product to suit a customer's needs.

continued

Personalisation occurs when the customer is a co-creator of the content of their experiences.

Cookies are used by the server-side connections to store and retrieve information on the client side of the connection. Using cookies the server can gradually gather a profile of the client machine's Web-based activity.

Adaptive customisation occurs when customisation is based on the design of filters that assist users to locate the best product for their purposes.

Electronic recommendation agents or **shopping bots** draw together a number of products from different suppliers and allow the consumer to compare the offerings from different merchants.

Collaborative filtering algorithms use the preference data collected from a consumer and seek other consumers in their database with similar preference patterns. Recommendations are made to the target consumer on the basis of the purchase behaviour of members of the group with a similar preference pattern.

Cosmetic customisation presents a standard product differently, through packaging, presentation and small changes to personalise a product.

Permission marketing envisions every customer controlling the customisation of the targeting and marketing communication behaviour of marketers. This reduces clutter for the consumer, lowers search costs and increases the targeting precision of marketing communications.

Transparent customisation is achieved when unique products and services are delivered to customers without the customer being alerted to any product changes; the product is automatically changed to reflect what is estimated to be the customers' needs.

Collaborative customisation occurs when organisations conduct a dialogue with customers to help them to articulate their needs, to specify the product that best meets those needs and seek to create that product for them.

ASSESSMENT QUESTIONS

1. How does an IT-based service experience differ from a service experience with a human service agent?

2. Identify and discuss, with reference to a specific website, the stages in the Internet shopping experience. How might the detailed processes be designed in order to maximise customer satisfaction with the experience?

3. How does the Internet shopping experience differ from the bricks-and-mortar shopping experience? Suggest the impact that these differences might have on consumer behaviour.

4. What are the benefits of an online customer service operation from a business's perspective? Critically assess whether such a service can also generate customer value.

5. Compare and contrast the avenues through which customer service and support can be delivered.

6. Write a policy-and-practice document to inform the use of e-mail in communicating with customers.

7. What do you understand by the concept of 'customisation'? Briefly outline some of the different types of customisation of products and marketing communication that can be used in Internet marketing.

8. Discuss the advantages and disadvantages of cookies as a basis for developing communication and relationships with customers.

9. Evaluate permission marketing as a concept.

GROUP ASSESSMENT 1 – CUSTOMISATION

Locate a number of examples of the different types of customisation listed in Figure 5.7 (p. 136). With reference to the specific service or product that the respective website is offering, explain the value that the business is able to add through customisation. Finally, draw your ideas together and identify the ways in which businesses can add value through customisation.

GROUP ASSESSMENT 2 – IT IN SERVICE DELIVERY

Review the points made earlier in this chapter on the use of IT in the service experience. Consider the transaction of booking a train ticket. You can now do this through the Web, through kiosks at major rail stations or through a human service agent. Discuss which of these each member of the group has used and why. If necessary, visit a rail station and evaluate a kiosk. Also visit one of the following websites: www.thetrainline. com, www.virgin.com/trains, www.thamestrains.co.uk. Observe how a human service agent uses IT to support service delivery related to the booking of train tickets. Evaluate the strength and weaknesses of the three different options for booking a train ticket.

GROUP ASSESSMENT ACTIVITY 3 – PLACING YOUR BETS

Gambling is an easy service to offer over the Internet, although concerns about the security of financial transactions can be uppermost in gamblers' minds. Will they ever be able to lay their hands on their winnings? What about using credit cards over the Internet? Which kinds of gambling are safest – sports betting, casino or poker? Visit a number of different gambling-related websites and prepare a critical report of the service experience associated with Internet gambling. Some useful sites to get started with are www.ladbrokes.com, www.thespinroom.com, www.flutter.com, www.casinotalk.com, www.gamblersanonymous.com and www.williamhill.com.

REFERENCES

Allen, C, Kania, D and Yaeckel, B (1998) *Internet world guide to one-to-one web marketing*. Wiley.

Baty, J B and Lee, R M (1995) Intershop: enhancing the vendor/customer dialectic in electronic shopping, *Journal of Management Information Systems*, **11**(4), 9–31.

Berthon, P, Hulbert, J M and Pitt, L F (1999) Brand management prognostications, *Sloan Management Review*, **40**(2), 53–65.

Bitran G and Lojo M (1993) A framework for analyzing the quality of the customer interface, *European Management Journal*, **11**(4), 385–96.

Brassington, F and Petitt, S (2000) *Principles of marketing*, 2nd edn. Harlow: Pearson Education.

Breitenbach, C S and Van Doren, D C (1998) Value added marketing in the digital domain: enhancing the utility of the Internet, *Journal of Consumer Marketing*, **15**(6), 558–75.

Bloch, P, Ridgway, N M and Sherrel, D (1989) Extending the concept of shopping: an investigation of browsing activity, *Journal of the Academy of Marketing Science*, **17**(1), 13–21.

Brynjolfsson, E and Smith, M D (2000) Frictionless commerce? A comparison of Internet and conventional retailers, *Management Science*, **46**(4).

Campbell, C (1997) Shopping, pleasure and the sex war, in P Falk and C Campbell, *The Shopping Experience*. London: Sage, pp. 166–76.

Cole, M, O'Keefe, R M and Siala, H (2000) From the user interface to the consumer interface, *Information Systems Frontiers*, **1**(4), 349–61.

Dawes, J and Rowley, J (1998) Enhancing the customer experience: contributions from information technology, *Management Decisions*, **36**(5), 350–7.

Dibb, S, Simkin, L, Pride, W M and Ferrell, O C (1994) *Marketing concepts and strategies*, 2nd European edn. Boston, London: Houghton Mifflin.

Douglas, M (1997) In defence of shopping, in P Falk and C Campbell, *The Shopping Experience*. London: Sage, pp. 15–30.

Economist (US) (2000) Define and sell, 26 Feb, **354**(159).

Falk, P and Campbell, C (1997) *The shopping experience*. London: Sage.

Gilmore, J H and Pine, B J (1997) The four faces of mass customisation, *Harvard Business Review*, Jan/Feb, 91–101.

Godin, S (1998) Permission Marketing, *Fast Times*, April–May, 199.

Hanson, W (2000) *Principles of Internet marketing*. Cincinnati, Ohio: South-Western College Publishing.

Hoffman, D L, Novak, T P and Chatterjee, P (1995) Commercial scenarios for the Web: opportunities and challenges, *Journal of Computer Mediated Communication*, **1**(3). Available at http://www.ascsc.org/jcmc/vol1/issue3/hoffman.html.

Hoffman, K and Bateson, J (1997) *Essentials of Services marketing*. Orlando: The Dryden Press.

Holbrook, M B and Hirshman, E (1982) The experiential aspects of consumption: consumer fantasies, feelings and fun, in H H Kassarjian and T S Robertson, *Perspectives in Consumer Behaviour*, 4th edn. London: Prentice Hall.

Hoque, A Y and Lohse, G L (1999) An information search cost perspective for designing interfaces for electronic commerce, *Journal of Marketing Research*, **36**(3), 387–95.

Jansen-Verbeke, M (1987) Women, shopping and leisure, *Leisure Studies*, **6**, 71–86.

Jarvenpaa, S L and Todd, P A (1997) Consumer reactions to electronic shopping on the World Wide Web, *International Journal of Electronic Commerce*, **1**(2), 59–88.

Jones, K and Biasiotto, M (1999) Internet retailing: current hype or future reality?, *International Review of Retail Distribution and Consumer Research*, **9**(1), 69–79.

Kotler, P and Armstrong, G (1994) *Principles of marketing*, 6th edn. Englewood Cliffs, NJ: Prentice Hall.

Li, H, Kuo, C and Russell, M G (1999) The impact of perceived channel utilities, shopping orientations, and demographics on the consumer's online buying behaviour, *Journal of Computer Mediated Communication*, **5**(2). Available at http://www.ascusc.org.jcmc/vol5/issue2/li.html.

Lohse, G L and Spiller, P (1998) Electronic shopping: the effect of customer interfaces on traffic and sales, *Communications of the ACM*, **41**(7), 81–7.

Lohse, G L and Spiller, P (1999) Internet retail store design: how the user interface influences traffic and sales, *Journal of Computer Mediated Communication*, **5**(2). Available at http://www.ascusc.org/jcmc/vol5/issue2/lohse.html.

Lord, C (2000) The practicalities of developing a successful e-business strategy, *Journal of Business Strategy*, **21**(2), 40–7.

Lovelock, C (1996) *Services marketing*, 3rd edn. Englewood Cliffs: Prentice Hall International.

Miller, D (1997) Could shopping ever matter?, in P Falk and C Campbell (eds) *The Shopping Experience*. London: Sage, pp. 31–55.

Miller, D (1998) *A theory of shopping*. Cambridge: Polity Press.

Moon, Y and Frei, F X (2000) Exploding the self-service myth, *Harvard Business Review*, **78**(3), 26–7.

Nel, D, Van Niekerk, R, Berthon, J-P and Davies, T (1999) Going with the flow: websites and customer involvement, *Internet Research*, **9**(2), 109–16.

Olaisen J and Revang O (1991) The significance of information technology for service quality: from market segmentation to individual service, *International Journal of Service Industries Management*, **2**(3), 24–46.

Peppers, D and Rogers, M (1997) *The one to one future*. Garden City, NY: Doubleday.

Prahalad, C K and Ramaswamy, V (2000) Co-opting customer competence, *Harvard Business Review*, **78**(1), 79–85.

Punj, G N and Staelin , R (1983) A model of consumer information search behaviour for new automobiles, *Journal of Consumer Research*, **9**(March), 366–89.

Rogers, E M (1962) *Diffusion of innovation*. New York: Free Press.

Rowley J E (1996) Retailing and shopping on the Internet, *International Journal of Retail and Distribution Management*, **24**(3), 26–37.

Rowley, J E and Dawes, J (1998) Enhancing the customer experience: contributions from information technology, *Management Decision*, **36**(5), 350–7

Rowley, J and Slack, F (2001) Leveraging customer knowledge: profiling and personalisation in e-business, *International Journal of Retail and Distribution Management*, **29**(9), 409–15.

Shih, C-F (1998) Conceptualising consumer experiences in cyberspace, *European Journal of Marketing*, **32**(7/8), 655–63.

Smith, A (1998) A grab for impulse shoppers, *Financial Times*, 18 Sept, 12

Solomon, M R *et al.* (1985) A role theory perspective on dyadic interactions: the service encounter, *Journal of Marketing*, **1**(49), Winter, 99–111.

Sterne, J (1996) *Customer service on the Internet*. Wiley.

Storbacka, K (1997) Segmentation based on customer profitability – retrospective analysis of retail bank customers, *Journal of Marketing Management*, **13**, 479–92.

Tauber, E. M. (1972). Why do people shop?, *Journal of Marketing*, **36**(Oct.), 46–59.

Underhill, P (1999) *The science of shopping. Why we buy*. London: Orion Publishing.

Venkatesh, A (1998) Cybermarketscapes and consumer freedom and identities, *European Journal of Marketing*, **32**(7/8), 664–76.

Ward, M R and Lee, M J (2000) Internet shopping, consumer search and product branding, *Journal of Product and Brand Management*, **9**(1), 6–20.

Wells, W D and Prensky, D (1996) *Consumer behaviour*. London: Wiley.

Yoo, B and Donthu, N (2001) Developing a scale to measure the perceived quality of an Internet shopping site (SITEQUAL), *Quarterly Journal of electronic Commerce*, **2**(1).

Online communities

After reading this chapter you will:

- Be able to evaluate critically the concept of online or virtual communities
- Be able to categorise online communities according to a variety of criteria
- Understand the central role of value creation to online communities
- Be able to discuss the creation and development of relationships in online communities
- Understand key factors in managing online communities

INTRODUCTION

There is considerable debate surrounding the potential contributions of online communities to the building of successful business models. In addition, online communities may have a significant societal impact. From a business perspective the concern is to balance the investment in establishing and maintaining an online community against the glittering promises of online communities. At a pragmatic level membership of an online community is seen as symbolic of a commitment to a website or brand and is exhibited through return visits to a website, repeat purchases and recommendations to other parties. Consumers might view community differently, and for them identification may be integrally associated with the various dimensions of the service experience whose delivery commences with the website and the placing of an online order. Many of these aspects of service delivery have been covered in earlier chapters that consider website design, marketing communication and customer service. This chapter seeks to explore how all of these threads might be drawn together, with an added ingredient to create a sense of belonging and community. The added ingredient is customer-to-customer relationships. Coupled with the business-to-customer, and possibly the customer-to-business, relationships that are the focus of relationship marketing, customer-to-customer relationships complete the complex network of relationships that might form the foundation for a community.

Customers' sense of belonging is likely to be associated with the relationship that they have with the organisation (possibly personalised through its service agents), shared values and culture, and their interaction with other members of the community. Community coupled with commerce, content and communication are widely discussed as the essential components of successful web presence. Online communities can provide a focus for social interaction in new arenas, unconstrained by geographical boundaries.

On the other hand, pessimists believe that online communities harm individuals and stifle true communities by isolating people from one another. People build shallow relationships on the Internet, which leads to an overall decline in the feeling of connection to other people and an increase in social isolation, depression and loneliness.

Although there are some well-established examples of online communities, such as The Well (www.well.com) and the communities associated with AOL, online community is a new concept for many businesses. Yahoo! has a club section (www.clubs.yahoo.com) on its site to allow individuals to create their own communities with message boards, chats, e-mails, online photo albums and other community information. Yahoo! has also purchased GeoCities (http://geocities.yahoo.com) which has 41 different neighbourhoods where subscribers can interact. NBCi (www.nbci.com) offers users the opportunity to build their own home page and set up chat rooms, message boards and other community tools, in exchange for accepting targeted e-mail advertising.

EXPLORATORY ACTIVITY

iVillage is a community website specifically targeted at women between the ages of 25 and 40. The site provides access to experts in different content areas, chat rooms, news and many other information areas of interest to women. iVillage was established in 1995.

Visit iVillage.com and fe-mail.co.uk and explore and compare the community features of each of these sites. Which of these sites do you think will be the most successful? Why?

WHY IS COMMUNITY IMPORTANT?

Community, coupled with commerce, content and communication are widely discussed as the essential components of successful web presence (for example, Hagel, 1999). Those organisations that control popular online communities are in a position to dominate business transactions over the Internet. In a marketing context, and in relation to the creation of virtual consumer communities, this philosophical stance on the significance of community can be viewed as an extension of the relationship marketing paradigm. At a more pragmatic level, community might be a strategy for sidestepping inadequate web search and navigation tools. Shoppers who are familiar with the site that they wish to visit are able to locate the site and, further, navigate within the site of their choice, and therefore neither customer nor supplier is exposed to the vagaries of search engine output. Hagel (1999) suggests that 'the scarce resource will be customer attention, and that the challenge will be how to maximise that resource' (p. 64). Further, a community makes it possible for businesses to collect and leverage knowledge about their customer base. Without some stability in the customer base any customer profiling may be transient. Similarly, personalisation of the offering depends on the knowledge gained from a continuing relationship with the customer. Once a virtual business has a community and preferably some knowledge about that community, it may also license its community to other businesses. So, for example, the advertising rates that a business can charge for placing banner ads on its website will depend upon the size of the audience that the site is expected to attract.

In summary, the interest in online communities from a marketing perspective is driven by the belief that the complex network of personal relationships and increasing identification with the group as a community provide a foundation for a very attractive business model (Hagel, 1999).

Whilst online consumer communities are a relatively new concept, online communities in which people communicated with each other on a regular basis through e-mail and other technologies, have existed for a long time. Early communities were formed by programmers and researchers to support their collaboration on programming of research projects. Later, interest-based communities and communities or teams within national and international organisations were formed. More recently communities that support commercial activities between organisations, and between organisations and individual consumers have developed. All of these different types of communities, with their vicarious different objectives, and orbits of control may be important to e-business. Kannan *et al.* (2001) argue that virtual consumer communities should increasingly take on the role of an intermediary in:

- Exchange relationships between community members
- Exchange relationships between community members and marketers and advertisers.

This intermediary role can create value for organisations and consumers and possibly also the community organiser, where this is a distinct third party.

Finally, although the discussion tends to feature virtual communities as separate entities, the boundaries around virtual communities are diffuse. Not only can members come and go, and are likely to be members of several communities, but virtual communities need to be considered alongside any real communities to which consumers belong. From the business perspective, the concern focuses on relationships with customers and between customers in a multi-channel environment. The online community is only one component of the customer's experience of the business.

WHAT IS AN ONLINE COMMUNITY?

Defining the concept of virtual community is a task that has engaged academics from various disciplines for many years. A small diversion from the pragmatic considerations of later sections in this chapter provides an opportunity to consider the multiple facets of the concept of online community.

There is a considerable literature on virtual and online communities in the contexts of learning and education, supplier networks, organisational development and knowledge management. This offers some key pointers about the nature, creation and management of virtual communities. However, there are two significant differences between these communities and customer communities: the nature of the contractual relationship between the customer and the organisation and the significance of team or peer communications. In marketing the emphasis has traditionally been on the organisation-to-customer relationship. Virtual customer communities need to embrace both organisation-to-customer, and customer-to-customer relationships. Indeed, Barnatt (1998) identifies key types of customer relationships as those with peer opinion leaders, industry experts and early adopters. Both organisation-to-customer and customer-to-customer relationships need to be two-way, and whilst business-to-customer relationships, within the context of a community associated with one organisation, are one-to-many or many-to-one, customer-to-customer relationships need to be many-to-many. Whilst this is convenient shorthand for understanding the organisational perspective on relationships, it is important to remember that this is not the customers' perspective. They will have many relationships with organisations and are likely to be members of many virtual communities.

The concept of virtual community, defined as any group of people who share a common bond yet who are not dependent on physical interaction and a common geographic location, is not new. Telephones and postal services supported virtual communities long before the advent of the Internet (McDonough, 1997). However, it is only relatively recently that tools for computer mediated communication (CMC) have permitted the construction of low-cost, online virtual community infrastructures with a global reach. Such technologies support virtual communities that consist of a web of many-to-many relationships in a way that was not previously possible. Several thousand virtual communities are now accessible over the Web.

Rheingold's (1993) definition of virtual communities has been much quoted:

> social aggregations that emerge from the Net when enough people carry on those public discussions long enough, with sufficient human feeling, to form webs of personal relationships in cyberspace (p. 5)

According to this definition virtual communities are driven by common social needs, which are strengthened by personal relationships that ensure some degree of loyalty between the members of the community. In commercial communities the mutual needs may be primarily commercial in nature and the communities may be mainly used for networking and building business relationships. These communities may lack the element of human feeling but there is significant information exchange and communication. Other authors also support the concept of virtual community (Turkle, 1996). However, amongst sociologists the definition of virtual communities has provoked much debate. A key theme in the sociological literature is reflected in the following quote from a discussion paper by the Critical Art Ensemble, Growing Virtual Communities, 'anyone with even a basic knowledge of sociology knows that information exchange in no way constitutes a community'. One position is that taken by Jones (1997) who explores the concept of community in the sociology literature, with particular reference to the relationship between physical space and community. This leads to discussion of cyber-place and virtual settlements. Tambyah (1996) discusses the effect that this new technological environment might have on people's sense of self and community. Other key issues are the balance between freedom and control, and security and vulnerability in this new context.

GROUP DISCUSSION ACTIVITY

Discuss the statement: 'information exchange in no way constitutes a community'.

Hagel and Armstrong (1997) have a concept of virtual community that is particularly useful in consumer marketplaces. They define virtual communities as computer-mediated space where there is an integration of content and communication with an emphasis on member-generated content. The other three defining characteristics of online communities are a distinctive focus on membership, the integration of content and communication, and a choice of competing vendor offers. Such communities have a social and commercial purpose. They serve not only as marketing feedback and new idea conduits, but also as a check on quality and social responsibility. In such communities, customers own companies rather than companies owning customers.

TYPES OF ONLINE COMMUNITY

A number of authors have proposed different typologies of online communities. Three of these are described here with a view to assisting in the development of an understanding of the diversity of online communities. In addition to the characteristics featured in these typologies, communities will be differentiated by cultural, experiential, language and geographical divides. Commercial communities should be delineated using any of the characterises that are normally used in segmentation and targeting in order to define a viable segment.

Hanson (2000) identifies two key types of virtual communities – personal communities and extended communities:

Personal communities are personal networks of social and business contacts. They are organised around small networks of individuals linked together by online tools, such as e-mail or a shared website. They are small and based on members who know each other.

Extended communities are more flexible in scope and scale. They are the communities that are created in business and consumer marketplaces as discussed below. They often have commercial objectives. Such communities capitalise on the strengths of many smaller personal communities, including both online and real world personal communities.

GROUP DISCUSSION ACTIVITY

Ask each group member to name the personal and extended online communities to which they have a sense of belonging or affiliation. Discuss the basis for the affiliation. Are any of these communities commercial communities? Note the great diversity of community membership and affiliation for any one person.

Armstrong and Hagel (1996) propose four types of virtual community, which are differentiated by the types of consumer needs that they satisfy. Communities can be transaction-oriented, interest-oriented, fantasy-oriented or relationship-oriented. Further, some communities fulfil several of these functions, and it might be argued that the more needs that are fulfilled the greater the attractiveness and cohesion of the community. All of these types of community can be organised for commercial or non-commercial purposes.

Transaction-oriented communities primarily facilitate the buying and selling of products and services and deliver information that is related to completing those transactions. These communities do not address the member's social needs. Examples of such communities include Virtual Vineyards, where consumers get information tips from the vendor and buy products at the website; Levis.com, where consumers can chat about the latest fashion; and Amazon.com, where visitors can get reviews about books from other readers. The organiser of such a community is usually the e-merchant.

Many B2B communities are transaction-oriented. Examples are virtual trade shows, which are online sites that show new products, technologies and services to current and potential buyers. A further example is the supply-chain networks that are organised to connect vendors and buyers. Various aspects of these supply networks are discussed further in Chapter 7.

Communities of interest are gathered around topics of common interest, and members typically have a significantly higher degree of interaction than in a transaction-based community. Interactions are on topics of common interest. Examples are the Well, the Globe.com and BioMedNet (www.bmn.com), a professional community for physicians. These communities usually have chat rooms, message boards and discussion groups to support extensive member interactions, and are characterised by a significant quantity of user-generated content. The content is owned and validated by the community. Any business that is able to engage with this type of community can benefit from an established community and member-generated content.

There are two main types of community of interest: those associated with leisure activities and those associated with professional groups. Leisure activities, such as music (rock groups, for example, The Backstreet Boys (www.backstreetboys.com), sport (for example, Manchester United (www.manutd.com)) and TV shows (for example, Coronation Street (www.coronationstreet.co.uk)), attract lively communities. Professional groups use online communities to share expertise and professional news. An example is Physicians online (www.po.com) which provides a forum in which physiscians can share both medical and business challenges. Agriculture online (www.agriculture.com) is designed to support farmers.

EXPLORATORY ACTIVITY

Locate and visit the website for your favourite music group or TV soap series. Make a note of the type of opportunity for interactions between fans.

Fantasy-oriented communities allow members to create new environments, personalities, societies and role-play. Examples include Sony.com and the fantasy communities within America Online. Members enjoy a shared virtual leisure experience in which they can escape from the real world.

Relationship communities are built around the life experiences of members and are often concerned with sharing and mutual support (see Figure 6.1). These life experiences are often very intense and lead to intimate sharing and strong personal bonding between members. Examples include Parent Soup (www.parentsoup.com), a site for parents with small children; Tripod (www.tripod.com) for people leaving college, facing their first job, the challenge of finding their first home, and associated lifestyle changes.

Figure 6.1 The Well

Home | Join | About | Conferencing | Members | Services & Help | Gift Store | Enter The WELL

If You Build It ...
What does it take to create and maintain a successful online community? Ask leading web designer Derek Powazek, author of **Design for Community**.

Love after 40
Do wrinkles, gray hairs and some extra pounds spell the end of youth's giddy passions? Do you even *want* to get on the roller coaster of romance any more? Join the discussion in **Boomers**.

Home | Join | About | Conferencing | Members | Services & Help | Store | Enter The WELL

Website Feedback

GROUP DISCUSSION ACTIVITY

Visit the Well website. Why do you think that this online community has been a success?

CASE CAMEO

THE GLOBE.COM (www.theglobe.com)

The Globe.com is an international online community, with a number of specific interest groups under its overall umbrella. Communities include those associated with Happy Puppy, and Kids Domain. Happy Puppy is a game site covering games on a wide variety of platforms. Kids Domain is an entertainment and education site for parents, grandparents, children and educators. It includes educational software, online games, crafts, contests and special holiday activities. The site also runs magazines, such as Computer Games Online, and online stores, such as the games stores Chips & Bits. The site can be personalised to show My Homepage, My Clubs, My Forums and My Settings.

EXPLORATORY ACTIVITY

Visit the Globe.com. Choose one of the interest groups and make a note of the opportunities for interaction that it offers. What value do visitors derive from this community?

Hanson (2000) proposes a further categorisation of online communities in terms of the strength of commitment to the community:

Communities of users simply share an experience of a product. They may provide helpful advice and share problems and complaints, but level of commitment to the community is low.

Communities of values exist when members actively participate and identify with the goals of the community.

Communities of requirement are so-called because members of the community are mutually dependent. The community has become essential to the effective functioning of a business or to the satisfaction of an individual member.

The vision of a dedicated online community is not realistic for every organisation. Encouraging active participation in online communities is not easy (Romm *et al.*, 1997; Cothrel, 1998). Successful online communities are likely to cluster around hobbies, professions and other topics that excite interest (politics, health, cars, investments and houses). Those businesses that are not likely to attract consumer-to-consumer communication or regular visits from customers are doomed. Barnatt (1998), when discussing financial services, proposes three different types of virtual community strategy, which may have applicability for other sectors:

1. Virtual community creation, as discussed above.
2. Collaboration with other organisations in the same sector to create a site with a wide range of industry provision, that offers the customer a wide range of products and assistance in choosing between them.
3. Piggyback on existing virtual communities, where the member interest and virtual community is really sustained by another organisation. Such communities may be information-dissemination communities, communities of interest, shop-talk communities or professional collaboration communities.

These last two models are likely to be important for many players in the e-marketplace whether or not they are leaders in their traditional marketplace. The important feature of both of these models is that they involve relationships with other businesses, and customer commitment to a virtual community that is not the community that is directly associated with the business that is seeking to function in the e-marketplace.

VALUE CREATION

Value is created differently for different stakeholders because members, community organisers and advertisers will all seek different benefits from participation in the community. All stakeholders must be able to take value from the community for it to continue. Without **value creation**, communities will not continue to exist. Value creation can be achieved through the information content or other products generated by and shared within a community or through the very existence of an identified group.

Value through community existence

A community brings together consumers with specific demographics and interests. This presents opportunities for transacting business and communicating messages about products and services that are of interest to consumers, and which marketers and advertisers value and are consequently willing to pay for. In as much as business transactions take place in communities, value is created. In addition, virtual communities can attract advertisement revenues, because they constitute a targeted audience. Value creation may also arise from the marketing information that is generated within communities. Typically, such information may include the demographics and psychographics of members, their attitudes and beliefs about products, services and issues, their behaviour in relation to business transactions within communities and information on the way in which they interact. Such information is a rich seam of marketing information if members are content to accede to its use.

This type of value is primarily of benefit to the community host and its partners, such as advertisers. Members benefit from value creation through one or more of the avenues below.

Value through content contribution and co-production

Members' input to the community consists of information content in the form of comments and feedback, elaborating their attitudes and beliefs and informational needs. Members may provide such content unsolicited or in response to queries by other members or the organiser of the community. Community organisers may also contribute their own content. For example, the organisers of BioMedNet provide content in the form of information on the latest medical research and techniques, which the physician members would find very useful. If the content is sufficiently valuable to members, they may be prepared to pay to become a member of a community and the community may become exclusive. Membership of communities associated with specific professional groups may also be restricted to members of that profession. Other communities exist to create new software products. Examples are the communities that are developing LINUX and APACHE server software. Co-production was discussed in Chapter 5.

EXPLORATORY ACTIVITY

Visit the website of LINUX (www.linux.com). Describe how this site creates customer value through community.

A virtual community can be created to enhance the stickiness of a website, and therefore the frequency with which customers return to it. In this role the community increases the traffic through the website, the time that a visitor lingers and their level of interactivity with the website. Alternatively a website might be used as an additional avenue for communication amongst the members of an established community. In this context, the purpose of the virtual community is to enhance the efficiency or effectiveness of the community and to better support it in the furtherance of its objectives.

Value through commerce

Since most organisations, including those in the public and voluntary sector have some commercial activities, websites are not simply about communication and information exchange, but also have commercial purposes and may, for example, sell some of their services to members of the community or others through their website. Alternatively, virtual communities may negotiate with suppliers for enhanced deals for their members. This is a role that has long been performed by membership organisations such as trade unions and professional bodies in relation to, for example, preferential insurance rates for their members. In the virtual environment, groups may come together in a more *ad hoc* way, as in the co-buying model, to negotiate a good price with suppliers.

The exact manner in which value is created in virtual communities also depends on who organises the community, and who owns or controls it. Transaction-oriented communities are generally controlled and organised by marketers, and the value is created mainly through transactions rather than through advertising revenues or content. The marketers also control the marketing information that such a community generates and have the potential to use this information to inform other business ventures, including bricks-and-mortar ventures. The information might also inform customer service, marketing research and other dimensions of the way in which the marketer shapes the relationship with customers. If the community is controlled and owned by members, the purpose is to benefit the members, and value is created through content exchange and or subscription fees. Alternatively, communities can be managed by organisations that specialise in managing virtual communities. The Case Cameos on Parentsplace.com and GEIS-TPN illustrate how such an intermediary role might evolve.

PARENTSPLACE.COM

A Californian couple started Parentsplace.com to create a meeting place for parents. They expected that the community would be self-supporting through the sale of child-related products to community members. As the community grew in the chat rooms and discussion rooms, the members were evidently more interested in their common interests, getting tips and information on child rearing, and the level of commercial transactions was low. Accordingly, in order to keep the community alive, the organisers adopted a business model of an advert-supported community. This was achieved by selling advertising space to advertisers and removing the retail section of the community.

GEIS-TPN

GEIS-TPN was a business-to-business community started by General Electric's lighting division in order to manage their supply chain efficiently by bringing suppliers to a Web-based transaction system. The supplier community grew, more buyers joined the community and, at the appropriate time, GE spun off the venture into a separate entity that helped both buyers and suppliers to build relationships and to transact business.

CREATING AND DEVELOPING RELATIONSHIPS IN ONLINE COMMUNITIES

Trust, commitment, sharing, culture and loyalty have all received attention in the marketing literature. The issue of relationships lies at the heart of the creation and development of online communities. The assumption is that the Internet will set new standards for relationships and relationship management, and will impact on both the breadth (period of time over which the relationship extends) and depth (the degree of interaction that the customer experiences). This section explores customer charters, the nature of relationships in commercial online communities, including the role of customer-to-customer interaction, relationship lifecycles and customer relationship management.

The two purposes of online communities are associated with the two types of relationship: social (customer-to-customer) and business (customer-to-business). As in all relational situations, this second type of relationship will be built through purchase transactions, and product and service delivery. The important factor, as in traditional retailing, is that there is something that pulls the customer to return to the site or, in other words, something of value or benefit. The basis of the relationship may be different for different businesses and, equally importantly, businesses may have customers who:

■ See no benefit, either in terms of special offers, convenience or the security associated with dealing with a new brand or supplier, and do not want a relationship
■ Seek benefits from social relationships
■ Seek benefits from business relationships
■ Seek benefits from both business and social relationships.

In all of these categories the significance of the benefits to the customer and his lifestyle will range across a spectrum.

Customer charters

Customer charters are used in various consumer and public sector contexts to define the offering from the organisation. They are the opener from the organisation to the relationship in the sense that they state the starting point from which an organisation will build a relationship. By making explicit statements in the customer charter the organisation also influences the consumer's expectations.

The Case Cameo shows some phrases from the Boots Online Customer Charter, which embeds messages about what Boots perceives to be important to customers.

A CUSTOMER CHARTER – BOOTS ONLINE CUSTOMER CHARTER

Boots Online Customer Charter outlines the philosophy that underlies the site:

'A site tailored for you'
'We put you in control of the site and how to access information'
'We give you services'
'And personalise information and products to match your interests'
'We offer . . . secure and safe online buying, and easy re-ordering'
'We put you in contact with people of similar interests'
'We'll give you several reasons to come back to our site.'

EXPLORATORY ACTIVITY

Visit a website of your choice. Locate the Customer Charter. What can you learn about the organisational values and approach to customers from this Charter?

Types of relationships

Relationship marketing suggests that there are different levels and types of relationship and increasingly emphasises the importance of recognising the type of relationship (if any) that the consumer wants. The need for satisfactory e-commerce experiences and dynamic content to encourage repeat visits is widely recognised, but these tactics are focused on attention and interaction and, potentially, further transactions rather than explicitly on relationship building (Berthan *et al.*, 1996; Breitenbach and Van Doren, 1998; Dholakhia and Rego, 1998; Loebbecke *et al.*, 1998). They create a context in which relationships may be strengthened, but they do not constitute partnership.

Revisiting Figure 1.1 (p. 4), each of the four stages in the development of e-commerce can be associated with different communication patterns. In the Contact stage, communication is one way, from the organisation to the customer. The Interact stage allows for two-way communication but, because this is a limited dialogue and neither party has committed to a business transaction, this might be best characterised as two times one-way communication. The Transact stage is where a two-way exchange, or dialogue, occurs and each party reveals more of the offering that they bring to a relationship. Only in the Relate stage does true integration of the customer into the community associated with the business start to take place, and the communication becomes web-like, with a many-to-many communication network. Individual interactions become less significant as the community of customers and the supplier move into a proactive partnership that forms the basis for the virtual community. It is important to recognise that community is only associated with the Relate stage.

Customer loyalty is usually taken to be an indication of the existence of a relationship and some commitment to the organisation on the part of the customer. Customer loyalty has been conceptualised as an interaction of attitude and behaviour. Dick and Basu (1994) propose four conditions related to loyalty: loyalty, latent loyalty, spurious loyalty and no loyalty, as shown in Figure 6.2:

- *Loyalty* signifies a favourable correspondence between relative attitude and repeat patronage
- *Latent loyalty* is associated with high relative attitude but low repeat patronage
- *Spurious loyalty* represents a low relative attitude with high repeat patronage
- *No Loyalty* is associated with a low relative attitude combined with low repeat patronage.

Other authors have proposed alternative categorisations of loyalty. Gabbott and Hogg (1998) suggest that bonding arrangements between parties (such as those that lead to loyalty) act as a form of glue. They propose six forms of glue: goal compatibility, trust, satisfaction, investment, social and structural bonding.

The wider literature on virtual communities demonstrates the significance of trust converted from other contexts into the virtual community. Initial

Figure 6.2 Categories of loyalty

		Repeat Patronage	
		High	**Low**
Relative Attitude	**High**	Loyalty	Latent Loyalty
	Low	Spurious Loyalty	No Loyalty

Source: Dick and Basu (1994).

commitment to a community may be transferred from the traditional retailing environment. There are three levels of membership or association that individuals can bring to a virtual community:

- Contractual, as with employees, who are required to use a website
- Membership of an organisation, such as a professional body, interest group, pressure group or church, which has already expressed an interest in affiliation to the community
- Simulated membership, such as is the case for holders of loyalty cards, and regular customers, in which the level of commitment is low, but the customer has accepted some association with the organisation in exchange for modest benefits, often in the form of discounts.

Commercial organisations may seek to build on commercial relationships and launch their own portal or they may seek to piggyback on one of the other community types above. This may involve rethinking how their offerings can be redesigned for different communities, which, in turn, implies a significant overhaul of marketing strategy.

Consumers will form a number of partnerships with selected organisations and they may pursue these in both online and real environments. One of the main challenges for researchers and managers is understanding the factors that influence entry to, participation in and continued commitment to online and probably more significantly, hybrid communities. Some recent authors have warned that consumers do not want relationships, or at best only form tenuous relationships, with selected brands or outlets. At this stage of development we do not know whether:

- Customers will exhibit reluctance to switch because trust is an even more important aspect in online commerce than in traditional commerce, or
- Customers will switch actively to get the best deal, using shopping bots, co-buying arrangements, and third party marketplaces to support this process.

Ultimately customers' propensity to switch is likely to be dependent upon product category and the nature of the decision making associated with a given product category. A further factor will be whether confidence and trust for that product category resides with the product brand (for example, Fisher Price) or with the e-merchant or intermediary brand (for example, Tesco, Yahoo!).

Customer-to-customer relationships

Online communities need to offer the opportunity for customers to give to and take from the community, and not just to complete a purchase transaction with a supplier or retailer. This involves offering customers the opportunity to interact with one another and to develop a web of relationships. Barnatt (1998) shows this as a wheel with spokes. In fact the web will be much more complex than this, since each customer will choose how many and which other customers to communicate with, and will make judgements on the value of other customers' inputs. She will have limited information on which to base these judgements, and is likely to use stereotypical categorisations. In this, people who, because of their professional status or longstanding association with the community, are viewed as experts or leaders will receive more audience attention than others. On the other hand, in global communities, there may be regional and national influences on networks.

Customer-to-customer interaction can normally have both negative and positive aspects in terms of the quality of the customer experience (Martin, 1996). Some of the potential challenges are illustrated by studies on the use of e-mail in workplace-based hybrid communities. Negative effects include flaming (McGuire *et al.*, 1987), dis-inhibition, de-individuation (Matheson and Zanna, 1989) and social abuses (Markus, 1994). In addition, odd effects may derive from members whose virtual identities are distinct from their real-life identities (Korac-Boisvert and Kouzmin, 1994). In virtual environments, although customer power may mean that customer-to-customer interaction may have negative effects for suppliers, such interaction will always be positive for customers. Every new member of a virtual community increases the usefulness or value of the community as a whole, for both new and existing members. The larger the community the more attractive it becomes to other members and the more attractive it is to retailers.

CASE CAMEO

HOTMAIL, RELATIONSHIPS AND VIRAL MARKETING

One of the most fascinating exploitations of real-world communities through the Internet is the free Web-based e-mail service offered by Hotmail to registered users. Hotmail has become the world's largest Web-based e-mail service since its launch with a spectacularly fast growth rate for its subscriber base.

Hotmail's approach is underpinned by viral marketing. Whenever a subscriber sends an e-mail to friends or associates, a short marketing promotion is inserted at the bottom of every e-mail. Viral marketing enables Hotmail to acquire customers at no extra cost. Hotmail adoption pattern is passed out through its existing network of subscribers. Hotmail can capitalise on the existing relationships between its subscribers and potential subscribers.

Relationship lifecycles

Members of communities will be at a variety of different stages in their relationships with the online community and its associated business. Hunt (1994) suggests that there are five stages in the process of developing a relationship.

1. *Choosing a partner (Introduction)* is the first stage during which customers make a careful choice of the communities and organisations with which they wish to engage. For organisations this phase could consist of establishing awareness of their existence through promotion, meetings with various stakeholders, special events and special offers. Stakeholders need to be persuaded that they may want to renew this initial contact.
2. *Structuring the relationship (Experimentation)* is the period during which the stakeholder and the organisation become better acquainted. Personal contacts, preferably at a variety of levels and between a number of individuals, are important during this stage of the process; understanding, knowledge and trust need to develop. Stakeholders need to be satisfied with the service quality and should be encouraged to extend their range of involvement with the organisation so that the relationship becomes more multi-dimensional.
3. *Devoting time to developing the relationship (Identification)* may involve diligent enquiries about service quality and customer satisfaction, seeking opportunities for creating value, building trust and ensuring commitment.
4. *Maintaining lines of communication (Continuous Renewal)* is the period during which the dialogues are well established. The stakeholders and organisations know what to expect of each other and they each understand their own role in the relationship. For the relationship to be continued, it needs to be able to change to accommodate any change in any of the parties. Both organisations and stakeholders may be subject to changing environments and changing competencies, and what they require from the relationship may change. Parties have mutual investment and loyalty and will strive to manage instabilities. Disruption in the relationship is painful.
5. *Parting on good terms (Dissolution)*. Although parties may be reluctant to terminate a good relationship, parting on good terms is important. Accordingly parting must be managed so that trustworthiness is not diminished. Happy memories may inspire valuable word-of-mouth recommendations to others and leave the door open for the development of other relationships in due course. Activities which offer opportunities for continued contact at a reduced level or support the development of an alternative relationship in which one or both parties fulfil different roles are helpful during the parting stage.

A model with similar stages was proposed by Tzokas and Saren (2002) (Figure 6.3). Each of these stages presents unique requirements and opportunities for those involved, and involves a different kind of trust. Another approach that focused on business relationships and identified

Figure 6.3   Stages in the relationship lifecycle

Stage	Introduction	Experimentation	Identification	Continuous renewal or dissolution
Key focus of stage	Exploration and initial mutual appreciation of capabilities	Action-based learning about each other	Dissolution of boundaries and new tasks	Inventing the future
Development agendas	Strategic fit Behavioural fit Cultural fit Purpose fit	Pilot projects Information sharing Joint activities Testing promises	Organisational and relational skills Openness	Creativity New horizons Integration potential
Type of trust	Calculus-based trust	Knowledge-based trust	Identification-based trust	Integration-based trust

Source: After Tzokas and Saren (2002).

parallel stages of courtship, engagement, housekeeping, negotiating differences and recognising that the relationship changes both parties.

New organisations or new contexts, such as the e-marketplace, with no established community or relationships will probably pass through each of these stages in turn. But this model of the stages of relationship marketing is a model of the stages in relationship building, and not a model of the lifecycle of an organisation or a community. Established organisations should have relationships in all of the stages in this process and need therefore to manage each of these stages in parallel. In discussing relationships in online communities it is important to think in terms of the stages in relationship lifecycles. Although the focus in e-business is currently in the establishment, or courting stage, of relationships, the other stages – development, continuance and parting – are equally significant. This requires a focus on member development and participation, value management and moderation or facilitation of relationships.

GROUP DISCUSSION ACTIVITY

Each group member is asked to identify a brand (digital or otherwise) with which they might be prepared to admit that they had 'formed a relationship'. Discuss the nature and basis of those relationships, with specific reference to the stage in the relationship lifecycle, using one of the models of the relationship lifecycle posed above. Make notes on what you have learnt about the interpretation of stages in relationship lifecycles from this process.

Customer relationship management systems

Customer relationship management (CRM) uses rich databanks of customer information to manage the relationship with customers. This may involve the customisation of marketing communications or the customisation of the product on offer. Customer relationship management systems support all stages of the interaction with the customer from order, through delivery to after-sales service. The objective is to use IT to enhance customer service. Many of the features of such systems have already been introduced in Chapter 4. CRM systems cover online ordering, e-mail, knowledge bases that can be used to generate customer profiles and to personalise service, the generation of automatic responses to e-mail, and automatic help.

Customer relationship management may also mean assessing the value of the customer (sometimes referred to as **customer lifetime value**) to the business and the consequent actions. Dissolution of the relationship may be initiated by the customer or the business.

Another perspective on customer relationship management derives strongly from the systems link between CRM software and data warehousing software. Coupled together these may be used to generate business intelligence. Using these tools it is possible to collect customer data with which special analysis and reporting tools can be used. Web data analysis using these tools is often outsourced to specialist business intelligence organisations. Examples of these are to be found at: www.oracle.com, www.informatica.com, and www.informix.com.

GROUP DISCUSSION ACTIVITY

Make a list of the ways in which customer relationship management systems can enhance customer service. For further information visit www.crm-forum.com, www.ft.com/crm and www.axciom.com.

MANAGING ONLINE COMMUNITIES

Hagel and Armstrong (1997) argue that virtual communities will only become thriving and profitable (are these the same thing?) online meeting spaces and trading arenas for both customers and organisations once they attain a critical mass of members, retailers, content and ongoing communication. Once this critical mass is reached, marginal returns for all will improve. Hagel and Armstrong speculate that community growth will depend upon good gardening:

- Seeding (encouraging innovation within)
- Feeding (providing resources so that communities can pursue their own desired directions)
- Weeding (pruning dead wood and removing obstacles).

Communities will evolve through stages, from virtual villages, to constellations of communities affiliated with one another, to aggregations of complementary core communities, and finally to 'integrated infomediaries' working on behalf of their members who control their own member profiles. Cothrel (1999) argues that coordinating virtual communities is an emerging discipline and suggests there is a role for community managers. This role involves member development, value management, and moderation or facilitation.

EXPLORATORY ACTIVITY

Reflect on the last few paragraphs and try to summarise the critical success factors that convert a thriving online community into a profitable community.

What devices can organisations use for creating such communities? How is the two-way dialogue that can act as the basis for a relationship initiated? First and foremost it is important to remember that actions speak louder than words or, alternatively, that an important part of a relationship is what the organisation does. Service delivery is key in this context, as well as attention to issues such as selective use of customer information, quality of products, and customer service that resolves problems rapidly and effectively. Active listening is key. This means providing arenas in which customers can 'talk', make requests and ask questions. Typical options in the consumer market-place include:

- Help desks available through telephone or e-mail contact
- Mechanisms for customer feedback
- Chat rooms
- Message boards
- Live expert advice
- Topic-specific clubs/pages/areas and forums.

Customers then expect responses or engagement. Examples of this might be:

- A 24-hour response guarantee for customer feedback comments
- Policy and guidance on the operation of, and if necessary intervention in, chat rooms
- Access to information on order status
- Immediate help-desk response
- Personalised promotion or communication on the basis of any customer profile information that the customer has agreed to provide.

All of these features also serve to lend a personality to the site, and to create an interaction experience that has some of the sense of an interaction with a human service agent.

Online communities are time-consuming to maintain, and any organisation engaging in virtual community creation, whether for commercial or non-commercial purposes needs to be prepared to invest the resources necessary to maintain an online community. Successful online communities are dependent upon content quality, member engagement, respecting member privacy and business viability.

Content

Content may derive from the community organiser or from community members, and community sites typically have elements of both of these. Some sites also have advertisements and content from other sources. All content must meet quality standards.

Often a key role for the community organiser is to check the depth and quality of content. The editorial staff have responsibility for maintaining and updating content, which places them in the role of publishers. Many sites, such as portals that are seeking to attract large communities, enter into an alliance with a publisher or other provider of content.

Member-generated content will often be of much more variable quality and accuracy, and it may be difficult to assess its authority. On the other hand, good member content is low-cost, reflects current member interests, yields multiple perspectives, and in controlled access communities (such as those associated with professional groups) may have high credibility.

Another problem with member content is that members can make unfounded negative or positive comments about their experiences with specific products or services. In most cases, virtual communities use a disclaimer which indicates that they are not responsible for the opinions expressed by members. This might not, however, be sufficient if contributions from some members are likely to undermine or disrupt the community. Intervention is necessary in the form of moderators in chat rooms or editors who monitor the nature and quality of input and interactions and take action against members who continuously disrupt the community. Real-time member content, such as postings to discussion threads or chat rooms, cannot be easily controlled without an expensive 'real-time' moderator. Verification of identity lends some control and limits unsolicited messages from non-members. Behaviour of members can be influenced by a code of behaviour of the type shown in Figure 6.4.

Figure 6.4 A Code of Behaviour

Yahoo! Clubs – Club Rules

A. You are solely responsible for your activities and the content of your transmission through Yahoo! Clubs. Yahoo! has no responsibility for the conduct or content of any club, the membership rules of the requirements of any club.

B. You agree not to use Yahoo! Clubs, create any club, club name, club membership rules, user ID, or other content, or otherwise transmit any information of material that:

- Promotes or contains any information that is unlawful, false or misleading, impersonates any person or entity, or that promotes illegal conduct or purposes.
- Promotes bigotry, racism, hatred, or harm of any kind against any group or individual
- Is or could be in any way harmful to minors
- Is harassing, libellous, invasive of another's privacy, abusive, threatening, vulgar, obscene, tortious, or otherwise objectionable. Or that infringes or may infringe the intellectual property right of another.
- Disrupts the formal flow of communication in any Yahoo! Club or otherwise negatively affects the other members of the club.
- Involves the transmission of 'junk mail', 'spam', 'chain letters', unsolicited advertising or other unsolicited mass distribution of email.
- Consists primarily of promotional and advertising materials or any other form of solicitation.
- Exists primarily for commercial purposes.
- Violates the rights of another.

Reproduced with permission of Yahoo! Inc. © 2000 by Yahoo! Inc. YAHOO! and the YAHOO! logo are trademarks of Yahoo! Inc.

Member engagement

Communities depend upon member contributions. Communities comprise people who make different types of contributions. In online communities there are severe constraints on the type of contributions that members can make but it might be salutary to remember that communities do not only need leaders – they also need followers, music makers, carers, artists, actors, legislators, politicians, critics, inventors and even the silent majority. Voyeurs or lurkers, who learn from others' contributions but do not make their own contribution, are non-participating members. Too many such members can lead to a scarcity of useful content in the community and the community becomes moribund without a sufficient level of interactivity. Non-participants with an interest in the community need to be encouraged to participate, sometimes through the use of economic incentives, or through the injection of topics for discussion. Active participants need to be acknowledged, possibly through rewards associated with status and recognition. Committed contributors might, for example, be 'promoted' to community moderator.

Respecting members' privacy

In order to enhance the quality of interactions in a community, it is normal for members to provide demographic, lifestyle and interest information to the community organisers. In addition, the online community can also generate significant information regarding members' interests through chat rooms and discussion groups where they interact with other members. Virtual communities can also track members' transaction information. Whilst all such information has value for marketers and advertisers, most members expect virtual communities to respect their privacy and safeguard their personal information and not let advertisers use the information indiscriminately. Members also expect privacy in dealing with other members. Any serious breach of privacy can lead to litigation, negative publicity and quite possibly the disintegration of the community.

Business viability

Advertisers expect value for any advertising fees and commissions. They derive value through access to the right target segment, forging long-term relationships with members and getting information on how best to meet members' needs. If virtual communities cannot deliver value to advertisers, revenue from this source will decline and the financial basis of the community may be undermined.

Critical mass is necessary to enhance the attractiveness of the site to advertisers, the community organisers and members. Critical mass needs to be juxtaposed to focus. Focus is also valuable. A focused community has content that meets the needs of its members and a community profile that is attractive for commercial purposes. In addition focused content will enhance the likelihood of the site being ranked highly by search engines and consequently it will be easier for potential members to locate the site. Focus can be difficult to maintain as a community grows. One particular challenge is that experienced members may resent the 'newbies'. They may feel invaded by newcomers who take over their discussion groups. Retention of these members is essential and tactics to ensure their retention need careful consideration.

Another factor that influences the viability of a community is frequent use by members. Quite apart from the effect that more frequent visits might have on exposure to marketing messages, frequent, and preferably longer, visits mean more time online, and thus more opportunities for relationship building as summarised in Figure 6.5.

Figure 6.5 Building exposure and relationships

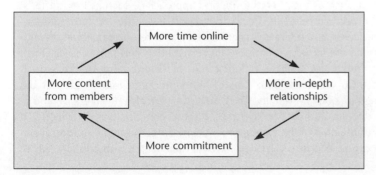

Evaluating online communities

Online communities must be evaluated in terms of their objectives. It is likely that at least some of their objectives will be coincident with the objectives for Internet promotion or the e-business in general. This will lead to the application of metrics associated with market share, sales and transactions. Such metrics are discussed in greater detail in Chapter 8.

Taking a more specific focus on community, appropriate metrics might include: access frequency, duration of visits, number of members, contribution level of members, involvement of members as moderators, quality and quantity of content, retention rate of members, joining rate and focus of the member profile.

CASE CAMEO

MAKING VIRTUAL COMMUNITIES REAL: WWW.SKIM.COM

When you join the online community of the Swiss clothing manufacturer Skim, the company assigns you a numerical ID, creating the equivalent of a Swiss bank account – numbered and anonymous. Every time you order an item of clothing, Skim prints your ID on it. Other members of the community can recognise you in public places, make a note of your number, go home, type your number into the site and send you an e-mail – still anonymously. Is this virtual for real?

CASE CAMEO

ONLINE COMMUNITY CREATION IN ACADEMIC PUBLISHING: MCB

MCB is a UK-based publisher of specialist journals that publishes around 150 academic journals, broadly in the business and management disciplines and information management. All print journals are available in electronic form and a few journals are published in electronic form only. These electronic journals and a host of other services are available through MCB's Emerald Intelligence + Fulltext service.

MCB has sought to redefine the publisher's role in the electronic marketplace. The Internet site provides a central infrastructure for content delivery, product information, sales support, operational information and the additional benefits that can be supplied by interactivity, community and customer-focused information resources. Many of its services, such as the Literati Club, and approaches, such as the Author's Charter, existed in print format. MCB seek to support a number of communities: writers, editors, reviewers and referees (as contributors to its resources), librarians and library consortia who are largely responsible for subscription and purchase. Each of these different communities fulfils a different role in contributing to the virtual community that MCB are seeking to create, although some individuals will be members of more than one community. Thus, an author can also be an editor, and a librarian can also be an author. Membership of these communities is defined by participation in a transaction of the type appropriate to the community. Authors have to submit an acceptable article, libraries have to take out a subscription. MCB mediates the community by creating an electronic (and non-electronic) environment in which each of the sub-communities has access to any MCB information that can assist in further contributions and the further strengthening of the relationships within the community. In addition to access to contents pages of journals and current awareness announcements, such as those that are delivered through Emerald, MCB supports a wide range of communication facilities that include virtual conferences, discussion groups and other resources. Different services are offered for each of these communities so that each community has its own unique window on MCB resources and activities. All of these services draw on MCB's core resources which, it is plainly evident, include its journals in both print and electronic form, advice from editors and other information, and also its community.

CO-BUYING – LetsBuyIt.com

CASE
CAMEO

LetsBuyIt.com is a pan-European business, based on the concept of co-buying. The company's first site was launched in Sweden in April 1999. Its geographical range now includes 13 European countries and currencies, including the UK.

LetsBuyIt.com is founded on the concept of co-buying. Co-buying means bringing together as many members as possible who wish to purchase the same product, so that LetsBuyIt.com can negotiate directly with the supplier or manufacturer offering the best price. The more people join the community, the lower the prices. Price advantages are possible due to the removal of the margins enjoyed by retailers and other intermediaries coupled with the advantages of buying in a group. Members are actively encouraged to tip-a-friend about co-buys, and there are many tip-a-friend links throughout the site. All co-buys are open for a limited period and members have to join the co-buy whilst it is active. Typically the co-buys displayed on the author's visit to the site closed within the month of the visit.

LetsBuyIt.com has launched an aggressive media-marketing campaign in order to attract members to its community and website. It seeks to build a community on the basis of shared commercial or purchasing transactions – the emphasis is on commerce, rather than communication or content. The concept and organisation have been created from the e-environment, but LetsBuyIt.com makes use of networks of friends and contacts, and encourages people to leverage their social networks in pursuit of the best deal.

CHAPTER SUMMARY

Online consumer communities are alleged to have a significant contribution to make to the success of e-business. An online community represents a group of loyal and committed customers, and may generate the level of stability that allows businesses to learn about and effectively profile customers both as individuals and in groups or segments. There are a number of different typologies of online communities: a key distinction is between transaction oriented communities and communities of interest. Businesses that cannot build their own communities may piggyback on communities of interest, or communities developed by business partners. Value in communities is created through the information content, or other products generated by and shared within a community, or through the very existence of an identified group. Community hosts need to be proactive in creating and maintaining relationships in online communities. Customer Charters and Codes of Behaviour can set out some of the ground rules. A key feature of customer relationships is commitment or loyalty. It is also useful to remember that relationships and therefore communities go through lifecycles and are dynamic.

KEY CONCEPTS

Personal communities are personal networks of social and business contacts.

Transaction-oriented communities primarily facilitate the buying and selling of products and services and deliver information that is related to completing those transactions.

Communities of interest are gathered around topics of common interest. There are two main types of communities of interest: those associated with leisure activities and those associated with professional groups.

Value creation is essential for all stakeholders if they are to participate in a community.

Customer charters define the offering from the organisation.

Relationship lifecycles have a number of stages including introduction, experimentation, identification, continuous renewal and dissolution.

ASSESSMENT QUESTIONS

1. Discuss the concept of online community.

2. Describe some typologies of online communities. Critique and compare these typologies in terms of how they inform our understanding of online communities.

3. Why is value creation important for online communities? What are the strategies that are available to generate value? Illustrate with examples.

4. Discuss the concept of relationships and its significance to online communities.

5. What is meant by a relationship lifecycle? Discuss the stages in one model of the relationship lifecycle and make proposals about the different kinds of marketing communications activities that are appropriate to different stages in the life cycle.

6. Explain the role that an online community host would need to play in order to manage an online community successfully and profitably.

GROUP ASSESSMENT 1 – EVALUATING ONLINE COMMUNITIES

Each group member is asked to join an online community in any area that matches her personal interests and participate in that community on a daily basis for a month. During this process each group member is asked to make notes of the activities and evaluate the performance of the community. At the end of the month compare notes with a view to the development of a group report that:

1. Identifies and critiques criteria for the evaluation of online communities from a user/member perspective.

2. Uses these criteria to evaluate the communities visited.

3. Offers a considered argument as to whether sustainable online consumer communities are a long-term strategic option for businesses.

GROUP ASSESSMENT 2 – RELATIONSHIPS

Produce an essay that critically analyses the differences and similarities between virtual relationships and 'real' relationships.

GROUP ASSESSMENT 3 – CREATING A COMMUNITY

Create the basis for a forum using one of the free community-creation services, such as those offered at www.delphi.com, www.discusware.com or www.idealbb.com. Write some acceptable user guidelines for participating in this forum. Critically evaluate the process of establishing a forum. Indicate strategies that you might adopt for attracting traffic to the forum.

REFERENCES

Armstrong, A and Hagel, J (1996) The real value of online communities, *Harvard Business Review*, **74**, 134–40.

Barnatt, C (1998) Virtual communities and financial services – on-line business potentials and strategic choice, *International Journal of Bank Marketing*, **16**(4), 161–9.

Berthan, P, Pitt, L F and Watson, R T(1996) The World Wide Web as an advertising medium: toward an understanding of conversion efficiency, *Journal of Advertising Research*, **36**(1), 43–55.

Breitenbach, C S and Van Doren, D C (1998) Value added marketing in the digital domain: enhancing the utility of the Internet, *Journal of Consumer Marketing*, **15**(6), 558–75.

Buttle, F (1996) *Relationship marketing; theory and practice.* London: Paul Chapman Publishing.

Cahill, D J (1998) Relationship marketing? But all I really wanted was a one-night stand, *Marketing News*, 14 Sept, **32**(19), 4.

Christy, R, Oliver, G and Penn, J (1996) Relationship marketing in consumer markets, *Journal of Marketing Management*, **12**, 175–87.

Cothrel, J (1999) Virtual communities today, *The Journal of AGSI*, **8**(2), 52–6.

Dholakhia, U M and Rego, L L (1998) What makes commercial Web pages popular?, *European Journal of Marketing*, **32**(7/8), 724–37.

Dick, A and Basu, K (1994) Customer loyalty: toward an integrated conceptual framework, *Journal of Marketing Science*, **22**(2), 99–113.

Erikson, T (1997) *Social interaction on the net: virtual community as participatory genre.* Proceedings of the thirtieth Hawaii international conference on systems science, **6**, 23–30, ed. by J F Nunamaker and R H Sprague. Los Alamitos, CA: IEEE Computer Society Press.

Figallo, C (1999) *Hosting Web communities: building relationships, increasing customer loyalty and maintaining a competitive edge.* Wiley.

Fournier, S (1998) Consumers and their brands: developing relationship theory in consumer research, *Journal of Consumer Research,* **24**(4), 343–73.

Fournier, S, Dobscha, S and Micj, D G (1998) Preventing the premature death of relationship marketing, *Harvard Business Review,* **76**(1), 42–50.

Gabbott M and Hogg G (1998) *Consumers and services.* Chichester: Wiley.

Gambetta, D (1988) Can we trust trust?, in D Gambetta (ed.) *Trust: making and breaking cooperative relations.* New York: Blackwell, pp. 213–37.

Gronroos, C (1996) Relationship marketing: strategic and tactical implications, *Management Decision,* **34**(3), 5–14.

Hagel, J (1999) Net gain: expanding markets through virtual communities, *Journal of Interactive Marketing,* **13**(1), 55–65.

Hagel, J and Armstrong, A G (1997) *Net gain: expanding markets through virtual communities.* Harvard Business School Press.

Hanson, W (2000) *Principles of Internet marketing.* Cincinnati, Ohio: South-Western College Publishing.

Hoey, C (1998) Maximising the effectiveness of web-based marketing communications, *Marketing Intelligence and Planning,* **16**(1), 31–8.

Hunt, S. (1994) *Seven Questions for Relationship Marketing,* Proceedings of the Marketing Education Group Conference, Keynote Address, University of Ulster, 4–6 July.

Iacobucci, D and Hibbard, J D (1999) Toward an encompassing theory of business marketing relationships (BMRS) and interpersonal commercial relationships (ICRS): an empirical generalisation, *Journal of Interactive Marketing,* **13**(3), 13–33.

Jevons, C and Gabbott, M (2000) Trust, brand equity and brand reality in Internet business relationships: an interdisciplinary approach, *Journal of Marketing Management,* **16**(6), 619–34.

Jones, Q (1997) Virtual communities, virtual settlements & cyber archaeology: a theoretical outline, *Journal of Computer Mediated Communication,* **3**(3), 26. Available at http://jcmc.huji.ac.il/vol3/issues3/jones.htm.

Kannan, P K, Chang, A-M and Whinston, A B (2001) E-business and the intermediary role of virtual communities, in S Barnes and B Hunt (eds) *E-commerce and V-business: business models for global success.* Oxford: Butterworth Heinemann, pp. 67–82.

Kaplan, S and Sawhney, M (2000) E-hubs: the new B2B marketplaces, *Harvard Business Review,* **78**(3), 97–108.

Korac-Boisvert, N and Kouzmin, A (1994) The dark side of info-age social networks in public organisations and creeping crises, *Administrative Theory and Praxis,* **16**(1) 57–82.

Kozinets, R V (1999) E-tribalised marketing?: the strategic implications of virtual communities of consumption, *European Management Journal,* **17**(3), 252–64.

Loebbecke, C, Powell, P and Trilling, S (1998) Investigating the worth of Internet advertising, *International Journal of Information Management,* **18**(3), 181–94.

Markus, M L (1994) Finding a happy medium: explaining the negative effects of electronic communication on social life at work, *ACM Transactions on Information Systems,* **12**(2), 119–49.

Martin, C L (1996) Consumer-to-consumer relationships: satisfaction with other consumers' public behaviour, *Journal of Consumer Affairs,* **30**(1), 146–69.

Massad, V J, Whitmyer, J L and Tucker, J M (2001) The deficiency of relationship marketing as a paradigm to explain e-commerce phenomena: the case of online auctions, *Quarterly Journal of Electronic Commerce,* **2**(3).

Matheson, K and Zanna, M (1989) Impact of computer mediated communication on self awareness, *Computers in Human Behaviour,* **4**, 221–33.

McDonough, M (1997) *Frequently asked questions: virtual communities.* Internal paper prepared for virtual community hosts at the Thomson Virtual Communities Laboratory.

McGuire, T W, Kiesler, S and Siegel, J (1987) Group and computer mediated discussion effects in risk decision making, *Journal of Personality and Social Psychology,* **52**(5), 917–30.

Moller, K and Halinene, A (2000) Relationship marketing theory: its roots and direction, *Journal of Marketing Management,* **16**, 29–54.

Newell, F (2000) *Loyalty.com: CRM in the age of Internet marketing.* New York: McGraw Hill.

Oliver, R L (1999) Whence consumer loyalty?, *Journal of Marketing*, 13 Dec, 33–55.

Prahalad, C K and Ramaswamy, V (2000) Co-opting consumer competence, *Harvard Business Review*, **78**(1), 79–93.

Preece, J (1998) Emphatic communities: reaching out across the web, *Interactions*, **5**(2), 32–43.

Reichheld, F F and Schefter, P (2000) E-loyalty; your secret weapon on the web, *Harvard Business Review*, **78**(4), 105.

Rheingold, H (1993) *The virtual community: homesteading on the electronic frontier.* Reading, MA: Addison-Wesley.

Romm, C, Pliskin, N and Clarke, R (1997) Virtual communities and society: towards an integrative three phase model, *International Journal of Information Management*, **17**(4), 261–70.

Smith, W and Higgins, M (2000) Reconsidering the relationship analogy, *Journal of Marketing Management*, **16**, 81–94.

Tambyah, S K (1996) Life on the Net: the reconstruction of self and community, *Advances in Consumer Research*, **23**, 172–7.

Turkle, S (1996) Virtuality and its discontents: searching for community in cyberspace, *The American Prospect*, **24**, 50–7. Available at http://epn.org/prospect/24/24turk.html.

Tsokas, N and Saren, M (2002) Competitive advantage, knowledge and relationship marketing – where, what and how?, *Journal of Business and Industrial Marketing*, forthcoming.

Williams, R L and Cothrel, J (2000) Four smart ways to run online communities, *Sloan Management Review*, **41**(4), 81–101.

The e-business enterprise

After reading this chapter you will:

- Understand the range of back-office functions that are necessary to support e-business transactions
- Appreciate the role of databases and Enterprise Resource Planning Systems
- Be able to discuss the functions of distribution systems
- Be able to evaluate delivery options
- Be able to evaluate payment options
- Understand the role and nature of virtual organisations
- Be aware of links between knowledge management and e-business

INTRODUCTION

Many of the earlier chapters in this book focus primarily on the customer interface, the establishment and maintenance of an effective dialogue, and possibly relationships with customers. This chapter explores aspects of the way in which an e-business needs to organise itself in order to deliver the promise and benefits to customers.

The impact on organisational structures, roles and activities is dependent upon the stage of e-business development (see Figure 1.1) and the extent to which the e-business venture is integrated with traditional business models.

In Stage 1 e-business, the ownership of Web-based activities lies largely with marketing departments and, since the site is primarily concerned with messages and information provision, the impact on other parts of the organisation may be minimal. As the site provides a richer and richer database, other departments are likely to need to take responsibility for maintaining the information on various parts of the website. Centralised templates and styles are necessary to keep the website consistent in appearance.

In Stage 2 sites, customers can interact through the site. Customers may go through a registration process and this may be used as a basis for passwords that control the information that a user can access. At this stage, the organisation needs to develop an information-access policy. Further, customer service must be in place to respond to customer comments and queries and, in general, Web presence starts to provoke the organisation to respond to customers, both in terms of maintaining the individual dialogue and of changing aspects of service and products in response to customers' comments. The organisation is drawn into closer engagement with the customer and needs to organise for this engagement.

In Stage 3, which features e-commerce transactions, activities associated with e-business start to permeate the entire organisation. As discussed further below, the supply and distribution chains need to be tightly coupled so that order fulfilment and delivery can be achieved as efficiently and effectively as the instantaneous nature of order placement might suggest to the customer.

In Stage 4, the relationship between the customer and the organisation becomes tightly coupled. Both parties need to consider what information they wish to share with the other party. Trust, security and legal and ethical issues become important to both parties in the relationship. Organisational production and logistics databases may be open to the customer and the customer may be in a position to compare details of intra-organisational performance with that of competitors. Further, they may share their perceptions with other customers. Customers start to feel some control and power, and are faced with the choice as to how they might exercise that power. They may do this by seeking a more personalised product or service, or by pursuing the lowest cost or fastest delivery option. In both consumer and B2B markets this type of customer power can push a business to rethink fundamentally its business models.

The impact of the Web on business models does not stop at the customer interface; ultimately it permeates the entire organisation. Organisations need to be prepared to change the way that they do things. As Figure 7.1 suggests,

Figure 7.1 Organising for the Web – impact areas

Systems	People
Enterprise resource planning systems	Structures and roles
Customer relationship management systems	Culture
Communication technologies	Virtual teams
Knowledge repositories	Learning organisations

this change focuses on both systems and people. This chapter explores some of the areas of impact. Other issues that are interlinked to the themes in this chapter are explored in Chapter 8 on strategy and Chapter 9 on protecting online societies.

BACK-OFFICE FUNCTIONS

Morath (2000) identifies the areas listed in Figure 7.2 as important in e-business. Earlier chapters have explored the functions of marketing and sales, and customer care. Here it is useful to visit some of the functional aspects of the back-office functions, including finance, that are necessary for successful e-commerce.

Back-office operations include order management, supplies and procurements, and packaging and delivery. The back office is effectively the factory of many e-businesses. Many will outsource production. The back office offers the infrastructure for working within a virtual organisation across organisational and regional boundaries. Virtual organisations are discussed at greater length below.

Order management starts with placing order creation in the hands of the customer. This reduces in-house time spent in order creation and reduces error rates. The order can then be automatically passed to the areas such as production and supplies that will contribute to its fulfilment. Customers can also engage in the process by being offered the opportunity to track orders. This functionality is particularly useful in business-to-business markets in which any delays may have implications for the customer's business and delays need to be managed.

Order fulfilment can be more difficult due to the tighter coupling of supply and demand. Surges in demand need to be managed. Normally such surges will arise from promotional activities or special events in the annual calendar (such as Christmas). Businesses need to monitor the effect of such activities on demand over a period of time until they are able to predict the effect that specific promotional activities will have on demand levels. They will then be in a position to match supply and demand.

Within the finance function, a key issue is the ability to receive money electronically. Further, those customers who do not pay by credit card may need to be assessed for permission for deferred payment and any receivables that are not paid on time need to be enforced.

Figure 7.2 Processes for e-commerce

Area	Activities covered
Marketing and sales	Product management
	Segmentation
	Approach management
	Results review
	Decision management
Customer care	Delivery
	Client feedback
	Customer relationship
	Suggestions
	Customer relationship management
Back office	Order management
	Production
	Supplies
	Packaging and delivery
Finance	Budgets and accounting
	Payables
	Receivables
	Risk management
	ERP

Source: Based on Morath (2000), p. 209.

All of the functional areas in Figure 7.2 must be tightly coupled. Staff must understand and respond to cross-functional dependencies and interactions.

DATABASES AND SYSTEMS

Effective data management offers a platform for the integration of functions within the business. Earlier chapters have identified various sources of data that flow into the e-business. In Chapter 4, the collection of data in respect of various web metrics was discussed. In Chapter 5 the collection of customer profile data in order to personalise the offering was explored. Other data from the marketplace may all be gathered into a data warehouse that forms the core of the database marketing process, as summarised in Figure 7.3.

In addition to performing a central role in understanding the marketplace, databases have become the hub of business systems control. Enterprise software systems, often referred to as ERP (**enterprise resource planning**) systems, link together the various aspects of a business that the central

Figure 7.3 The database marketing process

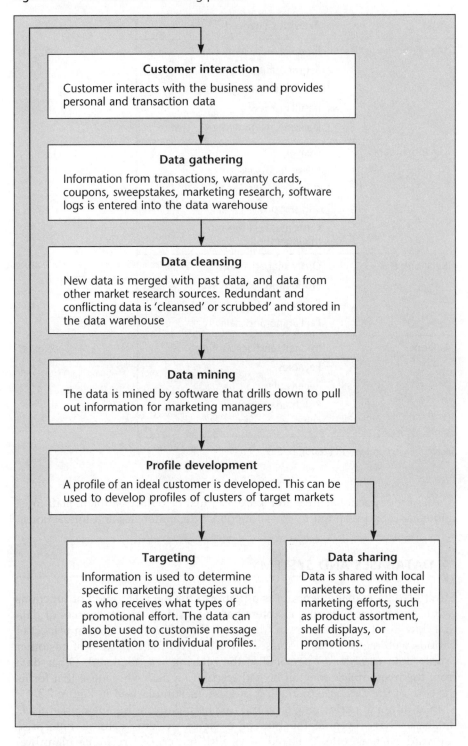

Figure 7.4 Enterprise Resource Planning systems and business system control

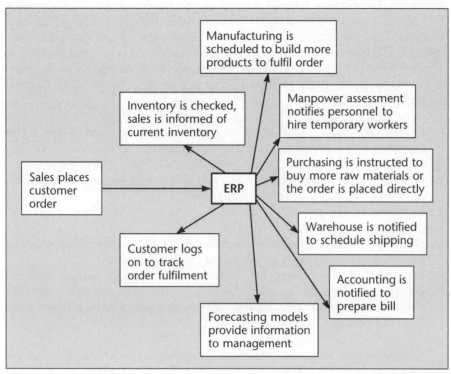

database serves. The system supports a wide range of clients from customers, the sales force, suppliers and management. Figure 7.4 summarises how the entry of an order into the system triggers a chain reaction through to other parts of the system. When a sales order is entered into the system, the ERP checks the inventory, schedules production, orders raw materials, notifies manpower to hire temporary employees, prepares the bill, schedules shipping, allows the buyer to track the purchase, and prepares reports for management on trends. This level of integration and sophistication is necessary at the systems level for a manufacturing organisation to be able to respond with agility.

DISTRIBUTION SYSTEMS

Organisations are critically dependent upon their distribution systems. They are not independent entities but are kept afloat by their unique network of collaborators and partners. Typically the producer interacts with consumers through a series of intermediaries and facilitators. These intermediaries and facilitators enable a transaction to take place between producers and customers. This combination of intermediaries and facilitators is described as a **channel**. **Intermediaries**, such as wholesalers and retailers, split large production runs into small amounts (breaking bulk) and thereby create an

assortment of products that is deemed to satisfy better a segment of customers. **Facilitators** help the flow of the transaction by physically moving the product, information or funds through the distribution channel. Traditionally, the distribution system makes the overall system more efficient. Different agents in the chain can concentrate on those functions in which they have special expertise, and which they can perform the most efficiently. Specifically channel members must perform the standard **channel functions**:

1. *Physical possession* – the good or service must be transferred to the customer using, where appropriate, warehousing and physical movement of the products from the producer to the customer
2. *Title or ownership flow* – title or ownership must be transferred when the customer purchases or receives the product
3. *Promotion* of the product – means of communication between channel members is essential for promotion
4. *Ordering system* – the channel member must also structure an ordering system, typically though an electronic ordering system
5. *Payment flows* – a system for payment must support the payment for goods when they are transferred. There is also some risk involved if the customer does not pay or, from the customer's perspective, if the product does not perform as required.

There are a number of characteristics of e-business that are challenging this traditional channel structure:

1. Transaction costs associated with channel functions are being lowered
2. It is sometimes easier for customers to make choices without an intermediary performing an assortment function
3. If the manufacturer is keen to engage in personalisation or mass customisation of products, the manufacturer may wish to form a direct relationship with the customer and the need to break bulk is less obvious.

Many authors have speculated on the potential disintermediation of traditional channel structures, and conflicts between channels in e-business and traditional wholesale and retail channels. Disintermediation and channel structures are discussed more fully in the next chapter, in the context of market structures and roles.

DELIVERY OPTIONS

Delivery is a key service phase of the transaction, in which customers discover whether merchants will fulfil their promises. They discover whether the goods will arrive to the specified schedule and whether they will be as specified in the online catalogue. Customers also need mechanisms for return or redress if the service or the product does not match their expectations. There are a number of different delivery options: digital delivery, postal and shipping services and van delivery.

Digital delivery

Information products, such as banking services, software products and digital music (for example, in MP3 format) can be delivered across the Web. There are only two constraints:

- The bandwidth of the network through which the customer receives the document
- The need for equipment at the user's end that supports the download, storage and utilisation of the delivered product.

Postal and courier services

Postal and courier services have received a further boost to their fortunes with the advent of e-commerce. They have already established efficient logistical systems for moving packages of varying sizes between locations and offer a wide range of services that support delivery to both business and consumer addresses. Such services have been optimised for delivery to commercial addresses and have needed to reshape their activities to accommodate increased levels of delivery to private addresses. For example, FedEx handles all the logistical operations and warehousing for a number of companies. The following Case Cameo summarises some of the services available from FedEx. All of the major transportation and delivery companies offer online tracking of services. Such services support international delivery. In the US consumer marketplace, the consumer is typically offered a range of different shipping options using different operators, as illustrated through the extract from Amazon.com in Figure 7.5. Such services are ideal for delivering relatively small, occasional items to consumers.

FEDEX WORLDWIDE SERVICES

CASE CAMEO

FedEx International First
A delivery before 8.00 am to nearly 5000 zip codes across the USA for those very urgent shipments where a mid morning delivery is simply not fast enough. Call FedEx to check service availability.

FedEx International Priority
An express time definite, door-to-door customs-cleared express delivery service for documents and dutiables to over 214 countries worldwide, designed for shipments of any weight where individual pieces may weigh as much as 68kg.

FedEx 10kg and 25kg Box
Both the FedEx 10kg Box and FedEx 25kg Box are packaging types with special rates for FedEx International Priority Service Shipments.

continued

FedEx International Extra HoursSM

For your next-day deliveries to the USA guaranteed by 3 pm to over 14,000 zip codes. It's "Extra Hours" because with our late pick-up, you get more time to prepare your packages.

Improved Next-Day Service Within Europe

Since September 27th 1999, FedEx offers an enhanced next-business-day service between hundreds of European cities, with later cut-off times and pick-up facilities (5–7 pm) and improved delivery times.

FedEx International Priority Freight

A flexible express delivery service for freight shipments of a maximum declared value of US$100,000 and almost unlimited total weight.

FedEx International Express Freight

Airport-airport cargo service for shipments of virtually any size or weight. Cargo reaches its destination, typically, in 1–3 days.

Figure 7.5 Shipping options for CDs

The following shipping options are available for you to select:

1. First class mail – this will be dispatched first class by Royal Mail. We have been advised by Royal Mail that packages sent by first class mail generally arrive within 1–2 days of posting.

2. Special Delivery – dependent on size these packages will be despatched by Royal Mail or Courier. Orders places by this method should reach you within 24 hours of despatch from our fulfilment centre. Please note that goods despatched on a Friday afternoon will normally be delivered the following Monday.

3. Lynx Courier – This method should be selected for larger, or more expensive deliveries. This is not guaranteed as a next day delivery service, though goods are usually delivered within 48 hours of despatch.

4. EU Standard/ Zone 1 Standard/ Zone 2 Standard – this will be despatched first class by Royal Mail. Upon entering the shipping country, it will enter the postal system of the country concerned. It is our experience that goods delivered using this method arrive within 7-10 days of despatch.

Source: HMV (www.hmv.co.uk).

From the consumer perspective, in the UK postal deliveries are often preferable to courier services because they deliver out of the Monday to Friday 9–5 slot, with early morning and Saturday deliveries. If the parcel cannot be delivered it can be collected from a local sorting office. Courier services are typically less flexible.

Delivery charges may be a significant element of the cost of acquisition of an item. It might be argued that these are modest compared with the time and transport costs associated with a trip to the shop, but they are more in evidence than these costs. Delivery charges depend on the mode of delivery chosen and modes with higher speeds of delivery typically cost more (see Figure 7.6).

The sting in the tail for delivery and its costs are return arrangements. Most businesses accept returns and refund the cost of the item. Return may be via post or courier collection. Costs of return vary considerably but might typically involve a handling charge of around 15 per cent of the price of the good.

EXPLORATORY ACTIVITY

Visit the websites of UPS and the Post Office. Examine and compare the delivery services that they offer for businesses.

VAN DELIVERY

Supermarkets need to deliver to customers on a regular basis and many individual deliveries will be bulky. Further, items will arrive in optimum condition if they are transported in chilled and cooled vans. Such vans also act as a mobile promotion of the Web-based service as they go on their delivery round. Personal interaction between the van driver or delivery agent and the customer may also be an important element of an ongoing relationship. Delivery to home addresses imposes a significant overhead, which was not present in the bricks-and-mortar model where customers took responsibility for picking, processing and delivery of their own groceries. Ultimately, the viability of the Internet option for supermarkets depends crucially on the value that customers place on the personalised delivery service. Customers may signal this value either through willingness to pay for the service or alternatively through a higher level of loyalty to specific retailers.

A key issue for customers is the delivery schedule. Tesco, for example, delivers in two-hour time slots from 10 am to 3 pm and 5 pm to 10 pm, Monday to Saturday, and from 10 am to 3 pm on Sunday. Charges for van delivery are also variable, but are typically a few pounds per order. Substitution is likely to be necessary for groceries when specific lines are out of stock. Customers typically specify substitutes, or allow the picker to choose them. Substitutes, in particular, need the option of a return.

CASE CAMEO

DELIVERY LOGISTICS

Supermarkets in the UK faced an interesting dilemma when deciding on the logistics of the delivery service associated with their e-tailing activities. Groceries are bulky items and typically a customer seeks a regular weekly delivery of a unique assortment of items that needs to be selected in accordance with his 'shopping list'. In addition, replacements and substitutes and produce of unacceptable quality may also require special attention and possibly additional customer service interaction. Tesco decided to base its delivery logistics on existing stores, arguably on the basis that it had already invested significantly in acquiring the optimal location of those stores to ensure easy access to and by customers. It was also able to roll out the e-shopping service more quickly using this approach. Sainsbury's, on the other hand, built special warehouses from which to make deliveries. These warehouses offered an opportunity to invest in the latest warehousing and picking technology but inevitably are not so numerous as retail stores.

GROUP DISCUSSION ACTIVITY

What are the factors that will determine whether delivery from stores or delivery from a warehouse is likely to be the most successful long-term strategy?

Figure 7.6 Comparing shipping costs

Distribution medium	Examples of products	Cost
Digital information	Airline tickets, journals, reports, banking transactions	Near zero
Digital entertainment	Digital audio and video	Consumer costs relate to time to transmit and local storage. Key seller costs are bandwidth charges
Hard goods	Books, CDs, clothes	Depends on weight, bulk and speed of delivery
Perishables	Groceries, meals	Potentially high cost due to personalisation, potential for spoilage, and the speed and mode of delivery required

Source: Based on Ward (2000), p. 371.

PAYMENT OPTIONS

Payment systems must:

- Be secure
- Be easy for buyer and seller to use and understand
- Be straightforward for banks to administer
- Accommodate different currencies
- Have low transaction costs.

Whilst these characteristics are applicable to all payment systems, business payment systems, as opposed to consumer payment systems, are more complex since they must accommodate:

- Multiple roles in the buying process, such as those of requisitioner, authoriser and purchasing department
- Support repeat orders and specialised and complex orders
- Exhibit a level of security that is consistent with the high value of some of the payments that will be made
- Fully integrate bank and payment authority into the system.

Although the dominant payment mechanism is via credit cards, there has been considerable experimentation with different types of payment system. The approaches discussed below illustrate some of the options that have been explored and the different types of systems that might be appropriate in different contexts.

Credit cards

Credit cards are widely used as a payment mechanism in the United States and to a lesser extent in the UK. However, the penetration of credit cards in some European and other markets is so low that credit cards are less acceptable as a payment mechanism in these marketplaces. Credit cards cannot therefore be regarded as a universal solution. Further, there has been considerable concern about the security of transmitting credit card numbers and transaction details over the Web. This has provoked the development and implementation of security approaches as discussed in Chapter 9. For example, through SET the merchant never sees the credit card number and cannot therefore be held responsible for inappropriate use of the number. In many respects, credit cards fulfil the requirements of a payment mechanism and they have the added benefit that they are an established and accepted standard. Tendering credit card details to numerous merchants may be perceived to increase security risk and is certainly tedious. Another option is to register with an intermediary, such as Pay2See (www.Pay2See.com). Merchants can then be referred to this intermediary and the shopper does not need to register with each merchant.

MasterCard has a range of corporate payment solutions cards, including MasterCard BusinessCard and MasterCard Corporate Purchasing Card. MasterSource, as described below, links payment and procurement solutions in a way that is suitable for B2B marketplaces and transactions.

In order for merchants to be able to offer payment they need a merchant account from one of the merchant services providers such as Barclays Merchant Services, NatWest Streamline Merchant Services, Midland Card Services or Lloyds Cardnet. These services coordinate the transfer of funds and in this intermediary role act to some extent as a verifier of the online payment. Not all e-merchants may be acceptable for registration with these services. Small companies, for example, trade on the Web using a Payment Solutions Provider (PSP) that funnels transactions through their merchant account. PSPs typically have an established track record of trading online.

LINKING PAYMENT AND PROCUREMENT – MasterSource

MasterSource is designed for businesses using any MasterCard corporate payment solution. The service combines Open Ratings predictive performance rating, based on criteria such as timeliness, responsiveness and reliability, with Dun & Bradstreet's information and technology solutions. MasterSource allows buyers to access reliable information on potential trading partners, thus increasing confidence levels and thereby increasing the number of transactions completed in B2B e-marketplaces.

EXPLORATORY ACTIVITY

Visit the MasterCard website. Write some notes on the types of payment solutions and services that it makes available for B2B marketplace transactions.

Electronic cash

Electronic cash is a pre-paid system. Consumers buy electronic tokens, and build up electronic funds prior to making a purchase (see www.cybercash.com).

Electronic wallets

Electronic wallets can be useful for making a series of micro payments online. Low value purchases, such as a single digital song or an article from a newspaper or journal, may only cost a few pence. A mechanism is necessary that ensures that the transaction costs of collecting payment for such items do not overshadow the value of the transaction. A software wallet requires a user to set up an online account to which he adds an amount of money. When transactions are undertaken, the wallet is debited (see www.ecoin.net). Another type of electronic wallet is operated by Internet Explorer. In this wallet a user keeps all of her credit card numbers, bank account numbers, and contact and shipping information in a file that can be used when the user wants to make a payment.

Smart cards

Smart cards use a micro controller chip embedded in the card. The cards can be purchased and reloaded from a bank account using an ATM-style machine. Various devices, including parking meters, vending machines and payphones, can read the card for payment. Information on individual purchases can be collected from the cards to track purchasing profiles. Smart cards must be inserted into a card reader before items can be purchased. As a Smart card slot is not a standard feature on a PC, applications of Smart cards are currently restricted to public access kiosks.

Digital cheques

Digital cheques are the same as conventional cheques except that, being digital, the signature also needs to be digital. These digital signatures use the public key/private key encryption techniques discussed in Chapter 9. The consumer fills in the cheque online and then sends it via a secure server to the recipient. The amount specified on the cheque is electronically withdrawn from the sender's account and deposited in the recipient's account.

Online payments

Online payments direct from bank accounts can reduce transaction costs. These may be appropriate in B2B markets and between organisations and governments for, say, tax payments.

Electronic payment systems

Electronic payment systems, that include both sending bills and making online payments, greatly reduce transaction costs. Such systems can be used to pay for small transactions, such as travel bookings, stationery orders, and parts and supplies, as well as large payments between businesses in respect of significant contracts.

Payment systems for businesses

A number of different initiatives are under development in relation to business payment systems. Open Buying on the Internet (www.openbuy.org) and the Open Trading Protocol (www.otp.org) are important developments to watch. The other option is the development of Internet-based EDI.

Paying offline

For customers and business sectors in which none of the above options are acceptable, another alternative is offline invoicing and payment, through credit cards, debit cards and cheques.

CASE CAMEO

OPEN BUYING ON THE INTERNET (OBI)

The vision of the OBI Consortium for the OBI specification is to facilitate the implementation of e-commerce solutions utilising interoperable standards-based Internet purchasing systems that offer:

- Universal, high-speed access
- Inexpensive, paperless information and transactions
- Platform-independent software and services.

Such a protocol is likely to have a number of business benefits including:

- Facilitation of the selection of strategic suppliers to leverage buying power and lower costs
- Integration of suppliers from sourcing through to payment
- Easy-to-use, efficient processes for the end-user
- Suppliers able to meet the unique requirements of each customer through one standardised approach
- Improved customer service levels
- Differentiation in the marketplace.

The consortium has 70 commercial members, including American Express, Ford Motor Company and BASF Corporation.

EXPLORATORY ACTIVITY

Visit the website of the Open Buying on the Internet (OBI) consortium and make notes on the latest developments in effective payment solutions for B2B marketplaces.

GROUP DISCUSSION ACTIVITY

Review the options for payment that have been outlined above and identify those that are appropriate for consumer online transactions. Visit the relevant websites cited above in the text. Develop a set of user-based criteria that can be used to evaluate and compare the options. These criteria are likely to incorporate some of the criteria outlined at the beginning of this section, but should also cover other perspectives.

VIRTUAL ORGANISATIONS

The same technologies that allow customers to communicate with and impact upon business, and that drive intermediation and disintermediation provide the platform for a fundamental review of the nature of business and organisation. Virtual organisations are viewed as one recipe for survival in fast-moving and turbulent business environments. Virtual organisations need to feature speed, flexibility and fluidity (Byrne, 1993), sometimes described as agility (Metes *et al.*, 1998). Internet technologies make it easier to form and re-form alliances, and to create blurred boundaries for the organisation. There are many definitions of a virtual organisation, but the following offered by Byrne (1993) highlights the role of information technology in the facilitation of alliances:

> A virtual organisation is a temporary network of independent companies – suppliers, customers, even erstwhile rivals – linked by information technology to share skills, costs, and access to one another's markets. It will have neither central office nor an organisation chart. It will have no hierarchy, and no vertical integration.

In comparison Turban *et al.* (1999) assert that the virtual organisation may be permanent or temporary:

> . . . . composed of several business partners sharing costs and resources for the purpose of producing a product or service. [It] can be temporary . . . or it can be permanent. Each partner contributes complementary resources that reflect its strengths, and determines its role in the virtual organisation. (p. 142)

EXPLORATORY ACTIVITY

Compare the two definitions of a virtual organisation. What are the differences and similarities?

A key dimension of both of these definitions is strategic alliances and partnering. The purpose of such alliances is to command speed and flexibility in order to:

■ Gain access into new markets or technologies
■ Break down market barriers to new products by rallying the required skills and expertise from groups, individuals and even rivals from outside organisational boundaries.

The opportunistic nature of such alliances suggests that they will generally be short-term and exist only until their objective has been achieved. The member companies may then disband and proceed to create new partnerships. In reality the permanence of alliances, and the way in which virtual organisations mutate will depend on the interdependencies between their members and the extent to which original objectives evolve into new shared objectives. Dynamic alliances are also volatile and potentially difficult to manage.

Marshall *et al.* (2001) suggest that virtual organisations need the following characteristics:

- Adaptability, flexibility and responsiveness to changing requirements and conditions
- Effectiveness in utilisation of resources
- Formation of business alliances with varying degrees of permanence
- Dispersion of component parts
- Empowerment of staff
- Stewardship of expertise, know-how and knowledge
- Low levels of bureaucracy
- Opportunist behaviours embracing change and uncertainty
- High infusion of IT to support business processes and knowledge workers.

The critical success factors for such organisations are:

- *A shared vision* (Wiesenfeld *et al.*, 1998)
- *Trust.* Lipnack and Stamps (1998) suggest that in the virtual organisation trust needs to replace the usual rules, procedures and policies that control behaviour in more traditional organisations
- *Shared risk*
- *Mutual benefits.* For members to be prepared to accept shared risk, they must experience shared benefits in terms of, say, reduced costs, increased revenues or increased market share (Friedman, 1998).

Any of these factors can change and the opportunism that led to the formation of the virtual organisation may lead to its untimely demise. When conflicts, misunderstandings or unforeseen events do arise the virtual organisation has few established procedures for negotiation and conflict resolution. The initial limited commitment to the relationship can mitigate against adequate information and knowledge sharing and effective trust.

GROUP DISCUSSION ACTIVITY

Discuss why, in the virtual organisation, trust needs to replace the usual rules, procedures and policies that control behaviour in more traditional organisations. Focus your discussion around a virtual marketing communications agency that specialises in website development for large corporate concerns. Each contract is large and draws in expertise from a variety of freelance designers, website creators and marketing consultants. Some contracts extend over several months or years but elements within contracts must be delivered to tight schedules.

Virtual teams are key components of virtual organisations. A **virtual team** is an evolutionary form of network organisation (Miles and Snow, 1986) enabled by advances in information and communication technology (Davidow and Malone, 1992; Jarvenpaa and Ives, 1994). In this context the concept of virtual implies permeable interfaces and boundaries, project teams that rapidly form, reorganise, and dissolve when the needs of a dynamic marketplace change, and individuals with differing competences who are located across time, space and cultures (Mowshowitz, 1997). Such teams are an essential way of working as companies expand globally, face increasing demands for fast product development, and use more globally-scattered subcontractors. Virtual teams promise the flexibility, responsiveness, lower costs and improved resource utilisation necessary to meet ever-changing requirements in highly turbulent and dynamic global business environments. This concept of a virtual team introduces further characteristics of virtual teams which need to be considered in the context of virtual business communities.

Virtual teams may be global. Computer-mediated communication allows members separated by time and space, and often culture, geography, history and futures, to engage in collaborative work. Individuals from different cultures vary in terms of their communication and group behaviours, including their willingness to trust others (Gydykunst *et al.*, 1997). One major dimension of cultural variability is individualism–collectivism as explored by Hofstede (1980). In individualist cultures, the needs, values and goals of the individual take precedence over the needs, values and goals of the in-group. In collectivist cultures, the needs, values and goals of the in-group take precedence over the needs, values and goals of the individual. In addition, compared with individuals from collectivist cultures, individuals from individualistic cultures tend to:

■ be less concerned with self-categorising
■ be less influenced by group membership
■ have greater skills in entering and leaving new groups
■ engage in more open and precise communication (Hofstede, 1980, 1991).

In general, individuals from individualist cultures might be more ready to trust others than individuals from collectivist cultures in all environments, but in particular in computer mediated communication environments. For the purposes of this chapter the key issue is that computer mediated communities will vary in the speed with which relationships are formed, the nature of the relationships and the effectiveness and duration of relationships.

KNOWLEDGE MANAGEMENT

Knowledge management is concerned with the management and exploitation of corporate knowledge. It is a holistic philosophy that drives organisations to optimise the utilisation of their knowledge resources. These knowledge resources include the databases discussed in an earlier section of this chapter, but also extend to implicit and embedded knowledge in workers' minds and competences. Internets, intranets and data warehousing offer powerful tools to support knowledge management. On the other hand, effective knowledge management has become essential for global organisations with permeable boundaries. No longer can organisations rely upon 'Joe in the paint shop' because:

- People in other countries may never have met, or be aware of the existence of, Joe
- Joe may leave the organisation and join a competitor or, alternatively, with changing marketplace dynamism may be downsized out of the organisation
- With new product categories, new technologies and new approaches to offering customer benefits, Joe's knowledge may become out of date.

The nature of knowledge management, and the related discipline of organisational learning has been discussed by many authors (for example, Pedler *et al.*, 1991; Nonaka, 1991, 1994, 1995, 1996; Dixon, 1994). Knowledge management has four interdependent strands: knowledge repositories, knowledge tools, knowledge cultures and the valuing of knowledge as an asset (Davenport *et al.*, 1998).

Knowledge repositories store both knowledge and information, often in documentary form. A common feature is 'added value' through categorisation and pruning. Repositories can fall into three categories:

- Those that include external knowledge, such as competitive intelligence
- Those that include structured internal knowledge, such as research reports, and product-oriented marketing material such as techniques and methods
- Those that embrace informal, internal or tacit knowledge, such as discussion databases that store 'know how'.

Knowledge access and knowledge tools, which provide access to knowledge or facilitate its transfer amongst individuals. Here the emphasis is on those tools and technologies that provide connectivity, access and transfer, such as video conferencing systems, document scanning and sharing tools. Telecommunications networks are central (Ruggles, 1997). There may be an attempt to create a repository of such knowledge or the emphasis may be rather on access to the individuals that hold or can provide the knowledge. Identified expert networks are often part of such projects. Success with improved knowledge access is not achieved without addressing organisational norms and values and confrontation of the relationship between knowledge and power.

Knowledge cultures develop so that the culture and other aspects of the organisational environment are conducive to more effective knowledge creation, transfer and use (Blackler, 1995; Mullin, 1996). This involves tackling organisational norms and values as they relate to knowledge (Choo, 1996). A range of different initiatives might fall into this category. These include:

- increasing awareness of the knowledge embedded in client relationships and engagements which, if shared, could enhance organisational performance
- focusing on knowledge-related employee behaviour with, for example, contributions to the organisation's structured knowledge base attracting significant rewards and bonuses
- implementing decision audit programs in order to assess whether and how employees were applying knowledge in key decisions.

In general this aspect of knowledge management is closely linked with specific types of virtual organisation and virtual team, and the way in which such teams can be encouraged to build trust and share knowledge, sometimes across national boundaries.

Knowledge assets are recognised as the value of knowledge to an organisation. Assets, such as technologies that are sold under licence or have potential value, customer databases and detailed parts catalogues, are typical of companies' intangible assets to which value can be assigned. Assessments of other knowledge can be made on the basis of knowledge that increases revenue and reduces costs.

Effective knowledge management is important to the success of businesses in online marketplaces. Since opportunities to capitalise on knowledge exist for all businesses in the e-marketplace, effective and rapid exploitation of knowledge assets becomes all the more important in this arena. On the other hand, most businesses need to integrate their approach to knowledge management across the business as a whole, rather than treat e-business as a separate endeavour. The interface between knowledge management and e-business is explored in the context of the four aspects of knowledge management.

Knowledge repositories – E-business transactions can generate a range of data. The challenge is to convert this data to knowledge, at various different levels. Intelligent agents (human or computer-based) may use this knowledge to personalise the product offering to individual customers. Managers may use the information to inform the future development of products, product portfolios and marketing strategies. Senior managers may use the information to assess the overall performance of the business and to identify new market segments and market directions. These different uses indicate that there are a number of different ways in which data needs to be converted into information before it can be integrated with information from other sources, including other parts of the business and competitive intelligence. These are not new problems, but do demand further consideration of the way in which data is fed into knowledge repositories, and how it is structured and analysed.

Knowledge access – Arguably the most interesting question associated with knowledge access in the e-business environment is the extent to which suppliers and customers are allowed access to the knowledge assets within the organisation's extranet. Indeed, using data extracted from this extranet, it is possible that 'partners' may be able to construct their own market intelligence, particularly if they have access to the knowledge assets or even just data on the business processes of more than one partner. In this way, each organisation would be in a position to compile a unique profile of its industry and the strengths and weaknesses of its partners, and make deductions about their likely future performance. Organisations need to covet their knowledge assets and heighten their awareness of their commercial value. Even access to such simple devices as price databases or delivery schedules might give organisational customers or suppliers an insight into trends in company performance that could have dangerous consequences for the future of an organisation.

Knowledge access is dependent upon knowledge infrastructures which embrace both the networks of access rights and security levels and controls, and the infrastructure through which knowledge can be accessed and shared. Knowledge management can only be implemented fully with intercommunicating systems, integration between e-business interfaces as shown to customers and the information systems used in business processes. For some organisations this will require a major reconfiguration of systems and associated information systems strategy.

Knowledge culture – As the discussion above suggests, a key aspect of knowledge management is knowledge creation and the surfacing and sharing of embedded and implicit knowledge. The data generated through e-business transactions is unquestionably explicit and so the issue of implicit or tacit knowledge does not arise in this context. On the other hand, the other issues that are much discussed in the context of knowledge cultures, such as knowledge sharing and trust, are key. The early e-businesses have recognised the difficulty in creating trust in relationships with customers in an environment where the tangibles are at an all-time low and the business medium is new. In addition to seeking to use established brands as the basis for relationships in an e-business, they have recognised the importance of product quality and service delivery. The real question is whether the culture that encourages openness, trust and sincerity can be sustained both within organisations, for effective knowledge management, and between customers and suppliers in the e-business environment.

Knowledge assets – Most e-businesses do not currently make a profit. Their value is not related to their profit but to their potential. In the growth phase of e-business the revenue is re-invested. Through this process e-businesses seek to create greater business potential and a stronger position in the e-business marketplace. This position is based to a considerable extent upon the knowledge that they have collected about their customer base and potential customer base in the e-marketplace or, in other words, their knowledge assets. Business value is unquestionably considerably influenced by the perceived value of knowledge assets, whether or not these are specified on balance sheets.

CHAPTER SUMMARY

This chapter has explored aspects of the way in which an e-business needs to organise itself in order to deliver its promise to customers. The level of integration between e-business and business processes is dependent on the nature of e-business activity. Transactions require tightly coupled back-office functions covering areas such as marketing and sales, customer care, order management, production, supplies, packaging and delivery, and financial functions. Many of these processes can be supported by database systems. Enterprise resource planning systems are sophisticated integrated systems solutions that embrace many business processes. Such systems need to support the transaction with the customer and the delivery of the product to the customer. Delivery options include digital delivery, postal and courier services and van delivery. Payment flow is achieved through payment solutions. Options include credit cards, electronic cash, electronic wallets, smart cards, digital cheques and online payments. Virtual organisations may often be responsible for delivering e-business innovation. Virtual organisations are viewed as one recipe for survival in fast-moving and turbulent business environments. Virtual teams are a key component of virtual organisations. Knowledge management is concerned with the management and exploitation of an organisation's knowledge assets. E-business is a knowledge intensive channel and the exploitation of knowledge assets is essential to competitive success. This involves attention to the four strands of knowledge management: knowledge repositories, knowledge tools, knowledge cultures and knowledge assets.

KEY CONCEPTS

Back-office functions are the functions that support the customer interface, including transactions. Typically they include marketing and sales, customer care, order management, production, supplies and financial systems.

Enterprise resource planning or **ERP** systems integrate the various business processes involved in satisfying an order.

Intermediaries such as wholesalers and retailers create an assortment of products that is deemed to satisfy better a segment of customers.

Open Buying on the Internet (OBI) is a specification to facilitate the implementation of commerce solutions utilising interoperable, standards-based Internet purchasing systems.

Virtual organisations are networks of independent companies, linked by technology to share skills, costs and access to one another's markets.

Virtual teams are project teams that form rapidly, reorganise and dissolve when the needs of a dynamic marketplace change.

Knowledge management involves processes and approaches for creating, harnessing and exploiting the knowledge assets of an organisation.

ASSESSMENT QUESTIONS

1. Explain how the nature of e-commerce involvement affects the business processes that are linked into e-business.
2. Identify the back-office functions that are needed to support an integrated e-business application. Use examples to elucidate your answer.

3. Critically evaluate the role of an enterprise resources planning system in business process control.

4. Describe the functions of marketing or distribution channels. Illustrate your answer with reference to a specific business sector.

5. Compare and contrast the various options for delivery of products and services that customers order through a website.

6. Outline the features required of e-business payment options. Compare and contrast three different payment solutions.

7. Differentiate between electronic cash, electronic wallets and digital cheques as e-business payment solutions.

8. Outline the essential differences in the characteristics of B2C and B2B payment solutions.

9. Critically analyse the concept of 'a virtual organisation'. Is this concept useful?

10. How can knowledge cultures contribute to e-business?

11. 'Customer data only becomes knowledge when the business knows the right questions to ask.' Discuss.

GROUP ASSESSMENT 1 – KNOWLEDGE MANAGEMENT TOOLS

Undertake a Web search using one or more of the major search engines to locate suppliers of the following software products: Enterprise Resource Planning Systems, Customer Relationship Management Systems and Knowledge Management tools. Describe the relationship between these systems.

GROUP ASSESSMENT 2 – DELIVERY AND RETURNS

Visit the websites of the following popular UK stores: Homebase (www.homebase.co.uk), Marks & Spencer (www.marksandspencer.com), Argos (www.argos.co.uk), Dixons (www.dixons.co.uk), Next (www.next.co.uk) and Woolworths (www.woolworths.co.uk).

1. Make a table of the delivery and returns options offered by these stores.

2. Is any standard pattern emerging in relation to issues such as:

- Payment for delivery
- Arrangements for returns
- Delivery time (for example, within 48 hours)
- Delivery slots available (for example, Mon–Sat, 8–8, two-hour slots).

3. Discuss the operational implications of offering each of the options that you uncover.

REFERENCES

Ashkenas, R, Ulrich, D, Todd, J and Kerr, S (1998) *The boundaryless organisation: breaking the chains of organisational structure.* San Fransisco: Jossey-Bass.

Blackler, F (1995) Knowledge, knowledge work and organisations: an overview and interpretation, *Organisation Studies*, **16**(6), 1021–46.

Byrne, J A (1993) The virtual corporation, *Business Week*, 8 February, 98–102.

Chesbrough, H W and Teece, D J (1996) When is virtual virtuous?, *Harvard Business Review*, Jan–Feb, 65–71.

Choo, C W (1996) The knowing organisation: how organisations use information to construct meaning, create knowledge and make decisions, *International Journal of Information Management*, **16**(5), 329–40.

Davenport, T H (2000) *Mission critical: realising the promise of enterprise systems.* Boston: Harvard Business School Press.

Davenport, T H, DeLong, D W and Beers, M C (1998) Successful knowledge management projects, *Sloan Management Review*, Winter, **39**(2), 43–57.

Davenport, T H and Prusak, L (1998) *Working knowledge: managing what your organisation knows.* Boston: Harvard Business School Press.

Davidow, W H and Malone, W S (1992) *The virtual corporation.* New York: Harper Business.

Dewan, R, Freimer, M and Seidmann, A (2000) Organising distribution channels for information goods on the Internet, *Management Science*, **46**(4).

Dixon, N (1994) *The organisational learning cycle: how can we learn collectively.* Maidenhead: McGraw-Hill.

Evans, P and Wurster, T S (2000) Click.BOOM: the next generation of e-commerce strategy, *Ivey Business Journal*, Mar/Apr, **64**(4), 35–41.

Friedman, L G (1998) The elusive strategic alliance, in P Lloyd and P Boyle (eds) *Web-weaving: intranets, extranets and strategic alliances.* Oxford: Butterworth-Heinemann.

Grewal, R, Comer, J M and Mehta, R (2001) An investigation into the antecedents of organisational participation in business-to-business electronic markets, *Journal of Marketing*, **65**(3).

Gudykunst, W B, Matsumoto, Y, Ting-Toomey, S, Nishida, T, Linda, K W and Hall, E T (1976) *Beyond culture.* Garden City, NJ: Anchor Books/Doubleday.

Hanson, W (2000) *Principles of Internet marketing.* Cincinnati: South-Western College Publishing/ Thomson Learning.

Heyman, S (1996) The influence of cultural individualism-collectivism, self construals, and individual values on communication styles across culture, *Human Communication Research*, **22**(4), 510–43.

Hofstede, G (1980) *Culture's consequences.* Beverly Hills, CA:Sage.

Hofstede, G (1991) *Cultures and organisations : software of the mind.* London: McGraw-Hill.

Introna, L (2001) Defining the virtual organisation, in S Barnes and B Hunt, *E-commerce and v-business.* Oxford: Butterworth Heinnemann, pp 143–52.

Jarvenpaa, S L and Ives, B (1994) The global network organisation of the future: information management opportunities and challenges, *Journal of Management Information Systems*, **10**(4), 25–57.

Klaus, H, Rosemann, M and Gable, G G (2000) What is ERP, *Information Systems Frontiers*, **2**(2), 141–62.

Kleindl, B A (2001) *Strategic electronic marketing: managing e-business.* Cincinnati: South-Western College Publishing/Thomson Learning.

Levy, M and Grewal, D (2000) Supply chain management in a networked economy, *Journal of Retailing*, **76**(4), 415–29.

Lipnack, J and Stamps, J (1998) Why virtual teams?, in P Lloyd and P Boyle (eds) *Web-weaving: intranets, extranets and strategic alliances.* Oxford: Butterworth-Heinemann.

Marshall, P, Burn, J, Wild, M and McKay, J (1999) Virtual organisations: structure and strategic positioning. Proceedings of the 7th European Conference on Information Systems, Copenhagen.

Marshall, P , McKay, J and Burn, J (2001) Structure, strategy and success factors for the virtual organisation, in S Barnes and B Hunt, *E-commerce and v-business.* Oxford: Butterworth Heinemann, pp. 171–92.

Matin, A , Gerard, P and Larivere, C (2001) Turning the supply chain into a revenue chain, *Harvard Business Review*, **79**(3), 20–2.

Metes, G, Gundry, J and Bradish, P (1998) *Agile networking: competing through the internet and intranets.* Englewood Cliffs, NJ: Prentice Hall.

Miles, R E and Snow, C C (1986) Organisations: new concepts for new forms. *California Management Review*, 18 (3) 62-73.

Morath, P (2000) *Success @ e-business: profitable internet business and commerce.* London: McGraw-Hill

Mowshowitz, A (1997) Virtual organisation, *Communications of the ACM*, 40 (9), 30–7.

Mullin, R (1996) Knowledge management: a cultural revolution, *Journal of Business Strategy*, Sept–Oct, **17**(5), 56–60.

Nonaka, I (1991) The knowledge creating company, *Harvard Business Review*, Nov/Dec, **69**(6), 96–104.

Nonaka, I (1995) *The knowledge creating company.* New York: Oxford University Press.

Nonaka, I (1994) A dynamic theory of organisational knowledge creation, *Organisation Science*, **5**, February, 14–37.

Nonaka, I (1996) The knowledge creating company, in K Starkey (ed.) *How organisations learn.* London: International Thomson, pp. 18–31.

Parr, A and Shanks, G (2000) A model of ERP project implementation, *Journal of Information Technology*, **15**, 289–303.

Pedler, M, Burgoyne, J and Boydell, T (1991) *The learning company.* London: McGraw-Hill.

Rao, B, Navoth, Z and Horwitch, M (2000) Building a world class logistics, distribution and electronic commerce infrastructure, *Electronic Markets*, **9**(3), 174–80.

Rosenbloom, B (1995) *Marketing channels: a management view*, 5th edn. New York: Dryden Press.

Ruggles, R (1997) *Knowledge management tools.* Boston, Oxford: Butterworth-Heinemann.

Stough, S, Eom, S and Buckenmyer, J (2000) Virtual teaming: a strategy for moving your organisation into the new millennium, *Industrial Management and Data Systems*, **100**(8), 370–8.

Tan, G W, Shaw, M J and Filkerson, B (2000) Web-based supply chain management, *Information Systems Frontiers*, **2**(1), 41–55.

Turban, E, McLean, E and Wetherbe, J (1999) *Information technology for management.* New York: Wiley.

Wiesenfeld, B M , Raghuram, S and Garud, R (1998) Communication patterns as determinants of organisational identification in a virtual organisation, *Journal of Computer Mediated Communication*, **3**, 1–21.

Willcocks, L and Sykes, R (2000) The role of the CIO and IT function in ERP, *Communications of the ACM*, **43**(4), 32–8.

E-business strategy

the Net's potential functionality is so broad . . . that we cannot and should not restrict our attention to a few narrow domains . . . it is like the proverbial blind men describing the elephant: different managers see different facets . . . but do not see the complete picture . . . we are navigating in uncharted waters (Venkatraman, 2000, p. 16)

LEARNING OUTCOMES

After reading this chapter you will:

- Appreciate the relationship between e-business strategy and other business strategies
- Be able to discuss the stages in strategy formulation
- Appreciate some of the key aspects of the business and environmental context as it impacts on e-businesses
- Be able to evaluate critically the routes to value creation
- Understand the role of alliances and intermediaries in e-business

▍ INTRODUCTION

Venkatraman (2000) argues that the power of the Web lies in the potential for the creation of 'new business models'. New business models are those that 'offer, on a sustained basis, an order-of-magnitude increase in value propositions to the customers compared to companies with traditional business models' (p. 18). Traditional companies cannot match the value propositions offered by these new business models without substantially altering their margin structures. The other challenge that they face is the incremental refinement of current business rules to create radically different rules. Businesses need to be prepared to contemplate new business models, even if they upset established alliances, and cannibalise stable revenue and margin streams. The Case Cameo on the music marketplace illustrates how far-reaching the impact of the Internet can be. Not all business sectors will be affected to this extent. Information-based sectors, such as publishing, media, travel, consultancy, education and training, and financial services, are likely to feel the blasts of the winds of change most powerfully, but no business can afford to be complacent.

CASE CAMEO

THE MUSIC MARKETPLACE

Universal, 13MG, Warner EM and Sony control about 80% of industry sales, and online distribution accounts for about 1% of sales (in the form of CDs). But the availability and increased acceptance of music players that use the MP3 format (MP3.com) are likely to create major disruptions in the marketplace. As more Internet merchants (including, for instance, Amazon) support the downloading of music onto MP3-compatible devices, every major record label needs to rethink its business model. Sony has decided to make a Walkman that will play MP3 music. Record companies need to rethink distribution, access, and pricing models just for a starter.

Source: Based on Venkatraman, 2000.

EXPLORATORY ACTIVITY

Update yourself on progress with MP3 by visiting the MP3 website (www.mp3.com).

▍ INTEGRATING E-BUSINESS STRATEGY

In common with any other business activity, e-business needs to be guided by a business strategy. **E-business strategy** is concerned with establishing business goals and objectives, and making decisions about how those objectives will be achieved. Strategic concerns affect the entire organisation and form the framework for future operational decisions and planning.

Strategy formulation for e-business has much in common with strategy formulation for other business contexts or functions. There is a danger that, in the race to capitalise on fast-growing e-business markets, businesses may forget the basics, overlook fundamental business principles and neglect adequate strategy formulation. All business strategy in e-business or otherwise is concerned to focus on questions such as:

- Which markets should we be in?
- What can our organisation offer that is distinct from that offered by competitors or even collaborative partners?
- Does the organisation have the skills, resources and other assets necessary to achieve objectives?
- How will our marketplace position change over the next five years?
- What will our competitors be doing in five years?
- What benefits will our customers expect in five years?

E-business marketplaces can change quickly and perhaps the five-year horizon might be a little ambitious, but longer-term vision is just as necessary in e-business as in any other business context. On the other hand, it may be necessary to review strategy more regularly and to regard strategy as dynamic and subject to evolutionary change in e-business contexts.

E-business strategy formulation must be aligned with other strategy formulation in a business. The relationship between e-strategy and other business strategies is dependent on whether the business is a pure-play or Internet start-up, or whether e-business is one of several channels through which the business delivers products and services. The extent to which e-strategy is integrated with other business strategies is also dependent upon the extent of integration of business activities. Some businesses have contained the perceived risk associated with e-business by creating separate companies for their e-business activities. Such a model inevitably leads to an independent e-business strategy.

Many early ventures into e-business, such as those associated with establishing a basic Web presence were relatively small-scale. If they were expected to have any impact on the business at all, this impact could be contained within the context of their marketing function and its associated strategy. However, service delivery and retailing and supply through e-business requires a much more significant investment and is likely to impact on a number of functional areas of the business. The greater the impact of e-business on the overall business, the more significant is e-business strategy, and the more important it is for the organisation to understand and clearly articulate the relationships between e-business strategy and other strategies. Typically e-business strategy needs to interface with, accommodate or be accommodated by:

- Corporate strategy
- Marketing strategy
- Information systems strategy
- Financial strategy
- Operations strategy
- Research and innovation strategy
- Production strategy (possibly).

The best model will vary with the nature of the business. E-business strategy may be embedded in one or more of the above areas or, alternatively, a separate e-business strategy may be formulated. The biggest danger of integrated strategies is that the e-business strategy may be incompletely articulated – inconsistencies between aspects of e-business in other strategies may not be tested out. A separate e-business strategy is appropriate when:

1. It is necessary to manage significant innovation in the development of e-business activity
2. E-business has a significant impact on business operations, customer relations and competitive market position
3. E-business is developed as a separate business function.

Whatever the level of integration between strategies, the strategy formulation process and issues such as the environmental context, the value chain, differentiation and market and channel structure must be considered.

E-business strategy must also link into plans for the execution of the strategy in any of the various functional areas on which e-business might impact. In particular the e-business strategy must inform the e-business plan. One part of this plan will be associated with the development, maintenance and review of the website, as discussed in Chapter 3. The e-business strategy must also embrace operations and service delivery. Bickerton *et al.* (1998) suggest that 'cyberstrategy' must encompass Internet, extranet and intranet strands as the business seeks to understand the impact on customers, suppliers and staff, and make plans in all of these arenas.

The way in which e-business strategy integrates with corporate and other strategies cannot be carved in stone. As discussed in Chapter 1 there are stages in the development of e-business. Figure 1.1 describes these stages in terms of functionality of a website and business function engagement (p. 4). An alternative perspective is to view these stages in terms of strategic stages of the business in e-business activity, as summarised in Figure 8.1. These stages take the business from the acquisition of e-business competence as a platform for development through to the optimisation of the contribution to core business.

GROUP DISCUSSION ACTIVITY

Visit the sites associated with Nestlé that are cited in the Case Cameo on p. 206. Discuss the roles that such sites play in the development of an Internet strategy for Nestlé.

STRATEGY FORMULATION

Strategy formulation is a cyclical process that involves auditing the market situation of the business, setting or revising objectives, establishing strategies to achieve objectives, detailed planning for the execution of strategies, plan implementation, evaluation of actions and, once one iteration of this cycle has been completed, going through the cycle again and again (see Figure 8.2). The next few sections explore the stages in strategy formulation and implementation.

Figure 8.1 Strategic development of e-business

Stage	Description of stage	Comments
1	Acquire e-business competence	Through key staff appointments or the establishment of partnerships for outsourcing work on the design, development and execution of an e-business plan and its associated technologies
2	Establish channel and acclimatise start-up community	Develop modest-scale applications that encourage employees, suppliers and customers to explore the new channel, and gradually encourage the use of Internet applications alongside, or as a substitute for, phone, fax and mail
3	Extend applications and increase community dependence	Develop applications where employees, suppliers and customers are pushed to engagement in the new channel, either because other options are removed or because the value proposition of the channel pushes them to make use of it. Supply chain management (SCM) and customer relationship management (CRM) solutions are often features of this stage
4	Optimise Internet contribution to core business	E-business contribution is fully mature, although continuing to evolve and subject to further enhancement. Potential conflicts between this and other channels become an issue that needs to be reflected in strategic perspectives

Source: Based on C Lord (2000) The practicalities of developing a successful e-business strategy, *Journal of Business Strategy*, **21**(2), 40–7.

Figure 8.2 The stages in strategy formulation and implementation

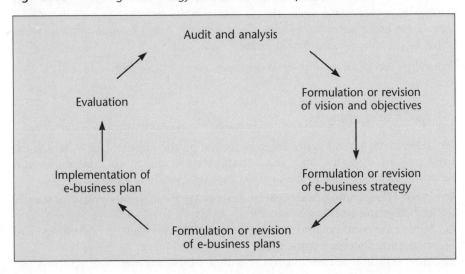

INTEGRATING INTERNET STRATEGY: NESTLE

Nestlé plans to invest $1.8 billion over the next three years to revolutionise the impact that Web technology will have on the business. The revolution will impact on business processes from the buying of raw materials, such as cocoa, to producing, marketing and selling products, such as Kit-Kat chocolate biscuits and instant coffee. The challenge for the Internet strategy is the scale of the transformation necessary in such an established business. With 134 years of tradition, revenues of $46.6 billion in 1999, 230 000 employees, 509 factories in 83 countries and a product range of 8000 different products, making an impact in such an organisation is a significant task.

Although Nestlé is a consumer-driven company, most of the changes will be invisible to consumers. Nestle.com does not plan to sell direct or bypass current links in the supply chain to its customers. Key changes will be in the way Nestlé buys, manufactures and delivers its products. The emphasis is not on leveraging the Web to reduce raw material prices or to eliminate distributors. Nestlé are instead interested in tying together disparate operations, creating partnerships with suppliers and customers to cut waste and moving food products more quickly from farm to factory to the family dinner table. Various initiatives have driven these changes. Since July 2000, store owners in the US have been required to order Nestlé chocolate and other products online at NestleEZOrder.com. This system slashes order-processing costs. Similar initiatives across most other countries in which Nestlé operates could trim 20% from world logistics and administrative costs. Such links also help to cut inventories. For example, in the UK, Sainsbury's and Tesco send in daily reports and demand forecasts over the Web to Nestlé headquarters, while Nestlé managers can check inventory levels on the supermarkets' computer systems.

Sharing information inside the company has also allowed buyers to exchange information on supplies worldwide. Only one buyer needs to collect the information and to pass it to other buyers across the world. This can also cut procurement costs significantly.

Nestlé anticipate that within two years 20% of their $2.4 billion annual advertising budget will be spent on the Web. This will mostly be used to fund sites such as VeryBestBaby.com, which offers articles about parenting and baby nutrition as well as banners advertising baby foods. Nestlé also has a site for coffee lovers and a Club Buitoni site for lovers of Italian food. These sites will help Nestlé to discover more about its consumers and inform innovation.

Source: Based on Nestlé: an elephant dances, *Business Week*, 11 Dec 2000, p. 16.

Audit and analysis

An audit is designed to encourage reflection on the marketplace in which the organisation operates and the organisation's ability to contribute and respond. Typically it may be focused around questions such as:

1. What is happening in the environment? Do these events pose any threats or opportunities?
2. What are our relative strengths and weaknesses in handling and exploiting the environment?
3. How effective are we in implementing e-business activity?

Typically question 1 is the focus of an external audit, which examines the marketing environment and the factors influencing development in that environment, as discussed below, coupled with competitors' activities, and their actual and likely future responses to changes in environmental factors, such as technological and sociocultural changes. Questions 2 and 3 might be the focus of an internal audit, which reports on previous performance in relation to aspects of the marketing mix, such as product offering, customer relationships and service quality.

External audits focus on the business and economic environment. The external audit considers customers and competitors. This is explored more fully in the section on environments below. Figure 8.3 lists some of the characteristics of competitors' websites that might be examined.

Internal audits examine the existing e-business activity and also the capacity for expansion of this activity if such expansion is likely to affect the business's capacity to fulfil its objectives. Existing activity can be evaluated in terms of business, marketing and promotional impact. Assessment of business impact requires attention to contribution to profitability, revenue and other financial indicators. Marketing effectiveness is concerned with issues such as retention, market share, brand presence and customer relationships. Promotion effectiveness in the Internet context is measured in terms of traffic, hits, transactions and customer feedback. A discussion of appropriate website performance metrics is included in Chapter 4.

Chase (1998) suggests that it is useful to identify best practice, worst practice and next practice. Next practice can be identified by looking at leading Internet companies, such as Amazon (www.amazon.com), Microsoft and Dell. Regular monitoring of suppliers, competitors and customer websites is useful and particularly important in business-to-business environments, where the businesses are highly dependent upon each other. The checklist in Figure 8.3 suggests some criteria for the analysis of websites.

SWOT analysis, otherwise described as an **opportunity** or **issue analysis**, is a widely used tool for structuring the information that may be gathered during an audit exercise. It encourages managers to summarise the position in terms of:

- Strengths
- Weaknesses
- Opportunities
- Threats.

Strengths and weaknesses focus on the present and past, and summarise 'where we are now'. *Opportunities and threats* encourage consideration of the present and the future, taking a more forward and outward-looking view of future strategic directions. They may summarise 'where we want to be', 'where we do not want to be, but might end up' or 'where we could be if we pursued certain courses of action'.

The gap between strengths and weaknesses, and opportunities and threats represents 'what we have to do to get there' and needs to be filled by managerial imagination, inspiration and leadership.

SWOT analysis may be conducted initially in the marketing audit and analysis stage, but reflection on marketing opportunities is intimately

Figure 8.3 Checklist for examining competitors' websites

- Layout of the site
- Amount of information
- Ease of access
- Any future plans
- Product specifications (comparative)
- List of distributors
- People (for likely recruits)

associated with the development or review of marketing objectives. SWOT analyses can be used at various stages in the marketing-planning cycle and are a particularly useful tool in workshops, which encourage the development of a shared understanding of the organisation's successes, failures and futures. The general opportunities and threats of e-business that were outlined in Chapter 1 offer a useful starting point for analysis, but each of these threats and opportunities will impact differently in different businesses and the options for converting opportunities into strengths and for threats to escalate to weaknesses will differ.

EXPLORATORY ACTIVITY

Visit a website of your choice and analyse the site using the criteria in Figure 8.3.

E-business vision and objectives

The desire to exploit strengths and opportunities, and to overcome threats and weaknesses gives a foundation for the definition and review of e-business objectives.

E-business objectives need to link closely with corporate objectives, vision and mission statements, and appropriate functional area objectives, such as those relating to marketing and information systems development. They state what is to be achieved through the e-business activity proposed in the plan. E-business objectives usually relate to one or more of:

- Improving corporate image
- Increasing visibility
- Improving customer service
- Achieving increased or maintaining market share
- Performing transactions
- Forming alliances in the supply chain
- Maintaining or improving profitability
- Establishing a position in a new marketplace
- Reducing costs, through increased efficiency.

E-business objectives must contribute to corporate objectives and sometimes it is difficult to disentangle the contribution to business success or failure from the Internet and other channels. For example, in the customer interaction with an online store, and a bricks-and-mortar store the customer may switch between online operation and bricks-and-mortar at any one of several stages in the interaction. The Case Cameo on purchasing a car demonstrates how a customer interaction with a business may traverse Internet and bricks-and-mortar channels. Those pure-play Internet businesses that do not need to concern themselves with physical delivery and major companies that are not yet engaged in transactions online can clearly differentiate e-business strategy and objectives from those for other business areas and functions. For all other businesses it will be necessary to integrate both objectives and strategy across e-business and other channels.

PURCHASING A CAR

In purchasing a car, customers might visit the website and examine prices, specifications and extras for models that might be of interest. They might be influenced by a direct mailshot for a new model of their existing car. Next, they might visit a selected number of showrooms to sit in the car, look under the bonnet, go for a test drive and discuss the purchase with the salesperson. They may then decide to place an order online, check the balance in their building society account online and order a cheque online. The cheque may be received through the mail and taken to the nearest car showroom for the dealer from which the car has been ordered online. The car is collected from this car showroom after exchange of payment and ownership and other documentation.

Further, the impact of e-business activities may vary significantly for different product types or different customer segments. It may be necessary to set different targets for business contributions to revenue or market share for different markets and different product categories.

Venkatraman's proposition that the articulation of a strategic vision for e-businesses in precise terms is doomed to failure poses an interesting dilemma for an integrated corporate strategy. Venkatraman (2000) suggests that strategic vision for e-business operations should be viewed as a continuous cycle involving building on current business models and creating future business models through **selective experimentation**. The aim is to balance the refinement of the current business rules while creating new business rues for the e-business agenda. The way forward involves new initiatives in special areas to allow the development of expertise and experience. By working with a series of separate initiatives or **strategic experiments** the organisation creates a collection of **building blocks** which can form the foundation for business transformation.

It is important to be selective with respect to objectives. The old adage that objectives should be SMART is worth rehearsing again in this context. **SMART** objectives are:

- *Specific*, or focussed, giving details of products and market segments
- *Measurable*, or quantifiable
- *Achievable*, within the contexts and resources available
- *Relevant*, in that they contribute to organisational success, and are aligned with corporate objectives, and
- *Timely* so that actions are taken at the right time to achieve market success; this involves judging market readiness.

Quantifying objectives makes evaluation easier because it provides specific targets and standards of performance against which outcomes can be measured. It also encourages much more precise thinking about objectives and is likely to produce more specific objectives. For example, the objective 'to raise awareness of an insurance broker amongst clients and potential clients' might be a broad objective but the generation of objectives which embed quantifiable measures requires consideration of:

- The specific market sectors in which awareness is to be raised, for example, consumer markets, industry sectors, job roles of individuals to be targeted
- The measures of raised awareness to be used, for example, more enquiries, more customers registered with the broker or more recommendations from satisfied customers
- How large an increase in these awareness measures is required
- The likely impact on any competitors and how this could be measured.

E-business strategies

An e-business strategy is the means by which an organisation seeks to achieve its e-business objectives. The main areas of focus are the definition of the target market and the marketing mix to be employed, including key messages and channels to be exploited. The choice of segments is influenced by the competitive structure of the market and thus by the competitors' various roles in the marketplace. The issue of competitive positioning has been explored earlier in this chapter. Typically the organisation has a range of strategic options which support the achievement of its objectives. Some options will be related to increasing volume, whilst others will relate to improving profitability in existing market segments. Typical options in this last category include reducing costs, increasing prices, streamlining operations and changing the product mix. The key feature of strategy is that it offers a clear statement of the basis for differentiation from competitors.

A key issue is the extent of dependence on the Internet within the company. Pure-play Internet companies, such as Yahoo! and Amazon are almost entirely dependent on the Internet, although more recently some of these businesses have sought to consolidate their position by opening bricks-and-mortar stores. Other businesses, such as Dell and Cisco who are big Internet players, now have Internet contributions to the business of over

50 per cent. The factors that affect the dominance of Internet activities in the business are:

- The level of customer access to the Internet
- Whether the Internet can offer a better value proposition than other channels
- Whether the product can be delivered over the Internet
- Whether the product can be standardised (so that the user does not need to view or interact with the purchase).

De Kare-Silver (1998) takes the consumer behaviour perspective in assessing the likely relative importance of bricks-and-mortar retailing and e-tailing. In addition to product characteristics, De Kare-Silver suggests that familiarity and confidence with the brand and consumer attributes, such as familiarity with the medium, may be very significant.

De Kare-Silver (1998) suggests that there are a number of strategic options for companies in relation to the importance of the Internet as a channel:

- Use the Internet channel for information provision only
- Use the Internet channel primarily for export markets
- Subsume the Internet channel as another channel in the existing business
- View the Internet channel as another channel
- Set up the Internet channel as a separate business
- Develop a mixed system using a number of parallel channels with clear objectives for the contribution from the different channels and the nature of their interaction
- Switch fully to the Internet channel, taking out retail outlets.

De Kare-Silver's categorisations are concerned with the Internet as a channel for interaction with customers and other businesses in the supply chain. Another classification considers the areas of the business in which Internet and traditional business merge or diverge.

Integration between the e-business arm and traditional business can be considered in relation to functional areas such as production, sourcing, logistics, marketing and human resources, and financial decisions, such as investment, funding sources and performance criteria. The choices can be arrayed along a spectrum with a subsidiary (spin-off) at one end and a seamless operation at the other end. Internet spin-offs are distinct business ventures, operating separately from a parent company, and in a way that might be more consistent with the cyber marketplace. There are pros and cons associated with both models. Figure 8.4 summarises the conditions under which spin-off, and seamless integration, are respectively the best option.

Effective management of Internet business alongside established business poses challenges for many businesses. The Case Cameo below illustrates the dilemma for Barnes & Noble, a major US bookseller, when faced with strong competition from Amazon.com. Many other organisations are also experimenting with ways to defend their market position whilst developing a Web business, for example, toysrus.com, walmart.com, tesco.com, sears.com. One of the challenges to complete translation to Web-based models has been the inability to identify a new business model with assured profitability. This is

Figure 8.4 To spin off or to integrate?

Spin-offs are best when:

■ The company is willing to explore new business models and needs to free itself of the constraints of current operations

■ The spin-off can be created without being constrained by current technology and earlier legacy operations

■ The company bestows the spin-off with freedom to form alliances, raise capital, and attract new talent

Integration is best when:

■ There is no meaningful way to separate digital and physical operations without confusing customers

■ Senior management is committed to redefining the entire business value proposition

■ The entire organisation can be mobilised to migrate to an e-business channel

---

most evident in publishing, where companies are hedging their bets and developing e-add-ons to paper-based publications. Examples in the newspaper sector are fortune.com and ft.com. Academic journal publishers, such as Academic Press and Elsevier, are also entering into licence arrangements with libraries that couple subscriptions for print and electronic versions together.

Some authors (Useem, 1999) have discussed the necessity of accepting the **cannibalisation** of existing business channels when establishing an Internet channel. Cannibalisation occurs when an Internet channel competes with other channels of the same business in such a way that it undermines the viability of established channels and business models. This is particularly likely to be an issue for information-based businesses, such as publishing and banking and financial services. These businesses, in particular, need to recognise that the Internet will cause a step change in their industry and that the traditional good-management practices of listening to shareholders and customers, and focusing investments and technology on the most profitable products work well in evolutionary markets but, for some businesses, the Internet requires a suspension of rationality. It may be 'right not to listen to customers, right to invest in developing lower performance products that promise lower margins, and right to aggressively pursue small, rather than substantial markets' (Useem, 1999, p. 126). Cannibalisation may mean encouraging an Internet spin-off company to charge lower prices or offer higher interest rates than the traditional channel.

EXPLORATORY ACTIVITY

Both eSchwab, a stock brokerage operation, and Monster.com have swamped and cannibalised their parent companies. Do a search using an electronic database that provides access to newspaper articles to collect further details on the growth and development of one of these two organisations.

COMPETING CHANNEL DILEMMAS: BARNES & NOBLE

Barnes & Noble are a significant US-based bricks-and-mortar book-store chain. The advent of e-bookselling, led by Amazon.com, has impacted on the bookselling market. Belatedly, in 1997, Barnes & Noble entered the online scene as Bn.com. By this time Amazon.com had already built a loyal following and, with little to differentiate the books sold by both merchants, Barnes & Noble had little option but to compete on price. This meant that B&N were forced to sell books online for as much as 30% less than those on its store shelves, thereby creating internal competition between its two channels. The relationship between these two channels is a big strategic dilemma for Barnes & Noble. It has, for example, only 4 million customers online, but tens of millions in its stores. Major assets in building Web presence are the in-store customer base, and the established brand. However, the full leverage of these assets would involve widespread promotion of the website in the stores. Why promote a website that offers heavy discounts and no sales tax in most states to customers who might buy at the full price? Some would argue that bricks-and-mortar stores seeking to translate their brand strength online must be willing to cross promote vigorously the two channels, but for businesses such as Barnes & Noble this involves a reconsideration of their entire business model.

Source: Based on How Barnes & Noble misread the Web, *Business Week,* 7 Feb 2000, p. 63.

GROUP DISCUSSION ACTIVITY

Outline the nature of the dilemma facing Barnes & Noble. Do UK bookshop chains, such as WHSmith, Dillons and Waterstones face a similar dilemma? Visit the websites of two UK booksellers and compare the services offered through those websites with the product range that is available in their stores.

Another key strategic issue is **market and product positioning**, which identifies and delineates the marketplace in which the business seeks to operate. Ansoff's matrix which summarises marketing opportunities in Figure 8.5, identifies the options for innovation in market and product positioning:

1. *Market penetration*, in which business channels are used to sell more existing products into existing markers. This is achieved through using the Internet as a marketing communications channel to increase awareness of products, brand and the company amongst existing and potential customers in an existing market. Customer service and other strategies that build relationships may also help to strengthen market penetration.
2. *Market development*, which uses the Internet to sell into new markets. SMEs have particularly used this approach to develop more strongly in national

Figure 8.5   Ansoff's matrix

		Product	
		Present	New
Market	**Present**	Market penetration	Product development
	New	Market development	Diversification

and international markets. When expanding into new markets businesses need to be able to manage operations in the new market, including delivery and any sales or support infrastructure. Some organisations, as a result of having a website, have discovered that they have some penetration into audiences beyond their traditional ones. For example, as a consumer-oriented retailer, Argos have identified a significant niche of business customers amongst website sales.

3. *Product development*, where new products are developed that can be marketed and/or delivered via the Internet. New information-based products, such as databanks and financial services products may fit into this category. Co-production (see Chapter 5), working with customers particularly in business-to-business markets, may support product development that meets customers' needs.

4. *Diversification*, where new products are developed and sold into new markets.

Ultimately, the business needs to establish its **unique selling proposition** (USP) for this new channel. This proposition underpins marketing communication and informs website design – it must be clearly evident to site visitors. The USP also acts as a guide to staff as to the purpose of the site. The USP in this context needs to be linked to the other USPs for the company and its products.

EXPLORATORY ACTIVITY

Examine the websites of the following organisations and try to identify their USPs: Yahoo!, Lancaster University (Lancaster.ac.uk), citv.co.uk, handbag.com.

Related to the USP and positioning of e-business products and services is the identification of target customers. Figure 3.1 (p. 49) identifies some of the potential audiences for a website. An understanding of these target customers will influence site design. Key customers to consider are those that have the biggest impact on the company's profitability. These customers could be:

- The most profitable customers
- The largest customers (possibly linked via an extranet)
- Customers who are difficult to target using other media
- Customers who are, or are not, brand loyal
- Decision makers within other organisations.

Communication with customers can be via intranet, extranet or Internet. The offering across these three environments needs to be integrated in order to avoid duplication of efforts and so that as many audiences as possible have a shared knowledge base. Figure 8.6 summarises some of the key questions in relation to the practicalities for the integration of marketing communications between the Internet and other channels. Large corporate customers may benefit from access to production schedules that indicate the status of, and progress with, their order. Similarly, if customer service agents have access to the same knowledge base as customers, they can assist customers in learning how to make effective use of that knowledge base. Johnson Tiles (www.johnson-tiles.com) has an extranet-buying service only available to its larger customers. The issue of knowledge bases is discussed more fully in Chapter 7. Bickerton *et al.* (1998) proposes a matrix that identifies different stages or levels of engagement with the customer, and the different opportunities for application of Internet, extranet and intranet, to fulfil these stages. The stages are:

- Presentation – describing access to information on the website
- Interaction – where two-way communication is possible
- Representation – where the customer engages in elements of co-production.

This model provides a framework for discussing the relationship between the different technologies, different functions possible through websites and different customer groups.

E-business plans

This stage is concerned with the detailed implementation of e-business strategies. The e-business plan specifies precisely actions, responsibilities, budgets and time-scales. The actions that need to be undertaken depend upon the Internet business objectives and the level of integration between Internet and business through other channels. A key consideration is the actions associated with the design, creation and maintenance of a website (as outlined in Chapter 3).

Roles and responsibilities for e-business activities depend upon partnerships and strategic alliances. Alliances are discussed in greater detail below. Coming closer to the website and the creation of an e-presence it is important to recognise that a number of partnerships need to be established and

Figure 8.6 Integrating marketing communications – some planning considerations

1. Will we use the site domain name or URL on all offline campaigns?
2. Will we update the site to be consistent with marketing messages in offline campaigns?
3. How will PR be handled by the website?
4. How will the medium be used to build relationships with customers? Will it contain personalisation facilities?
5. Will the site support sales staff meeting directly with customers?
6. How will customer service be supported – what standards will be adopted to provide a good standard of electronic customer service?
7. Will online sales be supported – are there plans for e-commerce?
8. Will the site be used to support trade shows?
9. How will the medium be used for sales promotions?

Source: Based on Chaffey *et al.* (2000), p. 158.

maintained in order to operate a successful website and associated e-business functions. Common partnerships include:

1. Design technology partnerships with internal departments or external companies that undertake site design, development and promotion. Marketing agencies or specialist new media agencies may be enlisted to support website development. The ISP chosen to host the site is another partner.
2. Promotion partnerships with media owners and advertising networks that drive traffic to the site.
3. Reciprocal promotion partnerships established with owners of another site in exchange for mutual promotion or co-branding.
4. Distribution partnerships to ensure products ordered through the Internet can be delivered.
5. Supplier partnerships to support availability of products and services. Special attention may need to be paid to issues of customer service if suppliers have some responsibility in this area.
6. Legal advice partners who advise on e-business legal and ethical issues.

A clear statement of the expenditure necessary to deliver the portfolio of e-business activities outlined in the plan is essential. Core costs identified in such a budget are likely to include those associated with:

1. Initial creation of the site
2. Initial promotion of the site
3. Ongoing maintenance of the site
4. Ongoing promotion of the site
5. Relaunch of the site.

These categories acknowledge that promotion needs to be budgeted for separately and involves an ongoing, and in many cases significant, expenditure. Relaunch of sites needs to be undertaken on an annual or bi-annual cycle (every two years) or, in some fast moving sectors, even more frequently. Budgets also need to be identified for any services that are delivered through the website, such as a help desk or after-sales service.

The cost of e-business activity relative to the anticipated effect on sales or service delivery is often a significant constraint in the model of e-business that can be supported.

Setting a budget for e-business activity is no simple task given the extent of change in this marketplace. Nevertheless, without a budget, costs are likely to escalate. The options are:

1. Starting with the previous year's budget – this assumes that there was a budget in the previous year and also that the previous year's budget is consistent with the proposed activities for the coming year.
2. Taking a percentage of company sales – a reasonable percentage may be difficult to achieve and, as discussed elsewhere, it can be difficult to estimate the impact of business activities on overall profitability.
3. Taking a percentage of the total marketing budget, typically starting as low as 5% and rising as the Internet business activities increase in impact.
4. Taking into account what other companies in the industry are spending. This approach makes sense in terms of matching competitors' presence but expenditures can be very variable.
5. Setting expectations about an effective online presence and funding these whatever it takes. In a rapidly-changing situation with little history, this approach, cautiously applied, may be the only option (obviously not favoured by accountants!).
6. Stepped budget, in which resources are gradually released as each stage in a development is implemented and results can be assessed. Results will be measured against preset targets.

Implementation of the e-business plan

Implementation involves delivering the actions associated with the plan, as discussed throughout the other chapters in this book. Schedules specifying activities are necessary to ensure that there is a shared understanding of the activities through which the plan is to be implemented.

Evaluation

Finally, it is necessary to establish how the outcome of any e-business activity can be evaluated and where the responsibility for that evaluation will lie. The processes associated with matching outcomes to projections and objectives need to be documented. Evaluation includes evaluation of individual e-business functions and activities, which culminates in an annual review of progress in meeting e-business objectives. Although an annual review offers an opportunity to take an overview, progress towards objectives should also be monitored over shorter periods of, say, one week, one month or three months. Failure to achieve interim targets should provoke a review of elements of the plan. The knowledge-based organisation will use this

Figure 8.7 Sections in an e-business plan

1. *E-business objectives* which, in the context of corporate objectives, identify the achievements that are sought through the e-business plan. Objectives may be expressed in terms of both business contribution and marketing impact

2. *Executive summary* indicating key points and directions

3. *Introduction* providing the context against which the plan may be constructed. Content might refer to key achievements from earlier e-business activities, competitor position or marketplace development. A key issue will be the way in which e-business interfaces with the remainder of the business

4. *E-business audit* which reviews the e-business position of the organisation and identifies opportunities for future development. Both internal and external audits should be evident. Marketplace, competitor and customer profiles are significant elements of the audit

5. *E-business strategies* which identify key strategic options that are to be pursued. This section will detail market and product positioning, value creation strategies, partnering arrangements, audiences and communication through Internet, intranet and extranet, channel choices and alliances, and promotional strategies. If appropriate, this section may be integrated with the next section on e-business plans

6. *E-business activity plan and schedule* which specifies in some detail the specific actions, responsibilities and time scales to be undertaken during the period of the plan. This section may include project management and plans for evaluating success or failure. Evaluation may be in terms of business contribution and marketing effectiveness measures

7. *E-business budget*, which indicates the resources necessary to implement the plan

evaluation process and the reports that emanate from the process as the basis for learning about strengths and weaknesses, effective promotional strategies, the quality of its relationships with specific target markets and the benefits that are sought by customers in specific segments. Feedback from experience in a marketplace is a very powerful, but high-risk, form of marketing research.

Figure 8.7 summarises the sections in an e-business plan using a parallel structure to that used throughout this chapter.

ENVIRONMENTAL CONTEXT

E-business environments are turbulent – they are changing rapidly and unpredictably. Both competitor products and market positions, and customers' perceptions of their needs may change quickly. This rapid and unpredictable change can present both opportunities and threats to an e-business – nimbleness and fast response are crucial. There are a variety of different views on the nature of the environment in which e-business functions. A helpful list (based on Pile (2000)) which has a strong customer perspective summarises a number of aspects of the environment in which all business is functioning, but whose impact is especially evident in the electronic marketplace:

1. *Customer expectations are ever increasing.* For example, customers expect a very much higher response rate on the Internet than they might have done five years ago.

2. *Customer sophistication is increasing.* Customers expect information at their fingertips and are more information literate. For example, when choosing a mortgage they expect to be able to talk with advisers, collect printed information, find advice in magazines and check the Internet.

3. *Customers expect multi-channel interaction with businesses.* Businesses must have the capability to deliver through all channels. For example, customers demand that banks have branches, telephone access, ATMs and Web presence. Customers want the flexibility associated with multiple channels. Customers expect what has been called the **Martini effect: Anytime, Anyplace, Anywhere**.

4. *Increasing competition and industry change.* Businesses with established brands can move into new sectors. This is particularly evident in the financial services industry which is essentially concerned with information processing. In the UK, Tesco, a food retailer, was the largest provider of credit cards in early 2000. Kwikfit, whose primary business is replacement of tyres and exhausts, quickly established a position as a significant provider of car insurance. Low barriers to exit mean that such organisations can move out of a market as quickly as they moved into it if conditions become less favourable.

5. *Disaggregation of the value chain.* The value chain is subject to further disaggregation in a number of industries, with businesses specialising in one element of the value chain. This may, for example, lead to the separation of retailing and manufacturing or, in the service sector, separation of the service supplier and the service delivery. So, in insurance, for example, the financial product may be designed by an insurance company to offer a financial service package to customers. The purchase of this product may be mediated by a financial services adviser. This means that the relationship between the insurance company and the customer is indirect and communication, in both directions, is filtered through the adviser.

6. *Globalisation.* Globalisation is more significant in some sectors than others. The benefits to be achieved from globalisation accrue to the manufacturer and not the customer. Globalisation is a supply-side issue rather than a customer issue; the customer wants a product and service experience that is consistent with his cultural view.

7. *Changing role of government.* Government's role in shaping the business environment is evolving. Although the picture is different in different parts of the world, typically they are pulling back from some of their traditional responsibilities for operating businesses, such as the postal services, and the railways, but increasing their involvement in regulation. Within the EU, Europeanisation is a key agenda.

8. *Nature and roles of channels are changing.* With the advent of electronic channels, the role of bricks-and-mortar and person-to-person outlets will

be re-assessed and change. Chapter 2 examined the different roles of the channels based on different technologies. Businesses need to think about the roles of the different channels in interfacing with their customers and design a multichannel experience that is under continual evolution.

9. *Technology change continues to accelerate.* Organisations need to be alert to technological innovation, and the potential impact of specific innovations on their business. All businesses will need to continue to make significant investment in technology.

10. *Market structure.* In the Internet environment, competitors move quickly in and out of markets. In assessing the environment it is necessary to be aware of:

- Well-known local or national competitors (including European competitors for British companies)
- Well-known international competitors
- New Internet companies, worldwide within sector and in other sectors.

11. *The valuations of individual companies and economic sectors are volatile.* This is evident in the significant market capitalisation of companies whose business models are rooted in the Internet (such as Amazon, eBay, and Yahoo!) and also in those companies that provide the technical infrastructure for the net economy (such as Intel, Microsoft, AOL, IBM and Cisco).

12. *Disenfranchisement* of those sectors of the population who do not have access to the latest technology or the ability to exploit it effectively. Further disenfranchisement is evident in sectors, such as banking, in which businesses are examining the profitability or customer-lifetime value of specific customers and are adopting tactics that will discourage or penalise less profitable or less valuable customers.

CREATING BUSINESS VALUE

The e-value business chain

Figure 8.8, based on Kleindl (2001), p. 223 depicts the stages in a typical business value chain and the impact of e-business on those changes. Each component in the value chain must add value in order to be successful as a business.

Figure 8.8 The e-business value chain

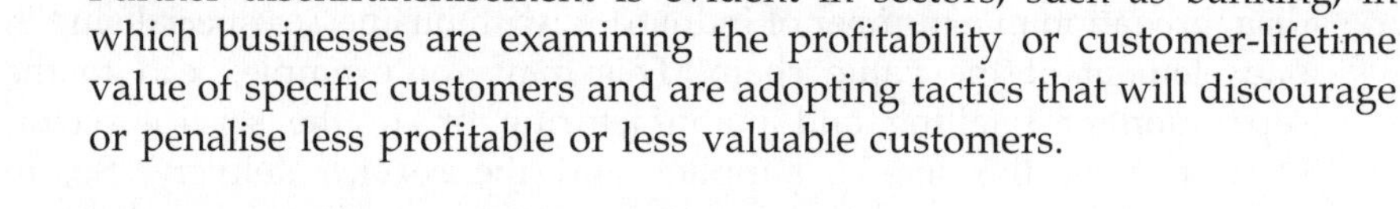

Supply $\Rightarrow$ Production $\Rightarrow$ Marketing $\Rightarrow$ Delivery $\Rightarrow$ Customer support

The steps in the value chain – supply, production, marketing, delivery and support – are the areas in which e-business has the potential to impact on business value. To gain a competitive advantage, a business needs to be able to perform some function in its value chain better than its competitors. The e-business value chain is concerned with the way in which information technology can be harnessed by businesses to generate competitive advantage. Information technology is allowing businesses to become more efficient through decreased costs in sales and marketing, and cost savings in more efficient manufacturing, research and development, and purchasing. A business can gain cost advantages through the use of extranets, enterprise resource planning software and e-commerce. Long-term competitive advantage is usually associated with customer value and customer satisfaction. The use of information technology in order to enhance the relationship with the customer may be achieved within marketing and sales or through customer support (as discussed in Chapter 5).

E-businesses may not always be able to create sufficient value alone but may prefer to engage in alliances or acquisitions in order to complete the e-business value chain. Whilst online-only merchants have a number of advantages over bricks-and-mortar businesses in the areas of established online brand names and mastery of the technology necessary to contact customers, they may have weaknesses in the delivery components of the value chain. E-businesses without warehouses have experienced difficulties in controlling the delivery of products. Bricks-and-mortar stores, on the other hand, are able to leverage the Internet as an alternative selling channel. Alliances allow partnering companies to pool expertise, enter new markets, share financial risks and get products and services to markets faster. In the computer industry, **co-opetition** is a new term for competitive models in which businesses that are competitors in some areas cooperate in other non-competitive areas.

Differentiation

E-businesses have to differentiate themselves from bricks-and-mortar businesses as well as differentiating themselves from other Internet businesses. Businesses have traditionally taken two paths to gain competitive advantage: cost leadership and differentiation.

Differentiation is concerned with identifying and delivering a product benefit or bundle of benefits that customers seek. Sources of differentiation can arise from any area of the market offering including product, branding, price, place, promotion, service quality and people.

Cost leadership is achieved by exercising tight control over production and distribution costs. This is normally achieved through:

- Economies of scale which allow fixed costs to be spread over several units. For economies of scale to have a significant impact they must be effected in an important part of the value chain
- Accumulation of experience which leads to the development of more cost efficient production and distribution methods

- Superior technology
- Operational logistics where, for example, feedback on actual sales levels can trigger additional production.

As discussed earlier, information technology can be harnessed to reduce costs at various stages in the value chain. The Net exposes the inherent weaknesses of high-cost competitors. For example, the cost of an Internet-based banking transaction is about one-fiftieth the cost of a human-teller transaction. In the computer industry, Dell has forced companies like Compaq, Sony and Toshiba to restructure radically their operations. Online travel agencies (for example, Lastminute.com and thetrainline.com) have sought to reduce the cost of booking. A key limitation of cost leadership strategies is that there is only one cost leader in any one marketplace, whereas differentiation allows a number of organisations to differentiate themselves in unique ways. In addition, cost leadership is often not sufficient to gain a long-term advantage because competitors can gain the same efficiency. This means that although cost leadership may provide a first-mover advantage, sustained advantage relies upon differentiation along other dimensions. These dimensions are normally associated with the creation of **customer value**. Strategies for the creation of customer value have been discussed in earlier chapters of this book. They are summarised here in order to compare their relative merits and limitations. Possible strategies include:

- Building brand names
- Creating and maintaining a portal
- Pursuing niche strategies
- Building and enhancing customer relationships
- Grabbing first-mover advantage through speed of innovation.

Building brand names

Brand names are important for recognition in e-business, and for the location of websites. They are also important in communicating values and other messages to customers. The main disadvantage of building a brand is the significant investment in marketing communications that is necessary to create brand awareness. Examples of attempts to build such brand awareness and to link it to website addresses are in evidence on the media, on billboards and on packaging, in stores and through literature. On the other hand, branding is more than placing a name before the public and needs to embrace the elements of the customer experience. Brands are an important tool in relationship building. The use of brands in e-marketing communication has been explored in Chapter 4.

Creating and maintaining a portal

Portal development is a special type of brand development, where the business seeks to succeed through the establishment of a portal which Internet surfers visit as their first port of call. Search engine sites, such as Yahoo!, are significant examples of portals but portals may also seek to add value and therefore enhance their attractiveness through association with communities and via a variety of other routes. Portals are attempting to offer an easy-to-use, all-in-one starting point for Web access. Individuals can rely on the portal to meet all of their needs if it provides a number of services, such as search, shopping, e-mail and games. Portals can generate revenue through e-commerce or through banner advertising and alliances. Traffic is key to successful portal development – advertising revenue depends on traffic. Portals are, however, expensive to maintain and require a significant capital and ongoing investment to achieve success. Portals have been discussed more fully in Chapter 5.

Pursuing niche strategies

Niche strategies allow a business to focus and to become an expert in one competitive arena. This is particularly useful for small businesses, which may be able to extend their presence from regional or national markets to international markets through Web presence. SMEs are currently using websites, intranets and e-mail, although their engagement with e-commerce is much more patchy. SMEs may also potentially benefit from customer relationship management, and increased business-to-business connections. In this later category of applications, SMEs can act as business intermediaries linking larger businesses with small suppliers. Online access to inventory and supplies helps to control costs. This approach can be particularly useful in the travel and tourist industry where the Web can be used to sell places and their associated services (such as accommodation and attractions). When businesses only have a presence in one niche and, particularly with business-to-business relationships, when that niche constitutes only one or two customers, the business can be very vulnerable to changes in the customer organisation.

Building and enhancing customer relationships

Customer relationship management allows businesses to build barriers to entry. Relationships with customers can be cultivated through marketing communications, customer service and building online communities. These have been explored extensively in Chapters 6 and 8. The biggest limitation of this approach is that relationships are a long-term strategy and it may take time for customers to settle with specific merchants. In the mean time their competitors will be doing their best to undermine customer loyalty. The business needs to be committed to a continuing presence in the e-market-place.

Grabbing first-mover advantage through speed of innovation

Speed has become a major factor in competing in turbulent environments. Being a pioneer offers the business a number of first mover advantages:

- *Lower costs* Development costs will be reduced by a shorter development phase for new products or business processes. Being first to enter the marketplace can also increase the business's or product's time in a lifecycle, so that there is an opportunity to spread development costs over a longer lifetime. In addition, pioneers have a longer period over which to gather experience and they may be able to leverage this experience to achieve greater economies of scale when the market grows.

- *Meeting current needs* The faster a business responds to the market, the more likely it is that information collected from market research still reflects the extant position. This will affect the business's ability to achieve significant market share.
- *Lower consumer risk perceptions* Established brands (such as those associated with first movers) are often perceived by customers to have a lower perceived risk than new brands; the longer a business has been established the lower the consumer's risk perception. In addition, the first mover has the opportunity to become the industry standard by which all entrants are compared. This, in turn, may allow the charging of higher prices.
- *Higher prices* Higher prices can be charged in some sectors because innovative buyers may be more price tolerant than customers who enter the market later.

On the other hand, it can sometimes be dangerous to be a pioneer. Pioneers often need to invest significant resources in educating the market and seeking a successful business model. Second movers can enter on the coat tails of first movers and benefit from their mistakes and investment in the creation of a market.

DISINTERMEDIATION AND RE-INTERMEDIATION

There has been considerable discussion about the impact of the Internet on channel structures. A channel structure is the path through which manufacturers deliver products and services to their customers. Typically, this channel structure, or distribution chain will consist of one or more intermediaries, such as wholesalers and retailers. If the value that an intermediary has traditionally offered to the distribution chain is undermined that business will be squeezed out of the distribution chain. Manufacturers may deal directly with consumers, or bypass a wholesaler and work directly with a retailer. This process of the removal of intermediaries in the chain between a producer and consumers is known as **disintermediation**. The elimination of channel members may reduce distribution costs, which can result in an improved proposition for the customer. The challenge for businesses under threat of being disintermediated is to identify a new value proposition.

Whilst disintermediation may be possible in marketplaces in which the manufacturer can identify a clear customer base, the range of offerings available over the Internet and the richness of the information base provides opportunities for buyers to consider a wide range of options and to gather extensive product and other information. Buyers need assistance is negotiating this information-rich arena. The role of providing this assistance is performed by new organisations, described as **cybermediaries** (Sarker *et al.*, 1996). Examples of such intermediaries are:

- Directories, search engines and shopping bots
- Malls (for example, Indigosquare.com)
- Virtual resellers (a business that owns its own inventory and sells direct, for example, Amazon, CDNow)
- Financial intermediaries (offering digital cash and cheque payment services)
- Online communities (for example, The Well)
- Evaluators in various sectors (for example, financial services, ScreenTrade (www.screentrade.co.uk), MoneyExtra (www.moneyextra.com), Utility Buy (www.buy.co.uk); travel, Co-op Travel (www.holidaydeals.co.uk)).

GROUP DISCUSSION ACTIVITY

Choose two of the intermediaries identified in the list above and make a table of the services that they offer to customers. In a second column in the table describe how this service might add value for customers and thereby justify the intermediaries' existence in the value/supply chain.

New players in channels and new channel structures may pose threats for existing channel structures. Businesses need to consider the effect that any new channel structure may have on existing supply and distribution relationships. The roles that channels can take are:

- A communication channel only
- A distribution channel to intermediaries
- A direct sales channel to customers
- Any combination of the above.

CASE CAMEO

ALLIANCES AND ACQUISITIONS: AOL

AOL has made a number of purchases to establish itself as the pre-eminent online portal site. In 1998, AOL purchased CompuServe and formed an alliance with China Internet Corp (an Internet service in Hong Kong). One of the largest Internet-related acquisitions was AOL's joint acquisition, with Sun Microsystems, of Netscape.

- AOL then controlled the NetCenter portal and the Netscape browser. It also acquired programming expertise from Sun.
- Netscape achieved fincancial stability.
- Sun acquired the Netscape e-commerce applications, Internet server software and a partnership with the largest portals.

Since these early alliances, AOL has diversified into alliances with other large retail or media players. Recent alliances include those with Wal-Mart (retailer), DirectTV (satellite television) and Time-Warner (media).

Businesses need to consider the impact on channel structures of the introduction and development of e-business activities.

There is discussion about the impact of the Internet on the quality and nature of business relationships. There are essentially two opposing views:

1. Networks may foster marketplaces in which it is easy to establish and easy to break business relationships, so relationships will become more *ephemeral*. The switching of suppliers that is implicit in this stance will be mediated by cybermediaries.
2. Networks may be used to lock in suppliers or customers. Switching will be prevented by high switching overheads or risk. EDI solutions certainly had the effect of locking businesses together because the EDI technology solutions were between specific businesses, but this technological fusion is less necessary with the open technology of the Internet.

These two positions reflect the technological possibilities. Business and marketplace factors will determine how businesses capitalise on these opportunities to form an appropriate collection of ephemeral and tightly linked business relationships that allow them to deliver customer value.

CASE CAMEO

ALLIANCES IN THE MEDIA: NBC.

NBC and other media companies have been cautious in entering the Internet market due to concerns about channel conflict. To put things into perspective, NBC sells around $100 million of TV advertising in a week – which exceeds Yahoo!'s annual advertising revenue. A further complexity is that other big media players had already established a Web presence when NBC decided to enter the marketplace. Disney has its ABC and ESPN networks and sports, news, and kids sites; the Mouse House has a stake in the search engine Infoseek; CBS has investments in CBS Sportline and CBS Marketwatch. On the other hand, NBC has recognised the need to understand and participate in this new channel. Television networks like NBC bring formidable assets but real liabilities to the Internet. Their brands and promotional platforms can drive traffic but TV networks are also concerned about protecting their core business. Does NBC really want viewers to collect their news from the computer rather than the television? NBC's primary offering on the Internet is content, including news, sports, personal finance, weather, entertainment, music, chat and local information. Nevertheless, NBC has developed an aggressive Internet strategy at little cost through the 1996 launch of MSNMC in a cable-and-online joint venture with Microsoft, and the purchase of a controlling interest in Snap, a fledgeling portal. Also, NBC has created online programming, and launched significant partnerships with TV-station affiliates. NBC has also acquired stakes in many Internet businesses, ranging from a popular music site to a new media production company to a technology firm that delivers Internet video.

Source: Based on M Gunther (1998), NBC sold media, but its Web plans are real smart, *Fortune,* **138**(4), 191–4.

EXPLORATORY ACTIVITY

Visit all of the websites mentioned in the above Case Cameo and investigate whether they are still in operation. What service is each currently offering to its viewers/visitors?

TYPES OF ALLIANCE

Alliances will create virtual organisations (discussed more fully in Chapter 7). There are a number of different ways in which organisations can work together or, in other words, there are a number of different models for alliances. These include:

Co-alliances of shared partnerships. Each partner makes equal contributions of resources, competences, skills and knowledge to the alliance to form a consortium. It is likely that the composition of the consortium will change in response to market opportunities or the objectives and competences of its members. Co-alliances often proceed on a project-by-project basis with intermittent reconvening.

Star alliances are coordinated networks of interconnected members incorporating a core surrounded by satellite organisations. The core is the leader and dominant player, and has the power to dictate the supply of competence, expertise, knowledge and resources to members. The fortunes of the alliance and its members are heavily dependent upon the fortunes of this dominant member.

Value alliances bring together a range of interrelated products, services and facilities that are based on an industry value or supply chain.

Market alliances are a development of value alliances. In market alliances, businesses work together on the manufacture, marketing, selling and distribution of a diverse, but coherent, set of products and services. As compared with the value alliance model, several value chains are likely to be involved.

BUYER BEWARE

Profits remain elusive in the e-marketplace, yet investors have bid the price of Internet stocks to extremely high levels and market capitalisation has been significant. E-business entrepreneurs who have sold out at the right moment have made fortunes. The stock market was buying on potential, and not reality, and that potential was often based on businesses with no identifiable

CASE CAMEO

PARTNERSHIPS FOR INFOMEDIARIES: MERRILL LYNCH

Merrill Lynch & Co is a large US-based financial services company. Its core business has been challenged by the growth of electronic trading and new entrants such as E*Trade. To counteract this Merrill Lynch is building an institutional portal, which is an array of websites for corporate investors. Through this portal investors can track their holdings and buy and sell a wide variety of stocks, bonds, futures and options. On the retail side, Merrill Lynch has launched Merrill Lynch Direct and is developing a major financial services portal. These ventures are supported by an ambitious collection of partnerships:

- Marketing partnerships – websites designed to drive traffic to Merrill websites include Microsoft Network, Multex, Third-age and Medialink.com.
- Content partnerships – news and data providers to Merrill's websites, to support stock market charts, spreadsheets, news and data and prospectuses online. Data providers include Standard & Poor, Dow Jones, ILX, New River and Intuit.
- Service partnerships to offer new services to clients, including Works.com, which offers automated purchasing for small businesses; Financial Engines, offering access to sophisticated asset allocation modelling; and D E Shaw, the developer of online trading software.
- Technology partnerships, including AT&T, Cisco, Compaq, IBM, Microsoft and Sun Microsystems, together with a collection of smaller providers.
- Business partners – Merrill has stakes in a range of alternate trading systems.
- Research & Development partnerships – significant sponsorship of activities at MIT.
- International partnerships – a portfolio of non-US media, technology and financial services companies.

Source: Based on Merrill's E-battle, *Business Week*, 15 Nov 1999 (3655), 256–68.

---

assets and no history of successful business performance. The market capitalisation of dot.coms crashed in 2000 and many of these businesses failed. In the longer term, investors need to make a rational evaluation of an e-business's strategy. They need, for example, to compare the fleet of foot Amazon.com with the more substantial Barnes & Noble. Amazon.com has one location, owns one main warehouse and collects money from its customers before it pays for merchandise. Further, it can easily expand its business model into other product lines. Barnes & Noble, on the other hand, has $2 billion in leases, pays for inventory, moves inventory to all of its stores, stacks it on shelves and has staff in over one thousand locations.

When they built the railroads across the United States, the largest profits were made by the pick-and-shovel manufacturers. Similarly, profits in e-business are likely to accrue disproportionately to those offering the products and tools of the e-business revolution such as hardware, software and telecommunications links. The major information-industry players have significant engagement with and commitment to the commercialisation of the Internet and the establishment of an e-commerce economy.

CHAPTER SUMMARY

E-business strategy is necessary in order to establish business objectives and the way in which those objectives can be achieved. The relationship between e-strategy and other business strategies is dependent on whether the business is a pure play or Internet start-up, an established business with multiple channels of which the Internet is one, and on the extent of integration of e-businesses and other business operations. Strategy formulation is a cyclical process that involves auditing the market situation of the business, setting or revising objectives, establishing strategies to achieve objectives, detailed planning for the execution of strategies, plan implementation and evaluation of actions. Key strategic issues are the extent of integration of spin-off, cannibalisation and market and product positioning. A key aspect of the e-business plan is the establishment of an appropriate budget in an unknown marketplace. In formulating strategy, businesses need to understand the environmental context. Business relationships are defined by the e-business value chain, which includes supply, production, marketing, delivery and support. E-businesses need to differentiate themselves and to gain a competitive advantage, either through cost leadership or through the creation of customer value. The Internet has the potential to impact on channel structures: disintermediation and the role of cybermediaries are live issues, as are the different approaches to the formation of alliances and partnerships in this marketplace. Finally, e-businesses navigate in uncharted waters and need to anticipate hidden rocks and be prepared to make diversions or to 'jump ship'.

KEY CONCEPTS

E-business strategy is concerned with establishing e-business goals and objectives, and making decisions about how those objectives will be achieved.

Strategic experiments are the basis for selective experimentation in new e-business marketplaces and allow businesses to develop expertise at the same time as collecting market intelligence.

SMART objectives are specific, measurable, achievable, relevant, and timely.

Spin-offs are distinct business ventures operating separately from a parent company. Internet spin offs create freedom for the Internet business to operate differently from the parent business, in a way that might be more consistent with the cyber marketplace.

Cannibalisation occurs when an Internet channel competes with other channels of the same business in such a way that it undermines the viability of established channels and business models.

continued

Market and product positioning identifies the marketplace in which the business seeks to operate. Innovation in market and product positioning is summarised by the four options in Ansoff's matrix: market penetration, product development, market development and diversification.

E-business plan documents the outcomes of the stages in the strategy formulation process including objectives, audits, strategies, activity plan and schedule and budget.

Martini effect is a term used to refer to the essential nature of Internet service delivery: Anytime, Anyplace, Anywhere.

E-value business chain comprises the steps of supply, production, marketing, delivery and support, which together are the areas in which e-business has the potential to impact on business value.

Co-opetition is a term for competitive models in which businesses that are competitors in some areas cooperate in other non-competitive areas.

Differentiation is the means by which businesses define for themselves a unique offering and market position. This, in turn, is the basis for a competitive advantage based on customer value.

Cost leadership is one means of differentiation which is based on exercising tight control over production and distribution costs. Cost leadership is generally a less successful approach than differentiation based on creating customer value.

Disintermediation occurs when businesses that have traditionally been part of the value or distribution chain for a given sector find themselves unable to offer value that justifies their continued existence in the value chain. Disintermediation is a threat for intermediaries such as wholesalers and publishers.

Alliances are ways in which businesses work together to create virtual organisations.

ASSESSMENT QUESTIONS

1. Critically discuss the integration of e-business or Internet strategy with corporate strategy and other functional strategies within a business.

2. How can SWOT analysis be used in the internal and external audits that inform e-business strategy? Illustrate your answer with reference to some of the opportunities and threats that arise in the Internet context.

3. Discuss the challenges associated with developing an Internet retail business as a parallel channel alongside a bricks-and-mortar business. Explain and illustrate with reference to examples of the concept of cannibalisation.

4. Use Ansoff's matrix to explore the approaches to product and market development that are available in e-business.

5. Outline the sections in an e-business plan and explain what each section has to contribute.

6. Review the range of expertise necessary to design and maintain a website, and indicate how these might lead to a complex network of alliances.

7. Why are budgets important in e-business? What are the challenges to budget setting in this context, and how might these challenges be navigated?

8. With reference to the e-business value chain, explain the ways in which value can be created in e-business. Illustrate your answer with examples.

9. What do you understand by the concept 'differentiation'? Summarise the range of strategies for differentiation that are available to businesses in the e-marketplace.

10. Explore the way in which business relationships may change in the e-business environment. Pay specific attention to the concepts 'disintermediation' and 'cybermediaries'.

11. Critically evaluate the different types of alliance that might be appropriate in e-business.

GROUP ASSESSMENT 1 – NEW BUSINESS MODELS

There has been much discussion of new business models in the Internet environment. Refer back to Chapter 1 for typologies of e-business models. Consider the section on alliances and partnerships in this chapter and the discussion of online organisation in Chapter 7. Choose an industry sector (for example, financial services, estate agency, travel or publishing) and prepare a critical account with examples that debates whether the Internet has generated 'new business models'.

GROUP ASSESSMENT 2 – CANNIBALISATION

Using an abstracting or indexing service, locate short articles in the professional and popular press about organisations that have faced the dilemma of parallel channels, with the Internet as one of those channels. Critically analyse how each of the businesses has differentiated these channels. Make reference to issues of differentiation and integration, perhaps through branding and marketing communications. Write this as a series of case studies. Draw together your findings to demonstrate the various approaches to differentiation of channels.

GROUP ASSESSMENT 3 – E-BUSINESS PLANNING

You have been engaged as a group of consultants to formulate an e-business plan for a major recruitment consultancy business that has significant experience in the placement of temporary and permanent office staff in the UK. The business is beginning to feel the effect of competitive offerings that make extensive use of the Internet. Your brief is to:

■ Review Internet activity in this business sector, and assess the competition.
■ Make preliminary proposals concerning the development of a USP for the Internet offering of this business.
■ Draft a project plan for the development of the e-business plan. This needs to reflect the stages in the plan, and the work packages that will be necessary to complete each of the stages.

GROUP ASSESSMENT 4 – MARKET RESEARCH AGENCIES

Visit a number of the websites of market research agencies and evaluate the type of services and information that are available. Write a report on your findings for a senior manager in a business seeking to develop its e-business activities and presence. Useful sites are Thomson (www.thomson-directories.co.uk), Mintel (www.mintel.com), MORI (www.mori.co.uk), A C Nielsen (www.nielson.co.uk), Euromonitor (www.euromonitor.com), Economist Intelligence Unit (www.eiu.com).

REFERENCES

Alt, R, Osterle, H, Reichmayr, C and Zurmuhlen, R (1999) Business networking in the Swatch Group, *Electronic Markets*, **9**(3), 169–73.

Amran, M and Kulatilaka, N (1999) *Real options: managing strategic investments in an uncertain world*. Boston: Harvard Business School Press.

Anderson, D (2000) Creating and nurturing a premier e-business, *Journal of Interactive Marketing*, **14**(3).

Bailey, J P and Bakos, J Y (1997) An exploratory study of the merging role of electronic intermediaries, *International Journal of Electronic Commerce*, **1**, 7–20.

Bakos, J Y (1998) The emerging role of electronic marketplaces on the Internet. Communications of the ACM 41, 35-42.

Banyopadhyay, S, Lin, G and Zhong, Y (2001) A critical review of pricing strategies for online business models, *Quarterly Journal of Electronic Commerce*, **2**(1).

Bickerton, P, Bickerton, M and Simpson-Holley, K (1998) *Cyberstrategy*. Oxford: Butterworth Heinemann.

Bornheim, S P (2001) *e-roadmapping*. Basingstoke: Palgrave.

Brynjolfsson, E and Smith, M D (2000) Frictionless commerce? A comparison of Internet and conventional retailers, *Management Science*, **46**(4), 563–85.

Burnham, B (1999) *How to invest in e-commerce stocks*. McGraw-Hill.

Chaffey, D, Mayer, R, Johnston, K and Ellis-Chadwick, F (2000) *Internet marketing*. Harlow: Pearson Education.

Chapman, P, James-Moore, M, Szczygiel, M and Thompson, D (2000) Building Internet capabilities in SMEs, *Logistics Information Management*, **13**(6), 454–60.

Chase, R L (1998) Creating a knowledge management business strategy: delivering bottom-line results, *Management Trends International*.

Chircu, A M and Kauffman, R J (1999) Strategies for Internet middle men in the intermediation-disintermedation-reintermediation cycle, *Electronic Market – the International Journal of Electronic Commerce and Business Media*, **9**, 109–17.

Chircu, A M and Kauffman, R J (2001) Digital intermediation in electronic commerce – the eBay model, in S Barnes and B Hunt, *E-commerce and v-business; business models for global success.* Oxford: Butterworth Heinemann, pp. 45–66.

De Kare-Silver, M (2000) *e-shock: the electronic shopping revolution; stategies for retailers and manufacturers,* 2nd edn. Basingstoke: Macmillan Business.

Dutta, S, Kwan, S and Segev, A (1997) Strategic marketing and customer relationships in electronic commerce. Proceedings of the Fourth Conference of the International Society for Decision Support Systems. Lausanne, Switzerland.

Feeney, D (2001) Making business sense of the e-opportunity, *MIT Sloan Management Review,* **42**(2).

Henderson, J R, Dooley, F, Akridge, J and Boehlje, M (2001) Distribution channel strategies and e-business in the Agribusiness industries, *Quarterly Journal of Electronic Commerce,* **2**(1).

Hensmans, M, Van den Bosch, F A J and Volberda, H W (2001) Clicks vs bricks in the emerging online financial services industry, *Long Range Planning,* **34**(2).

Kane, M (1999) Cybermediaries: the Net's new kings, *ZDNet Tech News,* 28 May. Available at http://www.excite.com/computers_and_internet/tech_news/zdnet/?article=zdnews3.inp.

Kaplan, S and Sawhney, M (2000) E-hubs: the new B2B marketplaces, *Harvard Business Review,* **78**(3), 97–108.

Kleindl, B A (2001) *Strategic electronic marketing: managing e-business.*Cincinnati, Ohio: South-Western College Publishing.

Leebaeret, D (ed.) (1998) *The future of the electronic marketplace.* Mass: MIT Press.

Leslie, K and Michaels, M (1987) The real power of real options, *McKinsey Quarterly,* 3, 4–22, and www.mckinseyquarterly.com.

Lord, C (2000) The practicalities of developing a successful e-business, *Journal of Business Strategy,* **21**(2), 40–7.

Markides, C C (1999) A dynamic view of strategy, *Sloan Management Review,* **40**, Spring, 55–63.

May, P (2000) *The business of e-commerce: from corporate strategy to technology.* Cambridge: Cambridge University Press.

Morath, P (2000) *Success@ e-business: profitable internet business and commerce.* London: McGraw-Hill.

Morgan, R F (1996) An Internet marketing framework for the World Wide Web (WWW), *Journal of Marketing Management,* **12**, 7575–775.

Pile, T (2000) *Staying in touch with the fundamentals.* Presented at Internet Marketing Workshop, De Montfort University, 8 December.

Porter, M (1980) *Competitive strategy.* New York: Free Press.

Senn, J A (2000) Business-to business e-commerce, *Information Systems Management,* **7**(2), 23–32.

Standing, C and Vasudavan, T (2001) Industry transformation in e-commerce: Web diffusion in travel agencies, in S Barnes and B Hunt, *E-commerce and v-business; business models for global success.* Oxford: Butterworth Heinemann, pp. 121–37.

Stepanek, M (1998) Rebirth of the salesman, *Business Week,* 22 June, 146–8.

Stroud, D (1998) *Internet strategies.* Basingstoke: Palgrave.

Teece, D J (1992) Competition, cooperation and innovation: organisational arrangements for regimes of rapid technological progress, *Journal of Economic Behaviour and Organisations,* **18**, 1–25.

Useem, J (1999) Internet defense strategy: cannibalise yourself: call it survival by suicide, *Fortune,* 6 Sept, **140**(5) 121–34.

Venkatraman, N (2000) Five steps to a dot-com strategy: how to find your footing on the Web, *Sloan Management Review,* **41**(3), 15–25.

Watson, R and Zinkhart, G (1997) Electronic commerce strategy: addressing the key questions, *Journal of Strategic Marketing,* 189–209.

Whinston, A B, Stahl, D O and Choi, S Y (1997) *The Economics of Electronic Commerce.* London: Macmillan.

9 Protecting online communities and societies

After reading this chapter you will:

- Be aware of the types of cybercrime that pose challenges for communities and organisations
- Appreciate that regulation and taxation pose many dilemmas in a global Internet environment
- Understand the role of data protection in relation to personal information
- Be able to reflect critically on the role of contracts
- Be able to review the approaches associated with the protection of intellectual property
- Understand the principles of, and the approaches to, security
- Be able to debate the issue of privacy
- Understand how trust can be cultivated
- Appreciate netiquette

INTRODUCTION

This chapter draws together a number of themes that are key to participation in, and commitment to, online communities and societies. Some of these issues require government intervention and legislation, but the greater responsibility in other arenas lies with large global organisations and businesses. As in other arenas, business and the state need to work collaboratively together to ensure that they are contributing to the creation of a society in which businesses can flourish and communities can optimise the quality of the life experience of their members. This is a complex process with many tensions and potential points of conflict between different interest groups. Some texts treat these issues as if they are problems for businesses to recognise, solve or negotiate. Some treat them as barriers to successful e-commerce. Here we regard them as elements in the rich fabric of a community or society that communicates and interacts in both real and virtual worlds. We see these potential sources of tension as issues for communities and societies, including those organisations that are embraced by those communities or societies, or have some impact upon them. The issues in this chapter will remain important and will always be resolved by a mixture of regulation, policy making, technology and good practice. None of them can be resolved by the next technological innovation or by a review of underlying business models.

This chapter does not seek to provide answers or offer detailed guidance but merely raises the issues so that the reader is alerted to the need to investigate further.

CYBERCRIME

Cybercrime is crime perpetuated over the Internet. The ease of engaging in Web transactions, communication, the low cost of entry for business or pseudo businesses and the global nature of the Internet make for rich pickings for cybercriminals. Many categories of business-related crime and crime against individuals that have been tried in the real world are particularly attractive to the cybercriminal because the remoteness of the Internet lends invisibility. The later sections in this chapter describe the approaches that governments, businesses and consumers can adopt in order to minimise crime and its effect on Internet commerce. For e-commerce to grow both businesses and consumers need to be confident that transactions and communication can continue without interference or risk. This can be achieved with a mixture of regulation and security measures. There are four main categories of cybercrime:

- *Hacking* – in which people illegally break into systems, generally with a view to either interfering with the operation of the system (for example, by redirecting mail) or to steal intellectual property, such as lists of customer contact details. Hackers can be excluded with effective firewalls that prevent access to unauthorised parts of systems. Another approach is to employ hackers to test out the security of a system.

- *Fraud* is defined as gaining others' assets by deception. There is a whole range of business scams that can be perpetrated on the Internet. These range from pyramid marketing, through Web auction to advance fee loans fraud. Laws and regulations usually exist to address this type of fraud.
- *Infringement of intellectual property* is straightforward because digital information can be easily copied, reproduced and passed to others. Encryption software can be used to protect against such infringements. This topic is explored later in the chapter.
- *Offensive material* which might be viewed as inappropriate or, particularly for children, harmful. Censorship is the long-standing approach to controlling the distribution of communications and images that a society feels to be inappropriate. The global nature of the Internet makes it easy to bypass traditional censorship mechanisms. Some control can be exercised through rating systems and software filters that control access to specific websites. Other controls are the responsibility of the users and, in the case of children, parents.

GROUP DISCUSSION ACTIVITY

Examine the types of cybercrime outlined above and discuss the consequences of each. Give examples of the context in which each of the different types of cybercrime might be perpetrated.

REGULATION AND TAXATION

E-commerce traders on the Internet have to do their best by a judicious blend of legal, technological and common sense measures (Burnett, 2000, p. 114)

Regulation and taxation have traditionally been matters for government to debate, legislate and take action on. This means that the traditional approach to regulation and taxation is hidebound by national boundaries and geography, and restrictions on business practices and taxation regimes vary throughout the world. On the other hand, international trade has a long history and laws have evolved so that transactions can take place legitimately between a supplier in one jurisdiction and a purchaser in another. The Internet promotes international trade in a way, and to an extent, that was not previously envisaged. Governments have needed to make speedy and important decisions on their positions regarding communication and commerce in this new space. This goes beyond the formulation of policies, laws and regulations to the institutions, and procedures for interpreting and enforcing such regulations. The Internet is often regarded as a wide frontier in which regulation, policies and conventions lag behind developments. The making of case law, which demonstrates how the laws and regulations are likely to be interpreted, also lags behind the specification of laws and regulations. Because the Internet and e-commerce are new, it is very difficult to predict the legal consequences of any action.

Jurisdiction

Both regulation and taxation are affected by jurisdiction. For example, if an employee of a German company posts a defamatory comment concerning an English companion on an electronic bulletin board of a US-based service provider, how do the different legal and regulatory systems operate in resolving this situation? Should any action for defamation be brought against the employee or the company, and in which country should the action be brought? The same dilemmas arise with transactions in which the parties to the transaction may be located in more than one country. The issue is not only which laws apply, but which legal actions are likely to lead to the most successful outcome, and whether the online merchant is equipped to fight a legal case in a 'foreign' jurisdiction.

Jurisdiction determines the laws and regulations that apply to a website. Since sites might be viewed in many countries in the world, it is impracticable to ensure compliance in every possible jurisdiction. In any case, what might be acceptable in one jurisdiction may not be so in another. For example, what might be considered 'free speech' in the US may be viewed as libellous, or contrary to cultural and religious practices in, say, Saudi Arabia.

One way of addressing some of these issues is to include a disclaimer stating that the site is subject to UK law and only open to business with UK residents (or whatever other jurisdictions the company wishes to work within).

Regulation

Business regulation embraces both statutory requirements and also regulations proposed through codes of practice by self-regulatory bodies, such as the British Advertising Standards Agency.

The USA has established some basic principles that can be represented by the following quotations:

> Governments do have a role to play in supporting the creation of a predictable legal environment globally for doing business on the Internet, but must exercise this role in a non-bureaucratic fashion . . . There should be no discriminatory taxation against Internet commerce. The Internet should function as a seamless global marketplace with no artificial barriers erected by governments. (US Department of Commerce, 1998, pp. 50–1)

Another important feature of the US government's position is the acknowledgement of the need for consistent principles:

> The legal framework supporting commercial transactions on the Internet should be governed by consistent principles across state, national, and international borders that lead to predictable results regardless of the jurisdiction in which a particular buyer or seller resides. (The White House, 1999)

The US government believes that Internet commerce will have a significant effect on US and world economies and has put in place the National Telecommunications and Information Administration (www.ntia.doc.gov) to work with other countries to keep government regulation out of e-commerce.

The NTIA has proposed five principles for governmental approach to global e-commerce:

1. The private sector should take the lead in developing Internet-based commerce.
2. Governments should avoid undue restrictions on Internet-based commerce.
3. Government intervention should be focused on ensuring competition, protecting intellectual property and privacy, preventing fraud, fostering transparency, supporting commercial transactions and facilitating dispute resolution.
4. Governments should recognise that the Internet is a unique medium and that it should have not have the same regulations as other media.
5. Electronic commerce should be facilitated on a global basis.

EXPLORATORY ACTIVITY

Visit the NTIA website and make a note of any important recent development on US government regulation of e-commerce.

The EU has embraced e-commerce as an evolutionary step in the development of the European market. The EU is acting to protect the competitiveness of the bloc within a general framework that adheres to similar principles to those proposed by the NTIA.

In the context of regulation, it is important to note that many existing regulations are inappropriate for e-business. Thus restrictions on opening hours have no relevance in this environment. However, on the contrary, there are a variety of other areas in which it is important that existing business regulation also applies in the Internet environment. These include:

1. *Advertising* In the US advertising is subject to regulation. Virgin Atlantic was fined by the US Department of Transport for failing to update flight prices and special deals information on its Internet site in breach of international air competition regulations. The British approach is essentially self-regulatory through the British Advertising Standards Agency (www.asa.org.uk). The British Code of Advertising Practice and the Sales Promotion Code set out a number of principles that must be complied with by all advertisers. These include the conditions that all advertisements must be 'legal, decent, honest and truthful' must not exploit the 'credulity, lack of knowledge or inexperience of consumers', and should not mislead through inaccuracy, ambiguity omission, or otherwise. The emphasis is on self-regulation, the main deterrent being that poor practice will lead to adverse publicity. Statutory controls exist in the form of the Control of Misleading Advertisements Regulations, 1988, the Trade Descriptions Act, 1968, and from the EU, the Misleading Advertising Directive, 1984. Organisations need to be aware of the advertising control regulations and conventions in any countries for which the website is intended.

EXPLORATORY ACTIVITY

Visit the BASA website and make a note of any items on the website relating to e-commerce.

2. *Financial services* are often highly regulated. In the UK, the Financial Services Act 1986 controls financial services provision and investment advertisements appearing in the UK, and affecting markets within the UK, whatever the location of the advertisers. Authorisation is required to conduct investment business in the UK. A website owner who is not authorised to sell financial services in the UK must ensure that the site has prominent statements to show that it is not intended for a UK audience.

3. *Defamation* The Internet provides ample opportunity for defamatory statements about individuals and organisations to be posted to a newsgroup, published by e-mail or otherwise. The practical difficulties associated with identifying and tracing the perpetrator, dealing with different jurisdictions and recovering damages from individuals with limited resources have led businesses and individuals who are seeking to protect their reputations to look to ISPs for redress. The ISP must protect itself by taking reasonable steps to ensure that its services do not promulgate such defamatory materials. Websites supporting online communities need to monitor bulletin boards and chat rooms, and ensure that there is a very evident code of behaviour. Organisations need to protect themselves against defamatory e-mails being circulated by their employees through guidelines for e-communication to which employees are expected to adhere. Similar principles also apply in relation to obscene, discriminatory or harassing communication or website content.

4. *Business communication* Under the UK Companies Act 1988, the name of the company must be clearly stated on all of its letters, notices and other official publications and documents. The Business Names Act also requires certain information to be contained in business communication. These requirements must be acknowledged and interpreted in the context of e-business communication.

GROUP DISCUSSION ACTIVITY

Visit twenty websites. Note the extent and nature of business details, contact points and addresses that are included on those websites. Discuss variations between the different websites.

Taxation

Focusing on taxation, tax jurisdiction determines the country that is responsible for taxing income from a transaction. Under the current system of international tax treaties, the right to tax is divided between the country where the enterprise that received the income is resident ('residence' country) and that from whence the enterprise derived that income ('source' country). The centrality of location to this taxation situation poses obvious problems. An EU Directive is seeking to resolve this by defining the place of establishment of a merchant who actually pursues an economic activity from a fixed physical location. The general principle that is currently being applied is that tax rules are similar to those applying to a conventional mail-order sale. For the UK, this is:

1. If the supplier and the customer are both in the UK, VAT will be chargeable.
2. Exports to private customers in other EU countries will attract either UK VAT or local VAT.
3. Imports into the UK from other EU countries will attract local VAT and imports from outside the EU will attract UK import tax.
4. Services attract VAT according to the location of the supplier. This is different from the position for goods. In particular, e-service suppliers that might otherwise be subject to UK taxes are motivated to find a lower tax location from which to operate. The UK gambling industry has exploited this position and is able to offer gambling at a lower tax rate than that applied in the UK.

This variation in tax rates between locations has caused companies to identify optimal locations from which to operate, described as location optimised commerce on the Internet (LOCI). Governments must respond to these commercial initiatives and look critically at their tax rates and policies. As e-commerce grows the issue of tax revenues will become increasingly important for governments. Nevertheless, the issues of extraterritoriality and privacy greatly complicate the implementation of any proposed tax regimes. With products that are physically shipped somewhere, governments have some chance of monitoring transactions. But with products and services that are digital the e-merchant may not even know where the buyer is located. This will especially be the case if the payment is made through e-cash, where an anonymous transaction can be made with third-party intervention.

In summary, the challenge for governments and businesses is to work together to monitor and develop a taxation situation in which both national and international taxation can work satisfactorily to generate appropriate tax revenues. Fragmented approaches with different countries or states acting unilaterally may lead to:

- Double taxation or unintentional non-taxation
- Excessive compliance burdens for businesses
- Opportunities for tax evasion.

EXPLORATORY ACTIVITY

Visit Amazon.com and Amazon.co.uk, and compare the taxation arrangements that are in evidence in relation to the two different national markets in which these subsidiaries operate.

EXPLORATORY ACTIVITY

Visit www.e-commercecommission.org, and learn more about the US Congress's latest position with regard to Internet taxation.

DATA PROTECTION

Data protection legislation has been formulated throughout the EU to control the use of personal data about living individuals that is held in electronic databases. Data protection legislation is the regulatory contribution to the protection of individual's privacy. In the UK, the Data Protection Act 1998 (superseding an earlier Act) requires that all personal data controlled by an organisation in the UK ('data controller') must be processed in accordance with specific statutory rules and rights. Its eight Data Protection Principles are enforceable by the Data Protection Commissioner, by criminal law enforcement authorities and by the Courts against a data controller who holds personal data that is accessed and used in an unauthorised way. Under the Act, personal data must be:

1. Processed fairly and lawfully
2. Accurate and up to date
3. Held no longer than is necessary
4. Secure
5. Not transferred to any country outside the European Economic Area unless that country ensures 'adequate level of protection' for personal data.

These principles apply to all personal data, including customer profiles and employee records. The last principle may have particular implications for global e-businesses. Exceptions to this principle apply when the subject of the data has given express informed consent or the recipient in the destination country has contractually guaranteed adequate protection. Data subjects must be informed of the purposes for which their personal data is held and used in advance of any processing – they must give 'informed consent'. Any secret collection of data (such as through a cookie) does not meet this criterion. Appropriate notices must therefore be displayed on the website so that the data subject can provide consent as required. Significantly, it is only recently that agreement has been reached with the USA about the transfer of personal data. Use of the Internet for the transmission of personal data as a separate purpose must be recorded as part of the official notification and there must be appropriate provisions in the contract with the third party in the other jurisdiction. Although Data Protection legislation technically only applies in the UK, the principles translate into other jurisdictions in the sense that they are a good basis for addressing many of the privacy concerns discussed later in this chapter.

EXPLORATORY ACTIVITY

Visit the website of the UK Data Protection Agency, and learn more about the registration process that businesses are required to complete.

CONTRACTS

A **contract** over the Internet is formed as for other contracts when an offer is made and an acceptance received. The merchant makes an offer through the website. The customer places an order and the merchant confirms receipt of the order. There needs to be a clear statement as to how offers and acceptance are to be communicated and received. This is part of the terms and conditions of supply. These should be brought to the attention of the customer, and the customer needs to be required to affirm that she agrees to these before, say, being allowed to move on to the next stage in an on-screen dialog. Specifically, when designing the appropriate web page, it is important to ensure that the customer cannot circumvent any 'Accept' dialog box and thereby avoid acknowledging terms and conditions. Figure 9.1 illustrates the range of issues that may be covered by 'terms and conditions'.

Figure 9.1 Terms and conditions

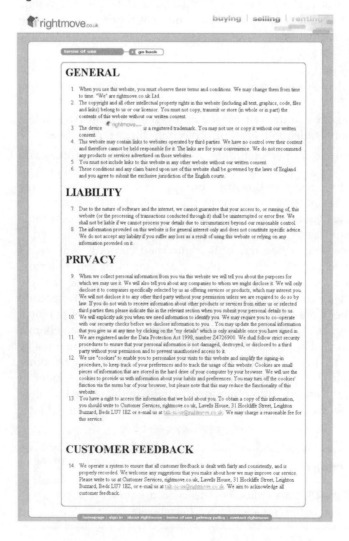

The laws of many countries have implied terms and conditions in contracts for sale and supply, whether or not they appear in the contracts themselves. For example, under UK law there are tests of reasonableness on limiting and excluding liability. Further, the supplier may not wish to deal with customers in certain parts of the world where there may be political or practical difficulties associated with delivery, payment or taxes. It may be desirable to implement technological restrictions to control access from such customers.

Consumer protection legislation in the UK also applies in the Internet environment. For example, under the Consumer Credit Act 1994, a consumer in any tripartite payment arrangement must be given copies of the agreement with the supplier within a certain time period, and also actually sign and return to the supplier a paper document.

May (2000) uses the practices of software vendors to illustrate one way in which this might be managed:

1. Software vendors sell the rights to use a piece of software; the vendor retains the assets of the intellectual property rights, and the customers pay a fee to enjoy the functionality offered by the software.
2. Every software licence has a statement of liability that bounds the vendor's liability.
3. Software licences declare the legal jurisdiction that will be used in the event of any dispute relating to the agreement. This is usually the home jurisdiction of the supplier.

The other issue is the rules of contract law and the things that need to be specified in any contract. The United Nations Commission on International Trade Law has recently completed work on a model law that supports the commercial use of international contracts in e-commerce. An EU Directive on the protection of consumers in respect of distance contracts (that is, those without the simultaneous physical presence of both the supplier and the consumer) requires suppliers to provide customers, in a clear and comprehensible manner (perhaps on a sub-page of the website), with the following information prior to the conclusion of any distance contract:

■ The location and identity of the supplier and, in the case of contracts requiring payment in advance, his address
■ The main characteristics of the goods or services
■ The price of the goods or service, including all taxes
■ Delivery costs, where appropriate
■ The arrangements for payment, delivery or performance
■ The existence of a right of withdrawal
■ The cost of using the means for distance communication, where it is calculated other than at the basic rate
■ The period for which the offer or price remains valid
■ Where appropriate, the minimum duration of the contract and whether the contracts for the supply of products or services are to be permanent or recurrent.

After the contract has been entered into, the supplier is required to provide written confirmation of the information provided.

Signatures are a key component of most contracts. Until recently, digital signatures did not have a status in UK law. However the EU Commission has also introduced a Directive on electronic signatures that gives electronic signatures the same legal status as written signatures.

GROUP DISCUSSION ACTIVITY

Each member is asked to visit one of the shops recommended by Shopsmart (www.shopsmart.com) and to make a note of the areas covered by the terms and conditions stated on the website. Compare the terms and conditions offered by different e-merchants. What are the common themes?

INTELLECTUAL PROPERTY

Laws and regulations concerned with the protection of **intellectual property**, such as books, documents, designs and trademarks, are important in protecting the creator of the intellectual property (the writer, designer or illustrator) from having her work hijacked, such that she is no longer able to benefit from this work. It has always been necessary to seek to protect intellectual property, but the Internet raises some new challenges. Intellectual property control is discussed in the context of copyright, patents, trademarks and domain names.

Copyright

Works that are protected by copyright include text, software, graphics, music and multimedia combinations. The issue of copyright is significant in online environments because with electronic information it is much easier and cheaper to produce a good quality copy than it is, for example, with print-based information or music imprinted on CDs. Owners of intellectual property have some difficulties in controlling downloading of information and its subsequent transmission to multiple users. Information, software and music are important e-business product categories. Further, organisations need to consider the copyright position of information that they provide on their website, such as pictures and graphics files, sound files, text and programs. Organisations must be clear about the copyright position of items on the website. In addition, all sites should contain a copyright notice and an explicit statement as to the extent to which material may be copied or circulated.

As with other legislation, the laws to protect intellectual property are unique to a specific jurisdiction, although the Berne Copyright Convention, managed through the World Intellectual Property Organisation, establishes widely acknowledged conventions that influence national legislation. The Berne Copyright Convention was extended to include digital applications in

1996. To illustrate the principles that need to be explored in every jurisdiction, we refer to UK legislation. In the UK a copyright owner has the exclusive right to control who is entitled to make or adapt copies of a work. The meaning of 'copying' covers the act of storing a work electronically in any medium, whether transient of permanent. Generally, without the owner's permission there is no right to print off or disseminate material published on the Internet.

The first **copyright owner** is the author of the work, unless the author is an employee creating the work during the course of his employment, in which case the employer owns the copyright. Where a third party, such as a consultant is contracted to produce a work, such as a website, the copyright remains with the third party, unless there is a written **transfer of rights**. If there is no transfer of rights it is important that there is a **licence** between the owner and the organisation, granting the right to distribute materials.

Many licences on the Internet rely upon **implied authority**. An author who makes copyright material available over the Web knows that it will be browsed, but this implied licence does not automatically extend to cover downloading, printing and transmitting the work. Licences can be used to inform visitors to a website of their rights in respect of the use of the on-screen work. The licence may also restrict usage to, for instance 'use for non-commercial purposes'. Many information-based sites will make some information available to attract Web users and then charge for additional information. Common sense dictates that information that is deemed to have commercial value should not be displayed, and the issue of copyright can be addressed in any licence agreement that is associated with the contract for access and use.

An interesting issue that has both copyright and liability dimensions are hyperlinks between sites. This link raises legal questions about the extent of

Figure 9.2 Technology for copyright protection

Technology	Description
Digital watermarks	Watermarks allow images to be sent over the Internet with visible watermarks over a page or with watermarks that will show up only after an image is copied.
Secure containers, and encryption	The file is encrypted by the publisher before being sent to the user. Once the publisher has received payment, it sends the user a key to unlock the product. Other users also need this key in order to be able to unlock the file.
Information metering	Through creating an audit trail of the whereabouts of a copy of a file, it is possible to assess who has accessed the material.
Copyright archive	This archive takes registrations of websites. It uses web crawlers and robots to search for the registered content and to identify copyright violations.

Source: Based on Kleindl (2001), p. 292.

liability for the content of the linked site and of copyright infringement where no consent has been obtained for including the hypertext link. The legal position on such links is unclear, but any attempt to control such links could have significant implications, especially for portals, subject gateways and cybermediaries.

The risk of copyright violation is a major impediment to the development of digital sales and delivery of software, electronic books, television programmes, and audio and video files. A number of approaches are being developed to give a greater level of copyright protection. These are summarised in Figure 9.2.

Patents

In England and Wales, patents protect novel ideas that are industrially applicable. Patents will not generally be granted for software-related inventions, methods of doing business, mathematical formulae or algorithms. Until recently there was a great deal of consistency in coverage between the UK and USA but recently the US Patent Office has changed its guidelines. Computer-implemented business methods may now be patentable in the USA, although the position is still somewhat fluid. Such patents are a relatively new phenomenon and e-commerce patents have yet to be challenged – the generic nature of many of them may enable competitors to formulate alternatives that achieve similar ends without infringement. Nevertheless, US patent clearance searches should now be considered for computer-implemented business methods relating to the Internet in order to avoid the risk of infringing a granted US patent. US patent protection should be a consideration for novel Internet business methods.

Trademarks, trade names, and domain names

A trademark confers exclusive rights on its owner within its jurisdiction. Trademarks are important business assets. Because they are intimately associated with brand and the values associated with the brand (see Chapter 4), the use of a trademark by another company may damage the original brand. Using a trademark to which an organisation is not entitled is known as '**passing off**'. In addition to the normal business threats posed by third parties using a trademark, the Internet presents a particular challenge for trademark owners, largely because of the relationship between registered trademarks and domain names, and the difficulty of applying globally the trademark protection normally afforded under national law and registration procedures. Organisations need to ensure that trademark registration extends to all countries in which the website might have an audience.

Memorable domain names are important business assets. Some might argue that the most valuable intellectual property in online business is the namespace. Domain names need to be registered with a registration authority. In the early days dealers in Internet names registered attractive names and names similar to those of major companies. In the UK, this practice is now deemed to be an infringement of the pre-existing trademark and is illegal. In practice, a new business should register its name as an Internet domain name immediately, and consider registering its trading name and brands as trade marks to cover online services in the territories in which its goods and services will be promoted and made available.

SECURITY

In discussions about e-commerce, security is often considered to be the most important issue that needs to be resolved. In reality much of this discussion confuses security with confidence that the transaction will be effected as the customer requests and expects, without any undesirable side effects. These side effects might be associated with the delivery of the service or product from the e-merchant, or they may be associated with the diversion or inappropriate use of information that the customer proffers in order to complete the transaction. Indeed security is often discussed in the context of payment, financial transactions, access to credit details and bank accounts.

Security is a particular challenge because the TCP/IP protocol that governs communication across the Internet was designed to be an open protocol, and is by its very nature not secure. This means that data transmitted from computer to computer can be intercepted, read and altered. Figure 9.3 summarises the security requirements for all computer systems. These include identification (Who is accessing the system?), access control (Is the user performing tasks and viewing data that he is authorised to access?), protection (Is customer privacy being respected?) and validity (Is the data accurate?).

Figure 9.3 Security requirements

Identification

■ Are new customers required to register?

■ Do customers register and are they given a password?

■ Does the organisation know customers' contact information?

Access

■ Which users are authorised to change the website?

■ Which pages in the website are users permitted to view?

Protection

■ Is customer purchase history and other information only passed to other companies with customers' permission?

■ Are credit card details secure and secret?

Validity

■ Is the data on the website correct?

■ What controls ensure that only those with permission can change the data on the website?

The management of security needs to focus on two interlinked but different dimensions:

■ Managing consumers' perceptions of risk
■ Technical devices for the actual management of risk.

Security is concerned with the management of risk and in particular with the trade-offs between accessibility and vulnerability. Businesses and consumers are accustomed to striking this balance in the real world, but both businesses and customers are unsure about how to make these trade-offs in the virtual world. Security in the e-commerce setting is principally concerned with protecting the privacy of transactional information and authenticating the credentials of transacting parties.

There is ample evidence to suggest that consumers feel apprehensive about giving their credit card details over the Internet, despite a demonstrably lower level of reluctance to tender such details over the telephone and willingness to allow a waiter to take a credit card out of sight in a restaurant. Customers need reassurance in the form of positive experiences, an improved understanding of the risks and how security measures can minimise those risks, and guarantees.

What are the risks and how can they be prevented? Secure systems need to exhibit the following features:

1. **Authentication** methods for ensuring that the parties to the transaction are who they claim to be, and for validating the identities of these parties.
2. **Nonrepudiation** protects the user by ensuring that the sender cannot legally deny having sent the message and entered into the transaction.
3. **Privacy and confidentiality** in relation to the protection of transaction data from access by an unintended or unauthorised recipient.
4. **Integrity** ensures that the message sent is that which is received and that it is not corrupted in transmission.
5. **Availability** such that the system and the data that it contains continue to be available for the purposes for which it was intended.

Hackers and others may seek to threaten system security for commercial or other gain by:

1. **Sending viruses** that might threaten availability and integrity.
2. **Spoofing**, or masquerading as someone else. There are two main types of spoofing. **IP spoofing** in which the spoofer seeks to gain access to confidential information by using false identification data such as the originating (IP) address. **Site spoofing** is used to divert customers from the retailer's site, to an alternative site.

Technical approaches to increasing security include encryption, digital signatures, public key infrastructures, SET and firewalls. All of these measures assume that it is necessary to know the identity of a business partner. In consumer marketplaces, this is not always necessary or possible; the retail store or the e-shop is taken on trust by virtue of its presence. The task of e-commerce security is not to protect messages exchanged during business transactions but to protect the parties involved in those transactions. Security is a much wider problem than simply being confident about those with whom you are doing business, but most consumers and businesses would regard this as an important opener to any business relationship or transaction.

Encryption

Encryption is concerned with coding data (using a key) before it is passed over an insecure medium, such as a radio wave or a telecommunications link. The receiver has a code (or matching key) that allows him to de-encrypt the message. The key used to encrypt a message is called the public key. The key used to decrypt a message is called the private key. Encryption is more secure if the two keys are different; this is described as public key encryption. When both keys are the same, the system is referred to as private key encryption.

Encryption makes the message secure during its transmission and is concerned with communications security. In an e-commerce context encryption is mainly used to scramble the details of an e-commerce transaction as it is passed between the sender and receiver. In this application, encryption makes it more difficult for fraudsters to read e-mail messages to which they should not have access, but it does nothing to prevent the fraudster from extracting credit details from the merchant's site, which is in any case a much easier task than extracting such credit details from e-mail transmissions over the network.

The most common encryption method is **SSL (Secure Sockets Layer)** and this is built into modern web browsers such as Netscape Navigator. SSL uses a private key to encrypt data that is then transmitted over the SSL connection. It is used to scramble customer and credit card information when it is transmitted across the Internet. The message, 'You are about to view information over a secure connection', is an indication that SSL is in use. Websites protected by SSL also carry a security symbol in the status bar, often in the form of a closed lock. A further indication of an SSL-secured website is that the URL commences with https. Since, with sufficient computing power, time and inclination, it is possible to decrypt messages encrypted using SSL, other methods of encryption are being developed. These include digital signatures, public keys and secure electronic transaction (SET).

Public key encryption (which uses both public and private keys) is usually used to secure small amounts of data such as credit card numbers. Private key encryption where the same key encrypts and then decrypts the message is used to transfer long messages and files between two trusted sources. **Pretty good privacy** (PGP) is a public key system. With PGP an organisation distributes a public key to all of the people from whom they wish to receive messages. These people use this public key to encrypt their messages. When the message is received, the organisation uses a private key, known only to it, to decrypt the message. A unique private key is generated from a public key only once and used by the recipient only for a specific transaction.

Digital signatures

Digital signatures allow the verification of the 'origin' of messages and thereby their authentication. In this context it is often said that digital signatures provide nonrepudiation, that is, the signer cannot later deny having sent a message. A digital signature scheme consists of two components. The signature algorithm creates a digitial signature for a given document and a **private key signature**. The verification algorithm takes the document, the digital signature and a **public verification key**, and returns a 'valid' answer if document and signatures have not been modified, and if the public verification key used to construct the signature corresponds to the private signature key. Otherwise an 'invalid' answer is returned. Thus, the 'digital' signature creates a link between a document and the public verification key, but it is important to remember that it does not link documents to people.

Public key infrastructures

Public key infrastructures (PKIs) are a means of associating public verification keys with persons. As such a PKI provides three aspects of security: confidentiality, authentication and nonrepudiation. This is achieved through the issue of certificates by **trusted third parties** (TTP), described at **Certification agencies** (CAs). A certificate is a valid copy of a public key of an individual or organisation together with identification information. Typical certificate information is:

- User identification data, typically name, URL of website and e-mail address
- Issuing authority identification and digital signature
- User's public key
- Expiry date of the certificate
- Class of certificate
- Digital identification code of the certificate.

Certification agencies (CAs) take responsibility for generating certificates, and managing public keys. This management requires procedures and protocols necessary throughout the lifetime of a key, such as generation, dissemination, revocation and change. Given that every organisation and individual involved in e-commerce and the use of this type of security might need a public key, the task of their management is massive. Further, the establishment of a CA requires complex trust building amongst various communities and stakeholders. It is anticipated that CAs might be banks and post offices. National laws on digital or electronic signatures thus need to be supported by regulations that control how CAs should operate and in particular the checks that the CA should perform. A *public key infrastructure* is then the entire collection of regulatory and technical measures for issuing and using certificates, and digital, or electronic signatures.

But, we are still not yet home and dry. These mechanisms link the document to a verification key and the verification key to a person. But, to hold the signer personally responsible for the document we need evidence that only the signer could have been in possession of the private signature key. The signature key could be produced by the CA and given to the person, but we need to be sure that the CA is secure for the lifetime of the key. Alternatively, the party may create its own key; then the CA will require evidence that the party is in possession of the private key corresponding to the public key included in the certificate. Whichever option is preferred, the question remains as to how the key is protected during its lifetime. All software, such as operating systems, web browsers and application packages that have access to the key, need to protect it. This requires that software is developed to high security standards and that users make use of the security mechanisms embedded in this software. Some would argue that this is an unrealistic expectation and that there remains a risk with this type of approach.

Secure electronic transaction (SET)

SET uses digital certificates and has been developed by a consortium led by MasterCard and Visa. By employing digital certificates, SET allows a purchaser to confirm that the merchant is legitimate and conversely allows the merchant to verify that a credit card is being used by its owner. It also requires that each purchase request includes a digital signature, further identifying the cardholder to the retailer. At the transaction level, SET works like this:

1. The customer selects items for purchase. Payment card details are entered on an order form that is sent to the merchant
2. Payment information is forwarded from the merchant to the acquirer
3. The acquirer decodes the customer's payment information and asks the card issuer for authorisation
4. When the card issuer accepts the request for authorisation, the acquirer sends the information back to the merchant, who then confirms the purchase to the customer
5. The purchase price is then deducted from the customer's account, as usual.

The acquirer is an intermediary who liaises between the bank and the merchant, to remove the need for the merchant to have the infrastructure to link directly to the bank. The whole transaction via the Internet is invisible to the customer and may be completed in under a minute. Before a consumer can execute such a transaction she needs to obtain a **digital wallet** or a plug-in so that she can communicate with a merchant via SET, and she needs to obtain a **digital certificate** from a CA (see Chapter 7). The certificate rests in the wallet at the relevant machine; the credit card details contained within the certificate can only be decrypted by the company that issued the card.

Although SET has been under trial for some years, it has yet to achieve the status of a widely accepted standard. It is a sensible solution that allows merchants to eliminate fraudulent card attacks, because card details are checked before the transaction is closed. One issue is the practical difficulty of issuing and managing certificates but, also, consumers and retailers have not been enthusiastic about SET.

A key difference between SSL and SET lies in the allocation of risk. SET makes the buyer responsible for proving her credentials, whereas, with SSL, the merchant takes responsibility for checking the buyer's ability to pay and that the credit card account being referenced belongs to the user initiating the transaction.

EXPLORATORY ACTIVITY

Visit the following three sites and compare the information that they offer on SET: www.mastercard.com/set, www.visa.set and www.setutility.com.

Firewalls

A firewall creates a barrier between an organisation's network and an external network, such as the Internet. The firewall can be a computer, a router or another kind of communication device. Firewalls only allow access to the secure network to users with specified characteristics. The ultimate firewall is complete physical isolation from external networks. Firewalls are used to prevent access by hackers who seek to obtain information about customers such as credit card details. They are also used to protect an organisation's intranet from unauthorised users.

PRIVACY

Privacy, as an issue takes on completely different dimensions in virtual businesses and online communities. Never before has it been possible for credit information, medical histories, criminal records, and purchasing habits to be so easily collected and transferred to other organisations. According to Kakalik and Wright (1996), the typical consumer is on more than 100 mailing lists and at least 50 databases. These figures are probably much higher today and the quantity of data that is kept on those databases about each individual has also increased.

Customers and citizens are concerned about maintaining as much control as possible over their own destinies. They are concerned that the information that they provide to organisations will be used in ways that they had not anticipated, maybe years later, and that the information, with varying levels of accuracy, may be passed to other organisations and other agencies, possibly with undesirable consequences for their credit rating, medical treatment opportunities, insurance premiums, employment and other life opportunities. What is the root of this concern? This lies in the asymmetric information availability between organisations and individual customers. The capacity to leverage the technology is far greater for organisations due to their much more significant resources. There are two key drivers in this asymmetry:

- *Economies of scale.* Organisations deal with a much higher level of transactions than the individual customer. This means that they have a much better base from which to gather knowledge about, and harness the potential of, the technology
- *Economies of sharing.* Consumer information now resides in giant databanks accessed by globally networked computers. Costs of data collection, data warehousing, data interpretation and data storage can be spread over different companies and over many applications. Individual consumers do not enjoy this level of networking.

Nevertheless, individuals who wish to preserve a level of privacy are not entirely powerless. Whilst these measures only offer a measure of control, they do reduce the transparency and ease with which an individual can be profiled. Strategies that enhance user privacy and control include:

- Operating under aliases in e-mail communication and membership websites
- Using a passport scheme that introduces anonymity at the level of the individual transaction
- Exercising judgement about the information that is provided (particularly in newsgroups and discussion sites), with whom to do business online and what transactions to perform online
- Exercising appropriate virus hygiene. Viruses do not only damage local systems, they can also siphon data to another host.

People are often relatively relaxed about the disclosure of personal information provided that their permission has been granted, the process is transparent and the information is being used for their benefit. Provided information is given voluntarily and customers are made fully aware of how it will be used, there is no privacy violation. Many e-merchants that keep personal profiles of customers are very careful to emphasise that the customer can choose what information he provides (apart from the basic contact details necessary for a transaction and delivery) and that he can view and, if appropriate, edit any details that the company is storing about him. This level of attention and sensitivity in relation to privacy is an important aspect of any successful relationship. Further, personal or business information is shared with a specified organisation or person for a specific purpose. Wider dissemination of the information or its use for purposes for which it was not given, can lead the customer to feel betrayed. Merchants that are seeking to build relationships, trust and communities also need to offer advice to community members about privacy. For example, Planet RX.com advises customers:

> Please remember that anything you post to the message board or chats becomes immediately accessible to the public. It's always a good idea to exercise caution and common sense when deciding to disclose any personal information. Please do not disclose any identifying information about others, such as names, addresses, occupations, phone numbers, place of residence or business, and anything else that could identify or bring unsolicited attention to another member.

GROUP DISCUSSION ACTIVITY

Visit a number of websites and collect their privacy policies. Compare and contrast these policies. Make a list of the undertakings that are embedded in privacy policies.

Consumer information is a valuable commodity in any marketplace. The success of e-commerce will depend upon consumer confidence that privacy is not being infringed. Privacy, and the way in which it is respected, could be a significant factor in the growth of e-commerce. One way in which businesses can demonstrate their commitment to privacy is through the use of a Privacy Policy, an example of which is shown in Figure 9.4.

Figure 9.4 A privacy policy

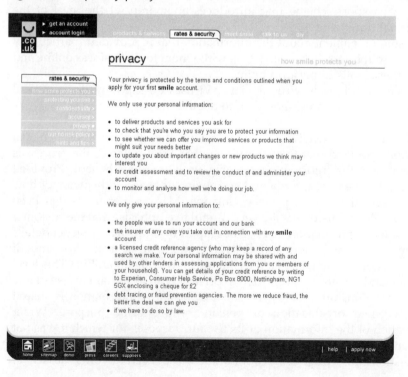

TRUST

The issue of trust is one that has been much discussed in the context of relationship marketing and in the literature on virtual communities and organisations. Trust needs to exist between all of the parties at each of the nodes in the supply chain. The bond of trust, especially in the depersonalised setting of the Internet, is very fragile (Hodges, 1997). Security and privacy policies and practices form the basis for a relationship that is founded on trust – but trust itself is much more elusive. Trust is the commodity that makes people and organisations comfortable and prepared to do business with one another, to share information and to participate in communities. Like other dimensions of relationships, trust should grow with positive customer experiences over a period of time and may be a factor that influences loyalty. Also trust with an organisation will often, but not always, transcend the channel. Issues of brand, loyalty and relationships have been discussed in Chapter 4. Figure 9.5 offers a few pointers on how to get started with trust. TRUSTe is a **trust agency** that acts as a third party. Organisations displaying the TRUSTe trustmark on their sites have undertaken to adhere to good practice in relation to trust and privacy, as indicated in the Case Cameo.

Figure 9.5 How to build trust

1. Tell people how you are using their information
2. Allow people to view the information that you are keeping on them
3. Allow people to change this information
4. Tell people how you will use the information and with whom you will share it
5. Embed all of the above points in a privacy policy, which is available on the website
6. Use 'branded trust' by registering with a trust agency, such as TRUSTe and display its trustmark on the website

CASE
CAMEO

TRUSTe TRUST AGENCY

For registration with TRUSTe businesses must disclose:

- What type of information the site gathers
- How the information will be used
- Who the information will be shared with (if anyone)

And they must agree to:

- Disclose information management practices in privacy statements
- Display the trustmark
- Adhere to stated privacy practices
- Cooperate with all reviews

TrustUK

TrustUK is a joint venture between the Alliance for Electronic Business and the Consumers' Association, endorsed by the Department of Trade and Industry. Early in 1999 the Alliance and CA participated in a series of consultations with the Performance and Innovations Unit (PIU) of the Cabinet Office and contributed to the proposals in respect of consumer trust and confidence online. The report that was the outcome of these consultations can be found at www.cabinet-office.gov.uk/ innovation/. The DTI's Consumer White Paper, *Modern markets: confident consumers*, contained plans for approval of online codes by a new body, TrustUK (www.dti.gov. uk/consumer/whitepaper).

TrustUK is an approval scheme for trade associations/subscriber bodies (code owners) whose members/subscribers are bound by an online code of practice. TrustUK does not approve web traders direct. Web traders need to register with a code owner. There are currently three code owners: the Association of British Travel Agents (www.abta.com), the Direct Marketing Associations (www.dma.org.uk) and the Consumers Association (www.which.net/webtrader). Web traders wishing to display the TrustUK e-hallmark must subscribe to, and comply with, a TrustUK approved e-commerce code of practice.

A web trader showing the TrustUK hallmark operates to a high level of commercial standards designed to:

■ Protect consumer privacy
■ Ensure that consumer payments are secure
■ Help consumers to make an informed buying decision
■ Ensure that consumers know what they have agreed to and, if necessary, how to cancel orders
■ Deliver the goods or services ordered within the agreed time period
■ Protect children
■ Resolve any complaints, irrespective of the location of the consumer.

BEING A GOOD NETIZEN

Netizens need to take care of themselves and others. In general, behaviour that is acceptable in the real world is acceptable in the virtual world, but the impact of some behaviours and how they translate into the online world may not always be obvious. This section introduces the issues of netiquette and concludes with a checklist that acts as a summary of many of the issues that have been dealt with in this chapter. The checklist offers a few simple guidelines for consumers to protect themselves during e-commerce transactions in the dynamic, exciting but strange and uncertain cyber world.

Netiquette refers to proper etiquette over networks, focusing specifically on communication behaviour. Codes of behaviour are sometimes outlined for online communities (as discussed in Chapter 6). Shea (www.albion.com/netiquette) suggests the following principles:

1. Be respectful of others online. Behave as if you were having a conversation with someone in person
2. Remember that the Internet is a global medium. Others online may have a culture, language or humour that is different from yours so jokes and sarcasm may not travel well
3. Respect the copyright on reproduced material
4. Do not send chain letters through e-mail. Chain letters are forbidden on the Internet
5. When in a chat group, observe the discussion to get a feel for the group culture before making comments
6. Use mixed case. UPPER CASE LOOKS AS IF YOU ARE SHOUTING
7. Keep file sizes small
8. Do not send large amounts of unsolicited information to people.

Rumour mongering and spamming are temptingly easy on the Internet. Rumours, whether true or manufactured can spread rapidly across the Internet, sometimes with devastating consequences for those cited in the rumour. Users should consider the possible consequences of passing on 'information', and check the reliability of their sources. **Spam** is the practice of sending unwanted e-mails to a large number of individuals. Spamming is much more attractive than junk mail because the spammer does not need to pay postage or other delivery charges. Spam is a problem in that it shifts the cost of the communication from the sender to the receiver. The receiver may be faced with sorting through many unwanted e-mail messages and in a business context this sifting might be very costly in terms of employee time. A number of software tools have been developed to filter spam on the basis of domain names. The Mail Abuse Prevention System (MAPS) allows complaints to be registered and mail to be blocked. **Flaming** is the process of sending angry e-mail messages, often from a false address. This may provoke the recipient to respond in like manner, and a negative exchange may ensue.

EXPLORATORY ACTIVITY

Visit the Mail Abuse Prevention System project website (http://maps.vix.com) and discover what is meant by a Realtime Blackhole List.

Netiquette also involves taking a responsible attitude to security. Figure 9.6 makes a number of practical suggestions for methods that individuals can adopt to protect themselves.

Figure 9.6 Security checklist

1. Look for the company's security policy and check its terms and conditions

2. Look for real-world contact details, such as a phone number and geographical address

3. Check that the site is secure before sending confidential information. Look for https in the toolbar or a padlock or unbroken key symbol

4. Keep records of any adverts, confirmation messages and e-mails to do with your order by printing them. If you do not automatically receive a confirmation of your order, e-mail the company and ask for it

5. Check your card statements carefully

6. Do not send confidential information such as credit card details via e-mail

7. Do contact the company if you have any unanswered questions

Source: Based on Consumers' Association (2001) Online insecurities, *Which*, March, 41–3.

CHAPTER SUMMARY

This chapter draws together a number of themes that are important for online communities and societies. Business and the state need to work together to ensure the development of a society in which businesses can flourish and the quality of life for individuals is optimised. There is a need to protect the individual from cybercrime in the form of hacking, fraud, infringement of intellectual property and offensive material. Governments have a role to play in supporting the creation of a predictably legal environment, which embraces regulation and taxation. In a number of areas existing legislation and regulation can be extended to the Internet environment. Jurisdiction of laws and regulations is a real challenge for e-businesses operating in global marketplaces. Data protection principles are designed to protect the privacy of citizens. Attention also needs to be directed towards contracts and terms and conditions as a basis for protecting those entering into transactions. The protection of intellectual property is important in a knowledge-based economy. This is achieved through copyright, patents, trademarks and trade names. Security in e-business must be addressed, especially in the context of e-commerce transactions that involve payment. Security can be enhanced through the use of encryption (often using secure sockets layer, or SSL), digital signatures and public key infrastructures. Privacy is linked to security in the sense that security allows individuals to keep things private. The information that individuals and businesses choose to release to other commercial parties depends significantly on trust. Trustmarks and trust agencies can help to reassure consumers. Finally, netiquette identifies some of the responsibilities of the individual in an online society.

Cybercrime is crime perpetuated over the Internet. It includes hacking, fraud, infringement of intellectual property and the distribution of offensive material.

Jurisdiction is the area of applicability of laws and regulations, including tax laws and regulations.

Business regulation embraces both statutory requirements and also regulations proposed through codes of practice by self-regulatory bodies, such as the British Advertising Standards Agency.

Data protection legislation controls the use of personal data about living individuals that is held in electronic databases.

Contracts underlie every business transaction. Both consumers and businesses need to be clear about the terms of the contract.

Intellectual property laws and regulations protect the creators of the intellectual property from having their work hijacked, such that they are no longer able to benefit from the work.

Authentication validates the identities of the parties to a transaction.

Spoofing is masquerading as someone else.

Encryption is concerned with coding data (using a key) before it is passed over an insecure medium, such as a radio wave or a telecommunications link. The receiver has a matching key that allows it to decode the message.

Secure sockets layer (SSL) is a common encryption method that is built into modern web browsers.

Certification agencies take responsibility for managing public keys that are used with digital signatures and public key infrastructures.

Trust agencies formulate codes of good e-commerce practice with which web traders wishing to display the agencies' hallmarks need to comply.

Spam is the practice of sending unwanted e-mails to a large number of individuals.

Flaming is the process of sending angry e-mail messages, often from a false address.

ASSESSMENT QUESTIONS

1. Describe the main categories of cybercrime. Give examples of some such crimes.

2. What challenges does globalisation pose for the regulation of e-business?

3. Review the categories of existing legislation and regulations that apply to Internet business.

4. Critically comment on some of the taxation issues that an organisation should explore when establishing an e-commerce site.

5. What is data protection, and why is it important?

6. Analyse the relationship between contracts and terms and conditions. Taking one business, produce a draft set of terms and conditions.

7. How can e-businesses protect their trademarks and trade names from 'passing off'?

8. Explain the following terms: copyright owner, transfer of rights, licence, implied authority.

9. What are the basic characteristics of a secure system?

10. How are the following concepts linked: Secure Sockets Layer (SSL), public key encryption and certification agencies?

11. Explain how the SET protocol operates.

12. Why do e-businesses need to deal with the issue of privacy? What measures can users take to protect their own privacy?

13. Why is trust important? What are the advantages and limitations of trustmark schemes?

14. What do you understand by the term netiquette? Why is netiquette necessary? Draft a code of behaviour to guide contributors to an online community that comprises the fans of a popular football club.

GROUP ASSESSMENT 1 – PROTECTING CHILDREN

Write a set of guidelines for parents who wish to protect their children from inappropriate use of the Internet.

GROUP ASSESSMENT 2 – EMPLOYEE USE OF THE INTERNET

Many Internet users have access to the Internet from their workplace. They may be tempted to use the Internet for booking holidays, ordering their shopping, listening to music and chatting to their friends, especially if they do not also have access at home.

■ Write an essay that discusses the personal and employment issues relating to employee use of the Internet.

■ Draft a set of acceptable use guidelines that would be appropriate for office employees in a major bank.

REFERENCES

Abel, S M (1998) *Trademark issues in Cyberspace; the brave new frontier.* Fenwick & West LLP. Available at www.fenwick.com/pub/trademark_issues_ in_cyberspace.html.

Ang, P H (2001) The role of self regulation of privacy and the Internet, *Journal of Interactive Advertising,* **1**(2).

Attaran, M and VanLaar, I (1999) Privacy and security on the Internet : how to secure your personal information and company data, *Information Management and Computer Security,* **7**(5).

Baig, E C , Aubin, T and Borrus, A (1997) Outlaw online betting? Don't bet on it, *Business Week,* 15 December, 44.

Bloom, P N, Milne, G R and Adler, R (1994) Avoiding misuse of new information technologies: legal and societal considerations, *Journal of Marketing,* **58**(1), 98–110.

Buckler, G (1998) Websites often put the bite on Net cookies, *Computer Dealer News,* **14**(39), 20.

Burnett, R (2000) Legal aspects of e-commerce, *Computing & Control Engineering Journal,* **11**(3), 111–14.

Cardinale, V (1998) A private debate, *Drug Topics,* **142**(20), 77–8

Cavoukian, A and Tapscott, D (1997) *Who knows: safeguarding your privacy in a networked world.* New York: McGraw-Hill.

Chou, D C, Yen, D C , Lin, B and Cheng, P H-L (1999) Cyberspace security management, *Industrial Management & Data Systems,* **99**(8).

European Initiative in Electronic Commerce (1997) Communication to the European Parliament. The Council, the Economic and Social Committee and the Committee of the Regions, 15 April. Available at www.ispo.cec.be/Ecommerce.

Evans, J (1997) Whose website is it anyway?, *Internet World,* September, 46–50.

Forcht, K A and Wex, R-A (1996) Doing business on the Internet: marketing and security aspects, *Information Management & Computer Security,* **4**(4), 3–9.

Foxman, E R and Kilcoyne, P (1993) Information technology, marketing practice and consumer privacy: ethical issues, *Journal of Public Policy and Marketing,* **12**(1), 106–19.

Furnell, S M and Karweni, T (1999) Security implications of electronic commerce: a survey of consumers and businesses, *Internet Research,* **9**(5).

Glanton, E (1999) Firm claims search engines abuse their names, *Marketing News,* 15 March, **33**(6), 16.

Golimann, D (2000) E-commerce security, *Computing & Control Engineering Journal,* **11**(3), 115–18.

Hawkins, S, Yen, D C, and Cou, D C (2000) Awareness and challenges of Internet security, *Information Management & Computer Security,* **8**(2).

Hodges, M (1997) Building a bond of trust, *MIT's Technology Review,* **100**(6) 26–7.

Hoogenboom, M and Steemers, P (2000) Security for remote access and mobile applications. Computers and Security: towards an integrated management approach, *Information Management & Computer Security,* **7**(5).

Huff, C and Martin, C D (1995) Computing consequences: a framework for teaching ethical computing, *Communications of the ACM,* **38**(12), 75–84.

Jones, M G (1991) Privacy: a significant marketing issue for the 1990s, *Journal of Public Policy and Marketing,* **10**(1), 133–48.

Kakalik, J and Wright, M (1996) Responding to privacy concerns of consumers, *Review of Business,* **18**(1), 15–18.

Kiely, T (1997) Obeying the laws of cyberspace, *Harvard Business Review,* **75**(5), 12–14.

Kleindl, B A (2001) *Strategic electronic marketing managing e-business.* Cincinnati, Ohio: South-Western College Publishing.

Koehler, J (1997) Privacy and emerging electronic payments, *Credit World,* **85**(6), 29–31.

Lessing, L (1999) *Code: and other laws of cyberspace.* New York: Basic Books.

Machlis, S (1997) Websites rush to self-regulate, *Computer World,* **32**(19), 2.

May, P (2000) *The business of ecommerce: from corporate strategy to technology.* Cambridge: University Press.

McCune, J C (1999) Big brother is watching you, *Management Review,* **88**(3), 10–12.

OECD (1999) *The economic and social impact of electronic commerce.* OECD, February.

Miyazaki, A D and Fernadez, A (2000) Internet privacy and security: an examination of online retailer disclosures, *Journal of Public Policy and Marketing,* **19**(1), 54–61.

Owens, A (1999) Taxing the Web, *Harvard Business Review*, **77**(4), 18.

Prabhaker, P R (2000) Who owns the online consumer?, *Journal of Consumer Marketing*, **17**(2), 158–71.

Roth, M S (1998) Customization and privacy, *Marketing Management*, **6**(4), 22.

Schneier, B (1996) *Applied cryptography*. Wiley.

Schwartz, D O (1998) Sharing responsibility for e-commerce and the privacy issue, *Direct Marketing*, **61**(2), 48–51.

Smith, R E and Wientzen, H R (1998) Privacy sound off: regulation vs self-regulation, *Internet Week*, 21 September, 35–40.

Tweney, D (1998) The consumer battle over online information privacy has just begun, *InfoWorld*, **20**(25), 66.

Turkle, S (1995) *Life on the screen: identity in the Age of the Internet*. New York: Simon & Schuster.

US Department of Commerce (1998) *The emerging digital economy*. US Department of Commerce.

Venkatesh, A (1998) Cybermarkets and consumer freedoms and identities, *European Journal of Marketing*, **32**(7/8), 664–76.

White House, The (1999) *A framework for global electronic commerce*. 1 July.

Whysall, P (2000) Retailing and the Internet: a review of the ethical issues, *International Journal of Retail and Distribution Management*, **28**(11).

Wright, B C and Carlin, G J (1999) Patenting methods of doing business, *Knowledge Management World*, March, 42–3.

Zgodzinski, D (1997) Buyer Beware, *Internet World*, March, 42–6.

Zugelder, M T, Flaherty, T B, Johnson, J P (2000) Legal issues associated with international internet marketing, *International Marketing Review*, **17**(3).

Some useful websites:

www.cib.org.uk/supersite/ecomm.htm (Chartered Institute of Bankers guide to e-commerce).

www.dti.gov.uk/infoage/index/htm (business in the information age from the Department of Trade and Industry).

www.ispo.cec.be/e-commerce/welcome.html (electronic commerce from the European Union).

www.e-commerce.gov (United States government electronic commerce policy).

www.eca.org.uk (E Centre UK (Association for Standards and Practices in Electronic Trade)).

Index